CREATING FOOD FUTURES

I dedicate this book to my daughters, Rozelle and Katinka, in the hope that the world they are growing into will remain one of beauty and wonder.
Cathy Rozel Farnworth

To my wife Susan and my sons, Gareth and Aled. Also to the memory of my parents, Richard and Marian.
Emyr Vaughan Thomas

Creating Food Futures
Trade, Ethics and the Environment

CATHY ROZEL FARNWORTH

JANICE JIGGINS
Wageningen University, The Netherlands

EMYR VAUGHAN THOMAS
The Open University, UK

GOWER

© Cathy Rozel Farnworth, Janice Jiggins and Emyr Vaughan Thomas 2008

All rights reserved. No part of this publication may be reproduced, stored in a retrieval system or transmitted in any form or by any means, electronic, mechanical, photocopying, recording or otherwise without the prior permission of the publisher.

Cathy Rozel Farnworth, Janice Jiggins and Emyr Thomas have asserted their moral right under the Copyright, Designs and Patents Act, 1988, to be identified as the editors of this work.

Gower Applied Business Research
Our programme provides leaders, practitioners, scholars and researchers with thought provoking, cutting edge books that combine conceptual insights, interdisciplinary rigour and practical relevance in key areas of business and management.

Published by
Gower Publishing Limited
Gower House
Croft Road
Aldershot
Hampshire GU11 3HR
England

Gower Publishing Company
Suite 420
101 Cherry Street
Burlington, VT 05401-4405
USA

www.gowerpublishing.com

British Library Cataloguing in Publication Data
Creating food futures : trade, ethics and the environment.
 - (Corporate social responsibility series)
 1. Food industry and trade 2. Nutrition policy
 I. Farnworth, Cathy II. Jiggins, Janice III. Thomas, Emyr
Vaughan
338.1'9

ISBN: 978-0-7546-4907-6

Library of Congress Cataloging-in-Publication Data
Farnworth, Cathy.
 Creating food futures : trade, ethics and the environment / by Cathy Rozel Farnworth, Janice Jiggins and Emyr Thomas.
 p. cm. -- (Corporate social responsibility)
 Includes index.
 ISBN 978-0-7546-4907-6
 1. Food industry and trade. 2. Nutrition policy. I. Jiggins, Janice. II. Thomas, Emyr Vaughan. III. Title. IV. Series: Corporate social responsibility series.

HD9000.5.F283 2008
338.1'9--dc22

2008020163

Printed and bound in Great Britain by
MPG Books Ltd, Bodmin, Cornwall.

Contents

List of Figures	vii
Liar of Acronyms	ix
List of Contributors	xi
Foreword	xv
Acknowledgments	xix

1 **Creating Food Futures: Trade, Ethics and the Environment**   1
   Cathy Rozel Farnworth, Janice Jiggins and Emyr Vaughan Thomas

PART I
THE BIG PICTURE: INNOVATIONS THAT ENABLE ACTION

2 **The Retail-Led Transformation of Agrifood Systems**   11
   Julio A. Berdegué and Thomas Reardon

3 **Regulation, Sovereignty and Accountability in the Food Chain**   27
   Megan Waples

4 **Innovation in Policy: The Common Agricultural Policy and Dimensions of Regime Change**   41
   Emyr Vaughan Thomas

5 **The Swedish Foodshed: Re-imagining Our Support Area**   55
   Susanne Johansson

6 **Growing Sustainable Communities: Understanding the Social-Economic Footprints of Organic Family Farms**   67
   Matthew Reed, Allan Butler and Matt Lobley

PART II
CASE STUDIES: INNOVATIONS IN STAKEHOLDER AND ORGANISATIONAL RELATIONSHIPS

7 **Balancing Business and Empowerment in Fair Fruit Chains: The Experience of Solidaridad**   81
   Irene Guijt and Edith van Walsum

8	**The FoodTrust of Prince Edward Island, Canada** Woody Wilson	97
9	**Beyond Profit Making: Combining Economic and Social Goals in the German Organic Agriculture and Food Sector** Martina Schäfer	109
10	**The Cornwall Food Programme** Roy Heath and Mike Pearson	123
11	**Ethics in French Wine Cooperatives: Part of a Social Movement?** Yuna Chiffoleau, Fabrice Dreyfus and Jean-Marc Touzard	131

PART III
CHANGING THE RULES OF THE GAME

12	**Impacts of the Supermarket Revolution and the Policy and Strategic Responses** Julio A. Berdegué and Thomas Reardon	149
13	**Supermarkets: A Force for the Good?** Robert Duxbury with Cathy Rozel Farnworth	163
14	**Mixing is the Way of the World: A New Social Label** Cathy Rozel Farnworth	175
15	**Responsibility in Value Chains and Capability Structures** Jérôme Ballet, Jean-Luc Dubois and François-Régis Mahieu	189
16	**Food, Environment, and the Good Life** David E. Cooper	203
17	**Conversion or Co-option? The Implications of 'Mainstreaming' for Producer and Consumer Agency within Fair Trade Networks** Stewart Lockie	215
18	**Towards a New Agenda** Cathy Rozel Farnworth, Emyr Vaughan Thomas and Janice Jiggins	229

Index   *237*

List of Figures

5.1	Contrasting dependency on land for food	56
5.2	The Swedish foodshed	59
5.3	Swedish food consumers' total agricultural land use	63
5.4	Different ways of estimating the foodprint for Sweden	64
6.1	The social-economic footprints of different farms compared	72
6.2	The different footprints of organic farms compared	74
8.1	Pork pricing	100
9.1	Social activities of organic enterprises in Berlin-Brandenburg	113
9.2	Activities related to passing on knowledge and experience by organic enterprises in Berlin-Brandenburg	115
Box 12.1	Family farmers as supermarket suppliers	150
Box 12.2	Cooperating to compete: Easier said than done	158
Box 15.1	A preventive mechanism: The social precautionary principle	198

List of Acronyms

ACF	Advocacy Coalition Framework
ASERCA	Mexican market promotion service of the Secretariat of Agriculture
BGMS	The Broads Grazing Marsh Scheme
CAM	Council of Agriculture Ministers
CAP	Common Agriculture Policy
CEC	Commission for Environmental Cooperation
CFP	Cornwall Food Programme
CFPU	Cornwall Food Production Unit
CHESS	Cornwall Healthcare Estates and Support Services
COPA	Comité des Organisations Professionelles Agricoles
CPU	Central Production Unit
Defra	Department for Environment, Food and Rural Affairs
DG	Directorate-General
ESA	Environmental Side Agreement to the North American Free Trade Act
EU	European Union
FDI	Foreign Direct Investment
FLO	Fair Trade Labelling Organisations International
FTE	Full-Time Equivalent
GAEC	Good Agricultural and Environmental Condition
GDP	Gross Domestic Product
GMO	Genetically Modified Organism
IFAT	International Fair Trade Association
IFOAM	International Federation of Organic Agriculture Movements
LACORS	Local Authorities Coordinators of Regulatory Services
LUPG	Land Use Policy Group
MS	Member States
NAFTA	North America Free Trade Agreement
NARAPs	North American Regional Action Plans
NHS	National Health Service
OECD	Organisation for Economic Co-operation and Development
PACA	Perishable Agricultural Commodities Act
PMRA	Pest Management Regulatory Authority
RCHT	Royal Cornwall Hospitals Trust
RDR	Rural Development Regulation

SEF	Social-Economic Footprint
SFP	Single Farm Payment
SPS Agreement	Sanitary and Phytosanitary Measures Agreement
TPA	Trade Promotion Authority Act (United States)
TWG	North American Free Trade Agreement Technical Working Group on Pesticides
UK	United Kingdom
URAA	Uruguay Round Agriculture Agreement
USA (US)	United States of America
VCA	Valle de Chira Association
WAFF	West African Fair Fruit Project
WTO	World Trade Organisation

List of Contributors

Jérôme Ballet is Senior Lecturer at the University of Versailles, St Quentin-en-Yvelines (UVSQ), France. His research topics are development economics, social responsibility and ethics. He is the Head of the Ethics and Socially Sustainable Development Unit at the Centre of Economics and Ethics for Environment and Development (C3ED), a mixed research unit at UVSQ. Jérôme is a founding editor of the web journal *Ethics and Economics*.

Julio A. Berdegué is Principal Researcher at Rimisp-Latin American Center for Rural Development, based in Santiago, Chile. He has worked extensively on understanding the rapid transformation of domestic and international food markets and value chains, and the welfare impact of such process on family farmers and rural small and medium enterprises.

Allan Butler is a Research Fellow with the Centre for Rural Policy Research at the University of Exeter, UK. He works on a range of projects requiring economic modelling or quantitative analysis. His main research interests include the economic modelling of agricultural systems; social network analysis; agriculture and bioenergy; organic farming and the relationship between the social, economic and ecological impacts of agriculture.

Yuna Chiffoleau is both an agronomic engineer and a researcher in sociology at the French Institute for Agricultural Research. She has specialised in rural development and network analysis. She thus works to highlight the nature and the role of the 'multiplex' social relations involved in innovation and learning processes within organisations, territories or markets. She applies her approach to research on wine and local food organisations and market building. Yuna is also very active in developing multi-disciplinary approaches for both theoretical and practical issues.

David E. Cooper is Professor of Philosophy at Durham University, UK. He has held Visiting Professorships in the USA, Canada, Germany, Malta and Sri Lanka. The many books he has written or edited include ones on environmental ethics, most recently *Buddhism, Virtue and Environment* (with Simon P. James).

Fabrice Dreyfus is currently the Head of the Institut des Régions Chaudes at the University Institute for Tropical Agrofood Industries and Rural Development at Montpellier SupAgro, France. As an agronomist he developed his early research on diverse agricultural production systems and related extension environments around the world. Later he shifted to sociology to address innovation processes, mainly in the French wine sector, with a special focus on skills development in the labour force, on knowledge dynamics among farmers' peer networks, and on cognitive interactions between farmers and scientists.

Jean-Luc Dubois is Director of Research at the Institute of Research for Development, and is assigned to the University of Versailles, St Quentin-en-Yvelines (UVSQ), France. His research topics are development economics, household livelihoods, poverty and social sustainability. He is the president of IMPACT, a French network supporting the design of public policies aiming at reducing poverty and inequality.

Robert Duxbury founded *True Food Values* to provide innovative solutions to the challenges faced by businesses and organisations involved in the supply of sustainable and ethical products. As a senior consultant with an international reputation in the organic market, he gained considerable commercial and technical experience working with Sainsbury's for over two decades after which he became Certification Director at the Soil Association. He is currently Vice President of the International Organic Accreditation Service.

Irene Guijt is an independent adviser, trainer and researcher focusing on learning processes and systems in (rural) development and natural resource management, particularly where this involves collective action and social justice concerns. Her recent PhD focuses on how monitoring triggers learning. Key publications include *Participatory Learning and Action: A Trainer's Guide* (co-author), *The Myth of Community: Gender Issues in Participatory Development* (editor with M.K. Shah) and *Negotiating Learning: Collaborative Monitoring in Forest Resource Management* (editor).

Roy Heath is Sustainable Food Production Manager for Cornwall Healthcare Estates and Support Services, UK. He is fortunate in that he not only has a job that he loves, but is also able to see the difference that his work makes both to local producers and the quality of the food on the patient's plate. He has had a unique opportunity within the NHS and has used it to maximise the impact of NHS spending on food within the southwest and Cornwall.

Susanne Johansson is a researcher and consultant working at the Centre for Sustainable Agriculture at the Swedish University of Agricultural Sciences, Uppsala. She has a doctoral degree in agronomy and works on sustainable food consumption and methodology to evaluate resource use in food systems and trade. In her doctoral thesis she developed the foodprint concept through devising methods to visualise resource use and environmental support for the food consumed in Sweden.

Matt Lobley is Assistant Director at the Centre for Rural Policy Research, University of Exeter, UK. His main research interests relate to the role of farm households in the management of the countryside, the environmental and social impacts of agricultural restructuring and the rural development potential of organic farming.

Stewart Lockie is Associate Professor of Rural and Environmental Sociology and Director of the Centre for Social Science Research at Central Queensland University, Australia. His research is focused on food, agriculture and natural resource management. Recent publications include the co-authored book *Going Organic: Mobilizing Networks for Environmentally Responsible Food Production*.

François-Régis Mahieu is Emeritus Professor of Economics at the University of Versailles, St Quentin-en-Yvelines (UVSQ), France. He has consulting and academic experience in several African countries, mainly at the University of Côte d'Ivoire as Head of the Department of Economics. His research topics are history of economics, development economics and ethics. He is a founding editor of the web journal *Ethics and Economics* and the President of the Fund for Research on Ethics and Economics (FREE).

Mike Pearson is Head of Hotel Services for Cornwall Healthcare Estates and Support Services. He is a passionate believer in the role that a large NHS Trust has to play in the sustainable development of the community that it serves. As director of the Cornwall Food Programme (CFP) in the UK, Mike is a great advocate of 'local food for local people', and is proud of the success of the CFP and initiatives that are taking it in new directions.

Thomas Reardon is Professor at the Department of Agricultural Economics, Michigan State University. He is a leading expert on the rapid expansion of supermarkets in developing countries and the effects of this process on the transformation of food markets and different types of agents along the value chains

Matthew Reed is a Senior Research Fellow at the Countryside and Community Research Institute in the UK. His specialist areas of research are the organic food and farming movement, social movements and the role of food in rural development. He is currently writing a book about organic food and farming as a global social movement.

Martina Schäfer is Assistant Professor of Sustainability Research at the Center of Science and Technology, Technical University of Berlin, Germany. From 2002 to 2007 she coordinated the interdisciplinary research group 'Regional Wealth Reconsidered' (www.regionalerwohlstand.de). Her main interests are sustainable agriculture and nutrition, sustainable consumption, sustainable regional development and the development of sustainability indicators.

Jean-Marc Touzard is a Researcher in Institutional Economics at the French National Institute for Agricultural Research. His line of research is focused on innovation processes in the agrifood industry and in agricultural cooperatives. In particular, he has carried out research programmes on the 'quality shift' in the French wine industry. He is currently working on the effects of agrifood innovations on sustainable development.

Edith van Walsum lived and worked as a field-based development professional in West Africa and India for over 15 years. She has worked as a consultant, trainer and lecturer and is presently Director of ILEIA (Centre for Information on Low External Input and Sustainable Agriculture), an international resource centre for sustainable agriculture. Her focus is on strengthening the capacity of farmers and organisations to develop ecologically sound and socially just agriculture, and on processes of scaling-up and mainstreaming of innovations in agro-ecology. Edith has published several papers and articles on these subjects.

Megan Waples is an attorney practising in Denver, Colorado. She has a BA in Environmental Studies from Brown University and a JD from University of Connecticut School of Law. She was previously a Program Associate at the Rockefeller Brothers Fund, where she focused on climate change and issues of global trade and governance, and an environmental management consultant.

Woodrow (Woody) Wilson originally comes from Johannesburg in South Africa. He has a wealth of experience as a packaged goods food marketer acquired over 25 years of international practice and experience. He is currently living in Canada, and is involved with the Sustainable Agriculture movement in that country. Establishing value chains is his speciality.

Foreword

Professor Jules Pretty OBE, University of Essex, UK

In the past two generations, the diets of most people in industrialised countries, and of an increasing number of those in developing countries, have changed enormously. We have undergone what Barry Popkin calls a nutrition transition – choosing diets high in refined cereals, sugars and saturated fats, and generally low in fruit, vegetables and fish. Large numbers of people now consume more food calories than they burn, along with too many simple sugars, saturated fats and an excess of salt. Ironically, just as food shortages had been largely conquered in industrialised countries, so has come a recognition that ill-health arising from food is now a major public health cost. We seem to know that diet and physical activity are critical determinants of physical and mental well-being, and can substantially increase life expectancy, yet we seem strangely unable to do anything about changing an inevitable slide into deep trouble.

The curious thing is that we do know that the Mediterranean diet identified by Ancel Keys in the 1960s is the gold standard. It is high in fruit, vegetables and carbohydrates, low in meat, some fish and olive oil (an unsaturated fat). Such a diet seems to make us well – or at least protects against ill-health. It is the source of the public health messages that encourage us to eat five fruit and vegetable portions a day. Again, we know about these targets, but cannot seem to do anything much about them. In many industrialised countries, only very small numbers of children eat at least the recommended amount of fruit and vegetable daily.

Diet-related illness now has severe and costly public health consequences. According to the Eurodiet study published in 2001, in the second half of the 20th century, most of Europe saw 'a very substantial increase in a number of chronic diseases in adult life. These become worse with age and are multifactorial. The principal factors, however, are diet and inactivity in coronary heart disease, strokes, obesity, maturity onset diabetes mellitus, gall-stones, osteoporosis and several cancers'. Worse still, it concluded that 'disabilities associated with high intakes of saturated fat and inadequate intakes of vegetable and fruit, together with a sedentary lifestyle, exceed the cost of tobacco use'. Some problems do arise from nutritional deficiencies of iron, iodide, folic acid, vitamin D and omega-3 polyunsaturated fatty acids, but much more serious is the excess consumption of energy and fat (causing obesity), sodium as salt (high blood pressure), saturated and trans fats (heart disease) and refined sugars (diabetes and dental caries). Diet is also a factor in about a third of cancer cases in industrialised countries.

Worryingly, it is not only North Americans and Europeans who are suffering from poor diets. In some developing countries, such as Brazil, Colombia, Costa Rica, Cuba,

Chile, Ghana, Mexico, Peru and Tunisia, overweight people now outnumber the hungry. Across the world, there are thought to be about a billion people overweight, of whom about half are obese. The likelihood of obesity is ten times greater for children if both parents are obese, and obesity during childhood tends to persist into adulthood. Childhood obesity also greatly increases the likelihood of acquiring type II diabetes in adulthood, and some have said that this generation of children may substantially pre-decease its parents. It is almost too much to bear. What can be done?

We eat every day, and only vote every four or five years (if we choose to or are allowed to). Yet eating is a vote for one food chain over another, thus affecting land management, transportation, manufacture, supermarkets and jobs, and so determining whether some will succeed and others fail. Yet our choices are not made with free will. We would like to think they are – but that is a mistake. Americans, for example, spend US$100 billion on fast food annually, and companies spend US$34 billion on advertising to persuade consumers to eat it. Today's half-hour television programmes in the US are four minutes shorter than they were a generation ago, to leave space for more advertisements, many of which are for food. Our choices are shaped by many local to global cultural influences – the quality of the soil, farm technology, hedgerow provenance, food advertisers and the global food trade. We must have food, and in having it we also encourage the system of production that brought it from land to larder. This means that the food system as a whole deserves description as another commons. It is something that belongs to us all – yet in an unrestrained or unregulated context, the tragedy is that we over-consume and under-invest in this commons. Worse, we appear not to appreciate the consequences.

When food is a commodity, there is little to stop over-consumption. There are no checks and balances to have us worry about the hidden costs of certain types of food production. Our current food system, despite considerable performance improvements in recent decades – it is faster, fitter and more streamlined – is still flawed. It simply is not working to the advantage of its 6.5 billion commoners. There is hunger at the tables of 800 million people. At the same time, there is obesity in hundreds of millions too. This cannot be right, yet, by our action, it already is accepted. However, collective action by producers of food, by consumers and by novel mixtures of both groups can make a difference. It is possible to create new forms of relationship, trust and understanding, leading to new cognitive constructions of food and its cultures of production.

The basic challenge for a more sustainable food and agricultural systems is to make best use of available natural and social resources. Farming does not have to produce its food by damaging or destroying the environment. Farms can be productive and farmers earn a decent living while protecting the landscape and its natural resources for future generations. Farming does not have to be dislocated from local rural cultures, as sustainable agriculture, with its need for increased knowledge, management skills and labour, offers new upstream and downstream job opportunities for businesses and people in rural areas. This suggests a logical need to emphasise agriculture's connections both to local ecologies and communities, and to consumers themselves.

This book constitutes a wake-up call: profound changes in food systems and production choices have taken place with very little input from civil society and surprisingly little oversight from national governments. These changes have pre-empted choices and removed sovereign control over food systems and production choices. If citizens and governments want to offer other choices and to bring into being other kinds of more sustainable and healthy food and farming systems, then they must act. This book shows how people are already addressing the challenges and have found effective and innovative ways forward that could be the source of, and inspiration for, much wider change – change that is practical, transformative and represents a better balance of interests and goals.

Acknowledgements

We would like to thank Professor Sten Ebbersten, Dr Lennart Salomonsson and Dr Ulrike Geber at the Swedish University of Agricultural Sciences for their tremendous encouragement at the opening stages of this book.

We would also like to thank Dymphna Evans and Martin West at Ashgate/Gower for their thoughtful support throughout. We thank the contributors for all their hard work, their responsiveness to comments and their willingness to share their new and challenging ideas. We are grateful to the reviewers of each chapter for the time they took to provide thought-provoking comments to the contributors. Some of the reviewers, all of whom wrote anonymously, are themselves contributors to the book. Their presence on the review team helped to ensure that this book maintained some internal cohesion. Other reviewers were invited as a result of their own work and interest in particular topics. Their presence helped to open up new spaces by adding fresh and provocative insights. The reviewer team was Hans Schiere, Irene Guijt, Martina Schäfer, Sara Lyons, Robert Duxbury, Jennifer Keahey, Penny Walker, Stewart Lockie, Laura Camfield, Veronica Tapp, Roger Farnworth, Elizabeth Cox and Harriet Friedmann.

Finally, we would like to thank our partners and our children for their patience and understanding over the past three years.

Chapter 1
Creating Food Futures: Trade, Ethics and the Environment

Cathy Rozel Farnworth, Janice Jiggins and Emyr Vaughan Thomas

Creating Food Futures

This book considers how we trade, process and purchase the food we eat. It draws on examples and evidence from throughout the world that indicate we are experiencing a global transformation in food supply and consumption that is placing our food security at risk. The authors ask whether there is scope for creating food futures that explicitly favour considerations beyond those of commerce and consumption. The essays challenge the idea that individuals and citizens are powerless in the face of rapid and transformational change in food systems throughout the world.

Yet as Berdegué and Reardon and Waples here highlight, the power of private commercial actors to determine how market-led transformations of food systems are governed has increased dramatically in recent years. Berdegué and Reardon argue that governments can and should mount a more decisive and urgent response in defence of the public interest because the playing field is far from level and a few players are vastly more powerful than others. Tansey and Rajotte (2008) demonstrate how intellectual property rules maintain the dominance of these powerful interests. Waples shows how trade rules and trade negotiations create and protect asymmetries along the food chain.

How willing are supermarkets to accommodate environmental and ethical considerations? Haverkamp (2007) has presented evidence that food chain businesses that create a proactive innovation strategy are paying more attention to environment-friendly product design with reduced cradle-to-grave environmental impact. However, Reed, Butler and Lobley in this book suggest that the adoption of environmental ethics in the supply chain does not necessarily ensure the adoption of a complementary concern for issues of equity and social responsibility in trading, a theme further explored by Schäfer. Duxbury reflects on the difficulties of this challenge in his analysis of his experience of introducing organic marketing to a major UK multiple retailer. In their essays, Johansson, Schäfer and Farnworth propose, with evidence, various tools and instruments that might stimulate and support such initiatives. In so doing they raise profound issues such as citizens' rights and individual and collective responsibility for social justice: issues that are something of a 'hot topic' if the spate of conferences and publications is anything to go by (see, for instance, Zoltitsch et al. 2007).

Guijt and van Walsum, Wilson, Chiffoleau, Dreyfus and Touzard, and Heath and Pearson 'get practical'. They show by means of case study analysis how suppliers and consumers are being brought into a different relation to each other in ways that make visible issues of environmental and social sustainability. They demonstrate what is achievable but also caution that much remains to be done. Thomas, Berdegué and Reardon, Ballet, Dubois and Mahieu, Cooper and Lockie take up the challenge of exploring how local innovations and initiatives can become mainstream in the marketplace. They variously explore different aspects of policy processes, livelihoods and food security, and return to the issue of democratic governance of food systems.

The issues addressed in this book have profound implications for people's lives everywhere in the world. Significant recent publications, on the basis of substantial evidence, show that our current policies, institutional arrangements and technologies for producing sufficient food for everyone and moving it to where people need and can access it, are inequitable, destructive of the natural resources that support food production and are a major contributor to the gaseous emissions feeding climate change (MEA 2004; CAWMA 2007; IPCC 2007). Our current arrangements for the production and transport of food do not have the resilience to cope with rapid changes in climate, increasing competition for land and water, the structural rise in food prices or future food demands. While there is no consensus on the ways forward, the case studies presented in this book contribute to the increasing evidence that local innovations are providing new models for how food systems might evolve in order to avert worst-case threats to food security and contribute to greater equity and resilience.

The contributors draw attention to often-overlooked or undervalued issues that have to do with institutions (the rules of the 'food game' and the procedures that govern it), the ways in which people give additional meaning and value to their food purchase choices and the processes of policy making in the public and private sectors. These issues and the processes by which they are constituted are invisible in most people's lives or taken as given and unchangeable. The failure of commercial law and public governance to keep pace with the rapid and widespread penetration of supermarkets into traditional food retailing is just one instance of the need to take stock and seek creative responses that engage the widest possible commitment to creating alternative food futures.

The overall message of this book is that 'business as usual' is not an option. Bold and committed action is necessary by public authorities to head off the corporate power that demonstrably harms small producers and restricts the choices of citizens and poor nations. The essays show how governments and donors could act more decisively to provide encouragement for diversity and innovation in food systems and to guide the decisions of private commercial interests and citizens toward productive but also more resilient, sustainable and equitable food futures. They show above all that individuals and groups of like-minded social entrepreneurs can make a difference.

Outline of the Book

The book is organised in three parts. Part I sets the global scene and identifies five major themes whose implications are further explored in subsequent chapters. The opening chapter by Berdegué and Reardon notes that although attention is given to change in export-oriented food trading, most food trade remains domestic. They demonstrate the dramatic pace of change in food retail markets and procurement systems that is taking place in the domestic food trade of developing countries. They analyse with great clarity the drivers and determinants of these changes and trace how supermarkets' changing role has an impact upon commercial law, regulatory and policy frameworks and the livelihoods of small producers and retailers. Undoubted gains in efficiency and wealth creation have been brought about at the price of concentrating power in the hands of increasingly dominant supermarket chains, the exclusion of asset-poor suppliers and retailers, a narrowing of citizens' choices and the restriction of public authorities' ability to regulate the emergent food system.

Waples takes the reader deeper into the details of trade agreements that affect food supply and food markets. She shows how decisions made in the course of trade negotiations are governing emergent food systems in ways that narrow the space for domestic regulation and the prospects of agriculture-led development in the national economies of poor countries. Typically, these decisions are made by those whose expertise does not lie in the sphere of food policy, let alone in farming, natural resource management or the role of agriculture and petty food trade in poor people's livelihoods in developing countries. Rather than acting to make food trade and the governance of food supply more equitable and resilient, the details of trade agreements are increasingly tending to disempower citizens and to forbid the deployment of policy instruments that in the past have served to protect and strengthen the public interest of weaker nations.

These opening two chapters raise the question of how it comes about that policy processes in democratic states have allowed market-led processes of change to become dominant beyond what a broader consideration of the public interest might consider prudent. Thomas considers this question by examining the food and agriculture policy processes of the European Union. He shows how the mind-numbing technocratic and bureaucratic detail and decision-making procedures militate against broad participation. The complexity of effecting change in policy regimes confers a degree of stability and balance. Over time, the development of broad consensus at political levels can bring about strong policy frameworks that drive change in particular directions. The downside is that the process excludes or at least reduces the potential for local experiment and innovation to drive change in any significant way. Even the language in which policy processes are voiced tends to exclude the non-specialist. Europe's citizens might indeed in the end find that their greatest power to create more meaningful, resilient and fair food systems has been reduced to their consumption choices.

Johansson, however, points out that the simplistic assumption that food purchases reveal what people want cannot be true because food prices do not reveal the full cost of production and supply; that is, prices generally do not include environmental and social costs. She turns to the development of a new instrument – foodprint analysis – that captures a wider range of costs and helps bring about an understanding of how, where and for whom these costs arise. The analysis is applied to data from Sweden to demonstrate how far domestic consumption has become dependent on producers elsewhere who might not receive a fair price, and on farming systems that might not be sustainable.

Part I ends with a contribution from Reed, Butler and Lobley, who consider the social-economic footprint of different types of farming systems. Their analysis shows that a shift to farming systems that sustain ecological functioning does not necessarily favour the viability of farming communities and rural livelihoods or provide the full range of values that consumers might want. They argue convincingly that while forms of production such as organic farming may mitigate the environmental costs of food production, they bring about change in the relations between consumers, retailers and consumers in complex ways that do not necessarily sustain the social or economic life of rural communities. The most entrepreneurial organic farmers may disturb existing social relations and economic networks as they evolve new forms of vibrant rural relationships, organic enterprises and non-farm businesses. Simplistic policy advocacy for 'organic' may not be the most effective approach to support rural communities' combined environmental, social and economic goals.

Part II addresses head-on the challenges raised by the first five contributors. It digs deeper into the detail of specific cases, innovations, tools and proposed mechanisms for change. It opens up spaces for reflection as well as warning of the struggles that still lie ahead. It seeks to inspire while realistically noting the changes that would be needed if local innovation and evidence of alternative ways forward were to drive wider system change.

Guijt and van Walsum open by asking if there is a necessary trade-off between business models of development in food systems and the values of fair trade[1] and empowerment. If values such as these are to be embedded in market relations then what are the concomitant changes required in the institutions that govern relationships along the chain of suppliers and retailers? Guijt and van Walsum trace, by means of case studies, who pays for the social innovations, such as those successfully initiated by the Fair Trade pioneer Solidaridad and others, that attempt to level the playing field and build concern for social equity into market relations. In questioning who benefits from such innovations, the authors show that much remains to be done in order to move towards greater equity between male and female participants in fair trade systems.

Wilson argues for the necessity of developing a mechanism to establish recognition in the marketplace for sustainable practices, and specifically considers how to establish a price premium for sustainable goods in highly competitive markets. The mechanism he proposes is to create a value-based identity that is recognisable by potential purchasers who have no direct connection to the actual place of production. Wilson explores the viability of this idea in relation to the experience of the FoodTrust brand in establishing an identity for produce from Prince Edward Island in Canada. His proposal contrasts with Cooper's suggestion in Part III that direct connectivity

---

[1] In this book we follow convention by using 'fair trade' to refer to the ethics of trade in general and Fair Trade to refer to the specific activities of those engaged in setting up and running trading enterprises under Fair Trade labels.

between producers and consumers must be restored if food systems are to become more resilient.

Schäfer digs deeper into the implications of restoring place-based livelihoods rooted in local food systems by considering the social footprint of organic food chains in the Berlin-Brandenburg region of Germany. As organic producers, processors and retailers have expanded beyond their initial niche they have come under increasing market pressure in competition with mainstream food chain actors. This has forced many to withdraw from a range of non-economic activities with which their earlier efforts were associated and that served to identify the ethical spaces that they created in the social lie of the region. She suggests a number of ways in which core business can be sustained under competitive market pressures without sacrificing the social benefits of non-market activities that sustain the ethical identity and added value of the social space created by the organic movement.

Heath and Pearson describe the activities of the Cornwall Food Programme (CFP). The CFP was developed to address the food supply needs of the National Health Service (NHS) in the county of Cornwall, UK. This innovative initiative is significant in the way that it demonstrates that, if sufficiently committed, public authorities can fight against the globalisation of food sourcing and can establish local and organic food sourcing initiatives. Not only has this initiative served to secure links to local suppliers, reduced food miles and generated a significant increase in local sourcing of food, it also has secured appreciable benefits for the Cornish economy in terms of jobs and reduced leakage of money from this economically poor county. On top of all this, it provides an inspiring example of how to work around the bureaucratic and restrictive public procurement rules to forge genuine innovation.

Chiffoleau, Dreyfus and Touzard trace the historical development of wine cooperatives in Languedoc, France, and show how the socialist ideal of 'one man, one vote' in cooperative governance has been buffeted by mass marketing and the industrialisation of wine production. New times demand new strategies and today the cooperatives' members are considering whether an 'ethical approach to corporate responsibility' might allow them to sustain their idealism in the face of market pressures. The authors' analysis points to a conundrum: while the ethical commitment of Fair and Ethical Trade producer cooperatives in the South to cooperative values is rarely questioned, European growers must 'earn recognition' to establish their collective identity as fair traders and ethical growers. Although the Languedoc wine producers aspire to solidarity with a wide range of stakeholders in distant places by means of a shared identity in a fair trade network, this obliges them to confront the difficulties of negotiating shared practices, common principles and establishing mutual trust in their enforcement.

Part III looks towards the future. It opens with a contribution from Berdegué and Reardon in which they pursue the implications of the supermarket revolution they outline in Part I. They stress that the window of opportunity in which public authorities can act to mitigate negative impacts on small, asset-poor producers and local entrepreneurs occurs at the early stages of the revolution, after supermarkets have gained their first foothold but before they have moved to penetrate the hinterland of the major urban centres. They highlight the regulatory actions that can be taken to ensure that relations between producers and suppliers do not become increasingly exploitative and they sketch a new role for policy actors in shaping food retail futures.

Duxbury offers a practitioner's perspective and provides us with a rare interview with an 'insider'. He reflects openly on his experience of working with a leading multiple retailer in the UK to introduce organic produce. His assessment of the emerging context is that supermarkets increasingly are willing to respond positively to changes in consumer demand for healthy produce with social value. He suggests that multiple retailers are probably already developing 'sustainability scenarios' that move adaptively towards ensuring food security under a range of climate changes and other shocks. Farnworth 'pushes the envelope' by considering how far ethical purchasing actually supports the social values of distant producers, especially when such values might not coincide with those of consumers, even of consumers who by choice opt for 'ethical consumption'. She offers a 'quality of life toolkit' as one option for bringing such issues to the surface and allowing consumers to co-create their values in alliance with the producers.

Ballet, Dubois and Mahieu take up the issue of responsibility that is implicit in the opening chapters to Part III. They call for a pre-emptive analysis by policy makers and researchers of the possible negative social consequences of emerging relations between suppliers and retailers in a food economy that is becoming globalised and suggest action to remedy or mitigate these. The authors draw on Amartya Sen's work on capability, understood as the substantive freedom to achieve alternative purposes that a person may value doing or being, in order to propose the notion of the 'capability of well-being'. From this they build a means of measuring how the values implicit in the material characteristics of food chains influence those involved in them. They urge the necessity of greater transparency and dialogue among stakeholders about what may be revealed through such measures and wider application of the precautionary principle in guiding the evolution of food futures.

Cooper takes a robust stand on the notion of 'the environment' as the key field of significance in food futures. He argues that the market disembodies and decontextualises relationships and commodities, yet all biological relations and food products have a home address, a biological point of origin and a material presence in a specific environment. He urges the necessity of widespread social and personal re-engagement with food practices that carry an appreciation of place. Market gardening and kitchen gardening are specific practices that Cooper sees as offering viable sites for engagement for largely urban populations. Such engagement offers the opportunity to rebuild an informed and intimate understanding of the mutual interdependence between the gardener and what he or she grows. Citizen-led urban food production can reveal the ways in which the survival of our social life is dependent on our mutual communion with each other through food and the natural systems needed to sustain food supply.

Lockie closes Part III by examining critically the thesis that fair trade offers a strong way forward. He raises profound ethical questions by pointing out that the rights of poor people to a livelihood have become subject to the personal consumption choices of others. Lockie points to a contradiction in the efforts to make fair trading practices mainstream in so far as such efforts work within and against the currently dominant rules of the market. In common with Farnworth, he argues that mainstreaming may turn out to hide the plight and values of poor producers in the South from Northern consumers, and could end up imposing universal standards that again remove diversity and suppress local place-based innovation. He goes on to suggest that organic and Fair Trade standards and certification processes, no less than supermarkets' supplier contracts, may impose norms and practices that exclude or disempower particular social categories. The acceptance of mass marketing and standardisation to meet mainstream market requirements also involves a hierarchy of control that removes local decision-making power and the potential to make alternative choices. Over time it may erode Fair Trade standards under pressure from mainstream markets' core business concerns – an issue also addressed by Guijt and van Walsum. In spite of his powerful criticism of the situation, Lockie is careful to balance his arguments with an assessment of the positive potential of mainstreaming strategies to reshape food futures by shifting norms and redesigning the playing field.

The book concludes with a chapter in which the editors bring together and consider the numerous questions raised by the vivid, engaging yet self-critical contributions of the authors. The urge to create new food futures necessarily creates dilemmas and tensions as innovative practice seeks to carve out a place in the mainstream. The editors highlight where opportunities for broad collaboration may exist as well as where more decisive action to head off socially or environmentally risky choices is needed. We hope the readers of this book will be inspired to take a hand in helping to create new food futures.

References

Barrientos, S. and C. Dolan (2004), *Ethical Sourcing in the Global Food System* (London: Earthscan).

Comprehensive Assessment of Water Management in Agriculture (CAWMA) (2007), *Water for Food, Water for Life: A Comprehensive Assessment of Water Management in Agriculture* (London: Earthscan, and Colombo: International Water Management Institute).

Haverkamp, D-J. (2007), *Environmental Management and the Dutch Food and Beverage Industry* (Wageningen: Wageningen Academic Publishers).

IPPC (2007), *Summary for Policymakers of the Synthesis report of the IPCC Fourth Assessment Report* (Geneva: International Panel on Climate Change), <www.ipcc.ch/ipccreports> accessed 2 January 2008.

Millennium Ecosystem Assessment (MEA) (2004), *Reports* (Millennium Ecosystem Assessment, coordinated by UNEP), <www.millenniumassessment.org> accessed 2 January 2008.

Tansey, G. and T. Rajotte (eds) (2008), *The Future Control of Food. A Guide to International Negotiations and Rules on Intellectual Property, Biodiversity and Food Security* (London: Earthscan).

Ton, G., J. Byman and J. Oorthuizen (2007), *Producer Organisations and Market Chains* (Wageningen: Wageningen Academic Publishers).

Zoltitsch, W., C. Winkler, S. Waiblinger and A. Halberger (eds) (2007), *Sustainable Food Production and Ethics* (Wageningen: Wageningen Academic Publishers).

PART I
The Big Picture: Innovations that Enable Action

Chapter 2

The Retail-Led Transformation of Agrifood Systems

Julio A. Berdegué and Thomas Reardon

When it comes to family farmers, in particular the poor, domestic food markets are of the outmost importance. Despite the attention paid by donors and governments to the food export market as a stimulus for pro-poor growth and poverty reduction in developing countries, the bulk of the agricultural output of developing countries is absorbed by domestic demand, with only a relatively small share destined for the international market (less than one-quarter in Latin America and certainly less than that in Africa and Asia; Berdegué et al. 2006). Only a tiny minority of small-scale farmers are engaged in the export market; even in Chile, a developing country whose agriculture is almost fully oriented to the export market, less than 5,000 family farmers are primarily dedicated to the production of agricultural export products (ODEPA 2002).

Donors and policy makers often believe that export markets are where the action is; for them, developing country food markets are stagnant waters where nothing much is happening. In fact, deep and rapid transformations are changing the structure, organization and dynamics of domestic food markets in these countries. It is here that the prospects of the vast majority of small farmers are being decided. Supermarkets are the central actors in this play; they are to a large extent also responsible for writing the script and directing the action.

Our purpose in this opening chapter is to discuss the trends in the spread of supermarkets in developing countries and to analyse the determinants of the 'supermarket revolution'.

Change in Food Retail in Developing Countries

Supermarkets have been around in a number of developing countries for half a century (Holton 1953, Galbraith and Holton 1965, Goldman 1974), serving upper-middle or rich consumers located mainly in large cities and consisting nearly exclusively of chains developed by domestic capital. In the 1990s supermarkets spread rapidly from their initial base to encompass other urban areas and socioeconomic strata, and offered a larger range of products. The massive entry of foreign chains was perhaps the most important spark that fuelled the 'take-off' and rapid diffusion.

Diffusion of supermarkets over regions and countries

The pattern of spread is taking place in three established waves; a fourth wave is gathering force. The first wave of take-off was experienced in the early to mid 1990s and included much of South America and East Asia outside China, South Africa and several of the former socialist republics of Central Europe and the Baltic region. In these countries the average share of food retail held by supermarkets went from approximately 10–20 per cent in the 1990s to 50–60 per cent in the early 2000s (Reardon and Berdegué 2002). The frontrunners included Argentina, where supermarkets' share in food retail had reached 60 per cent by 2002 (Gutman 2002), 75 per cent in Brazil (Farina 2002) and 55 per cent in the Czech Republic (Dries et al. 2004). It took these frontrunners only ten years to experience the supermarket diffusion that had taken five decades in the USA and the UK.

A second set of countries perched at the tail end of the first wave. They include Costa Rica and Chile, where supermarkets' share in food retail in 2002 was approximately 50 per cent (Alvarado and Charnel, 2002; Reardon and Berdegué 2002, Berdegué et al. 2005); in South Korea it reached 50 per cent in 2003 (Lee and Reardon 2005), approximately 50 per cent each in the Philippines and Thailand (Manalili 2005, Thailand Development Research Institute 2002), and 55 per cent in South Africa (Weatherspoon and Reardon 2003).

In the second-wave countries the share of supermarkets increased from about 5–10 per cent in 1990 to 30–50 per cent by the early 2000s. Examples include Mexico (56 per cent share of supermarkets in total retail; ANTAD 2005, Reardon et al. 2006a), Ecuador with 40 per cent in 2003 (Alarcon 2003), Colombia (47 per cent share; de Hernandez 2004), Guatemala (36 per cent in 2002; Orellana and Vasquez 2004), Indonesia with 30 per cent (Rangkuti 2003), and Bulgaria with 25 per cent (Dries et al. 2004).

The take-off in third-wave countries occurred only in the late 1990s or early 2000s, with supermarkets' share reaching about 10–20 per cent of national food retail by around 2003. Supermarkets for instance in Kenya (Neven and Reardon 2004), Nicaragua (Balsevich et al. 2006a) and Vietnam (Phan 2004) each acquired 20 per cent of the urban food retail market.

China and India are fascinating third-wave cases. They were the foremost destinations in the world for foreign direct investment (FDI) in the retail sector in 2004 (Burt 2004), with India ranking first and China second in the AT Kearney 'Global Retail Development Index' in 2005 and 2006 (Hindu Business Line 2006). Modern retail in China takes roughly 10 per cent of national food retail and 30 per cent of urban food markets (Hu et al. 2004a). The national share in India is less than 5 per cent, although the exact share is difficult to establish, with McKinsey (2001) reporting 2 per cent and Singh (2004) only 0.4 per cent. The market is still quite traditional and fragmented (Anand and Nambiar 2004). It is somewhat anomalous that China and India are latecomers in the third wave because their demand-side characteristics (income, absolute side of the middle-class population, urbanisation rate, share of women in the workforce) are similar to those of many countries in the second wave. The main reason for the lag is the severe constraints on retail FDI that were progressively relaxed in China only in the 1990s and partially relaxed in India in 2000.

China had no supermarkets in 1989 and food retail was nearly completely controlled by the government. By 2003 the supermarkets were generating US$71 billion a year in sales. Their share had climbed to 13 per cent of national food retail and 30 per cent of urban food retail, growing at the fastest rate in the world at 30–40 per cent a year (Hu et al. 2004a). The progressive liberalisation of retail FDI started in 1992 and culminated in 2004 as a provision of China's accession to the World Trade Organisation (WTO). FDI drove intense competition in investment among foreign chains and between foreign and domestic chains. The wholesale sector also expanded during the 1990s.

India is perhaps a decade behind China in FDI liberalisation. The Indian government in 2006 allowed single-brand foreign firms to own 51 per cent of retail joint ventures. But multiple-brand firms such as Wal-Mart and Tesco are still barred as sole enterprises at the retail level, although they can set up wholesale operations and they may enter joint ventures. Industry observers note that the major global chains expect that liberalisation will continue: since 2004 major investments and joint ventures have been announced by such major global and regional players as Wal-Mart, Carrefour, Tesco, South Africa's Shoprite, Hong Kong's Dairy Farm and Germany's Metro (CIES 2005, PlanetRetail several dates in 2004, and 2006). Reliance Industries, the largest private company in India, in October 2006 launched one of the most dramatic retail investments ever in the developing world. It announced it would make an investment of US$5.6 billion over the next five years (note that this is some 25 per cent larger than the already massive yearly rate of Wal-Mart investment in Mexico), building thousands of supermarkets, hypermarkets, discount stores and building thousands of so-called agrihubs in an 'attempt to build and forge strong and enduring bonds with millions of farmers' (PlanetRetail 2006f). This in turn has spurred other competitive domestic investment.

Geographic spread within a country

Supermarkets tend to start in large cities and then spread to intermediate cities and towns and out to small towns in rural areas. The richest and largest market is entered first because of the highest profit per capital invested. Competition and saturation of the initial base drives investment by the chain into a series of subsequent markets. The gross return declines but there are cost savings resulting from economies of scale and innovation in the procurement system (discussed below). Often the multinational chain acquires or initiates a joint venture with a large domestic chain and both buy up smaller local chains operating in the various regions of a country. The competition from the larger chains in turn pushes intermediate city-based chains to extend into the cities' hinterland towns, where they seek refuge from the increasing competition in their base market. This process accelerates the diffusion of supermarkets into an expanding geographic frontier.

Examples of this pattern are given for Argentina in Gutman (2002), Chile (Faiguenbaum et al. 2002), Central and Eastern Europe (in Dries et al. 2004, Dries and Reardon 2005), China (Hu et al. 2004a), and Indonesia (Natawidjaja et al. 2006).

Reardon et al. (2006b) review illustrative evidence of supermarket chains' expansion into small rural towns in Bulgaria, China, India, Indonesia, Mexico, Poland, South Africa and Vietnam. The upshot is that what begins as a transformation of big-city retail ends as a transformation of small rural town retail.

Diffusion of consumer segments and socioeconomic strata

Supermarkets apply the same business logic to increasing their customer base, focusing first on upper-income consumer segments, then moving into the middle class and finally into the markets of the urban poor. The penetration rates beyond the initial core of a chain's operation (large-city, upper-income segment) depend on several inter-related factors: the more advanced the general penetration, the broader the diffusion; the degree to which the procurement system of the leading chains has been modernised (leading to cost reductions that can be passed on as price reductions to win over poorer consumers, while maintaining profits); and the product category (with broader diffusion in processed products, less in semi-processed and least in fresh products), as discussed further below. Thus, for example, the typical small store of the Lianhua chain operating in the small towns in the hinterland of Zhejiang in China (that is, a first-wave internal zone in a third-wave country), carries cheap dry goods for poor consumers while a Carrefour hypermarket in Shanghai carries a full line of fresh products that would rival its stores in Paris.

Diversification of shop formats As modern retail spreads, the shop format tends to diversify to facilitate the differentiation among consumers and locations. For example, in order to penetrate the markets of inner cities and small towns where space is limited and the product assortment can be narrow, chains use discount stores, convenience stores and small supermarkets. For instance in 2006–7 in Mexico Wal-Mart and Soriana opened small-format supermarkets in the smaller towns. In contrast, chains use large supermarket and hypermarket formats to penetrate suburbs and large cities where transportation is available. Zoning regulations condition these choices. Tesco, for example, has been opening small-format city centre stores in downtown Bangkok, where it cannot open hypermarkets. Chains also open small, focused stores offering hard discounts and convenience stores to compete with traditional neighbourhood shops on price. A typical example is that of the southern Indian supermarket chain Trinethra that in October 2006 (PlanetRetail 2006g) opened a chain of Trinethra Quick Shops selling the 3000 types of products that represent 70–80 per cent of its supermarkets' sales.

Diffusion of product categories

Supermarket penetration is most prominent and starts earlier in processed food because of economies of scale in procurement as well as direct relations with processed food manufacturers. In China supermarkets very quickly took over staples and packaged food retail in the top 60 cities between the late 1990s and the early 2000s (ACNielsen 2002), as they had done in Hong Kong in the 1980s (Goldman et al. 1999) and in Argentina in the 1980s and 1990s (Gutman 2002).

Next come semi-processed foods (such as dairy products, meat and fruit). Supermarket chains again have advantages over family-run stores and wet market operators (suppliers of perishable fresh produce) because of economies of scale and their relations with major processors and packers. Goldman et al. (1999) point this out in the case of Hong Kong where supermarkets gained market share quickly in the 1980s and 1990s in fruit and meats but had difficulties making major headway in fish and vegetables. For chicken in Argentina (Gutman 2002) and beef in Chile (Faiguenbaum et al 2002) and in Costa Rica (Balsevich et al. 2006b) supermarkets quickly penetrated the commodity markets where large chilling facilities and arrangements with the processors lower the costs for the chains compared to traditional butchers. Market shocks may further increase supermarkets' share. Phan and Reardon (2006) show that there was a large shift in consumer poultry purchases from small shops and wet markets to supermarkets when avian influenza emerged in Vietnam. Supermarkets also take over the retail of dairy products rapidly and provide a major boost to dairy market development and product diversification (for China, see Hu et al. 2004b; for Russia, Dries and Reardon 2005; for Zambia, Neven et al. 2006; for Poland, Wilkin et al. 2006; for Chile, Faiguenbaum et al. 2002; for Brazil and Argentina, Farina et al. 2005).

Supermarkets have the lowest market share and the slowest penetration in fresh vegetables. This is also the case in developed countries such as the USA and France (Levenstein 1988; Codron et al. 2003). The shares of supermarkets in overall food retail compared to fresh produce are in Guatemala 35 per cent and 10 per cent respectively (Hernández et al. 2007); in Mexico, 56 per cent and 25 per cent (Reardon et al. 2006a, ANTAD 2005); in Brazil, 75 per cent and 50 per cent (Farina 2002).

Determinants of the Diffusion of Supermarkets in Developing Countries

The inter-country, inter-regional and intra-country diffusion patterns described above are roughly correlated with four factors: socioeconomic, related to the demand side of retail services; foreign policies driving FDI that condition the supply side of retail services; domestic policies affecting supermarket diffusion; and procurement system modernisation affecting the supply-side of retail services.

Demand-side drivers

There are two sets of demand-side factors that influence demand for supermarket services in developing countries. First, increasing rates of urbanisation from the 1960s and the entry of women into the workforce outside the home increased the opportunity cost of women's time and their incentive to seek shopping convenience and processed foods in order to save home preparation time. This has been reinforced by growth in the ownership of refrigerators, resulting in an increased ability to shift from daily to weekly or monthly shopping. Growing access to cars and improved public transport further support this trend.

Secondly, real per capita income growth along with the rise of a middle class increases demand for processed foods. This offers an entry point for supermarkets as they can offer greater variety and lower costs than traditional retailers because of economies of scale in procurement and the concomitant arrangements with large processors.

Supply-side drivers: foreign direct investment

The hitherto missing element in the post-1990s rapid take-off was the removal of stringent policies against retail FDI. Starting in the early 1990s there was a series of partial or full liberalisations of retail FDI. Often such provisions were included to some degree in structural adjustment programmes and bilateral or multilateral trade agreements such as the North American Free Trade Agreement (NAFTA). Sometimes the removal of the barriers occurred well after trade liberalisation, as in Indonesia, the Philippines, and Thailand; it was resisted for some time as local retailers prepared for the opening that then occurred in 1998 in Indonesia and in 2000 in the other two countries (Cabochan 2005 and Manalili 2005).

The dominant pattern so far has been for the investment to flow from Western European and US global multinationals – mainly Carrefour (France), Wal-Mart (USA), Ahold (the Netherlands), Metro (Germany) and Tesco (UK). These five companies taken together have roughly US$600 billion of sales a year. A secondary but important flow has come from chains that from the global perspective are in the second rank but which often are leading chains in a particular market, that have invested in emergent retail multinationals in their own or nearby regions. Examples include Japanese, Thai, Taiwanese, and South Korean retailers moving into China, Chinese retailers into Vietnam, Hong Kong retailers into the rest of Southeast Asia and India as well as China; Slovenian retailers into Southeast Europe; Chilean retailers into Argentina; Turkish retailers into Russia; South African retailers into the rest of Africa and India; Indian retailers with plans now to enter Africa and the rest of South Asia.

The reasons for retailers to undertake FDI are several. First, multinationals based in Western Europe and the USA in the 1990s faced highly saturated and contested home markets after a period of intense consolidation. Multinationals from developing countries faced a similar situation; they often combined expansion into secondary cities with investment in neighbouring countries as a way of maintaining profits and occupation of prime retail sites as a strategy for dealing with the ingress into their regions of global multinationals.

Secondly, by moving from saturated to less-contested markets supermarket chains secured a far superior profit rate at entry. Gutman (2002) reported that Carrefour, for example, earned profit rates three times higher in Argentina than in France. The capital advantages and access to much cheaper international credit (see Shwedel 2003 for the Mexico case) of global multinationals over domestic firms meant that a large chain might enjoy several years of high profits before the market was saturated by global competitors and the limited number of large local chains. The multinationals also had access to best practices in retail and logistics management, some of which they developed as proprietary innovations.

An upshot of the intense investment competition is that the supermarket sector is increasingly and in most cases overwhelmingly foreign owned and consolidated.

The so-called multinationalisation of the sector is illustrated by the case of Latin America, where global multinationals constitute roughly 70–80 per cent of the top five chains in most countries; the top five chains in each country have taken 65 per cent of the supermarket sector, and 60 per cent of the Latin American food market is controlled by supermarkets. The consolidation has taken place mainly via foreign acquisition of local chains and secondarily by larger domestic chains absorbing smaller chains and independents. The end result is that about 40 per cent of all the food retailed in Latin America is sold by a handful of companies, most of which are large multinational corporations. The process continues to deepen in Latin America, exemplified by Wal-Mart's expansion from the USA into Mexico and Central America so that this single firm now constitutes the unchallenged dominant force in an increasingly integrated food system that extends from the US border with Canada to the Panama Canal.

Supply-side drivers: modernisation of retailers' procurement systems

As retail FDI poured into developing countries over the past decade, domestic chains made competitive investments and the surviving traditional retailers strove to compete on cost and quality. The growing intensity of competition meant that survivors had to reduce costs in order to penetrate the mass market and raise quality to hold on to and deepen the market among middle-class clientele. A crucial instrument in cutting costs and increasing quality was the modernisation of procurement systems.

The procurement system of early supermarkets did not differ much from that used by traditional retailers. Each store procured its own products or one store was used as an entrepôt for a few neighbouring stores; products were procured from the traditional wholesale markets; retailers relied on spot markets rather than on contracts with suppliers; and retailers relied on public quality and safety standards where these existed. Wholesalers continued to hold dominant positions. This system had significant disadvantages from the perspective of the supermarkets: low or no standards for quality and/or safety, inconsistent volumes and quality and high transaction costs related to the use of many small brokers. In response the supermarkets drove rapid innovation, characterised by four central trends: a move towards large, integrated procurement catchment areas; use of specialised wholesalers and logistics firms; increasing use of contracts and preferred suppliers; and evolution of private standards and/or private enforcement of public standards. We now briefly discuss each in turn.

Extension and integration of procurement catchment area   As the number of stores in a given supermarket chain grows there is a tendency to shift from a fragmented, per-store, procurement system to a distribution centre serving several stores in a given zone or district and eventually the whole country. The catchment area of a distribution centre or set of centres usually starts as a geographic zone (such as northeast China) and then broadens to several distribution centres representing a centralised system for procurement over all zones in a country (such as Soriana's five distribution centres in Mexico).

The process of integration and centralisation relies on fewer procurement officers, increased use of centralised warehouses, centralisation of procurement decision making and in the physical distribution of produce. Centralisation increases efficiency by reducing coordination and other transaction costs (although it may increase transport costs by extra movement of the actual products). China Resources Enterprise (2002), for example, noted that it saved 40 per cent in distribution costs by combining modern logistics with centralised distribution in its two large new distribution centres in southern China.

The next step is to set up a system of distribution centres to allow coordinated procurement over a set of countries, a special form of intra-firm trade that usually forms part of the progressive entry of a global multinational into the countries of a given sub-region. Examples include Tesco's entry into Thailand, Korea and then China, and Ahold's entry in the early 2000s into Costa Rica, Nicaragua, Honduras, El Salvador and Guatemala through partnership with two regional multinational chains.

Shift from traditional to specialised wholesalers and logistics firms The second trend is a shift from exclusive reliance on spot markets (in particular, traditional wholesale markets and brokers) towards growing use of wholesalers specialised in a product category and dedicated to the supermarket sector as a main or the main client. These specialised wholesalers are able to cut costs and enforce private standards and contracts with suppliers on behalf of the supermarkets. Examples from Thailand are given in Boselie (2002), from the Philippines in Digal and Concepcion (2004), in Indonesia in Natawidjaja et al. (2006) and in Central America in Berdegué et al. (2005).

As noted in the case of Bimandiri (Natawidjaja et al. 2006) these wholesalers are expanding their operations beyond their point of origin to follow the expansion of the supermarket chains they supply. Examples include Hortifruti, which has become a multinational wholesaler supplying the supermarket chain CSU as it moved from its Costa Rica base into Nicaragua and Honduras, and Bimandiri, which has been expanding from its base in west Java into other parts of Indonesia, accompanying Carrefour's market expansion (Natawidjaja et al. 2006).

Retail chains increasingly outsource logistics and wholesale distribution functions by entering joint ventures with other firms. An example is the decision by Wu-Mei of China (CIES 2002) to build a large distribution centre operated jointly with Tibbett and Britten Logistics, a British multinational. Ahold's distribution centre for fruit and vegetables in Thailand is operated in partnership with TNT Logistics of the Netherlands (Boselie 2002).

Shift from spot market to implicit contracts or preferred supplier lists There is mounting evidence of chains and/or their specialised wholesalers entering into preferred supplier relationships with processors and farmers. The arrangements constitute informal contracts (Hueth et al. 1999). Chains and/or their specialised wholesalers tend to make this move where there is the greatest need for quality and consistency and where farmers or processors are associated or are individually large (thus lowering transaction costs). Research on preferred supplier systems is in its infancy and there are no systematic calculations yet available of the share of producers operating under such contracts. It is likely that they are still a minor proportion of the total number of producers supplying supermarket channels (see Boselie 2002 for Thailand; Manalili 2005 and Digal and Concepcion 2004 for the Philippines; Hu et al. 2004a for Shanghai; Dries and Reardon 2005 for Russia).

The contract is established when the retailer (via their wholesaler or directly) lists a supplier, the act of listing constituting an informal but effective contract (Hueth et al. 1999) and delisting carrying some tangible or intangible cost. Contracts serve as incentives to the suppliers to stay with the buyer and over time make the investments necessary to meet the retailer's specifications regarding the products supplied. The retailers are assured of on-time delivery and the delivery of products with desired quality attributes.

The contracts sometimes include direct or indirect assistance for farmers to make investments in human capital, management, input quality and basic equipment. Evidence is emerging that for many small farms these assistance programmes are the only source of such inputs and assistance; this is especially the case where public systems have been dismantled or coverage is inadequate.

There is evidence of interlinked product and factor markets emerging under the stimulus of preferred supplier contracts. Output and credit markets become linked when the listing of a farmer by a supermarket serves as collateral for credit. The Metro chain in Croatia, for instance, by informing the bank that their strawberry suppliers would have contracts with Metro, secured from the local bank the funding needed by farmers for greenhouse investments

Private standards and private enforcement of public standards The fourth trend is the increase of private quality and safety standards that have been developed and implemented by supermarket chains and large-scale processors as well as through the private enforcement of public standards (Reardon et al. 2001). This trend is a crucial aspect of the imposition of product standards that serve to coordinate supply chains by standardising product requirements across suppliers who may be located in many regions or countries, thereby enhancing efficiency and lowering the transaction costs of the supermarket chains' operations.

The private standards of a given chain may be designed also to ensure (at a minimum) that public standards are met in all the markets in which the retail chain operates. Often in the case of regional and global chains the private standard is set at the international level of the chain and imposed in the various countries that supply products either for the local stores of the chain or for the overall chain. This has led to an international diffusion of private standards.

The marked heterogeneity of retail procurement modernisation The degree of change in retail procurement systems varies greatly, reflecting the heterogeneity of incentives and capacity of the chains, products and countries involved. In some contexts the change process is in its infancy and in others is well advanced. The main patterns are as follows. At first, procurement modernisation is in general confined to the leading four or five chains per country that have the capacity to undertake the investments required. Because of the cost reduction afforded by the changes, late adopters can become non-competitive and targets for the many mergers and acquisitions occurring yearly. Once a procurement innovation is made, bringing a concomitant spike in profits and dip in costs compared to competitors, late adopters are taken over and competitors push hard to catch up. Frontrunners must again innovate if they are to stay ahead, thus propelling successive waves of technological and organisational change in procurement systems.

Diffusion of any change in the system varies also by type of product, typically occurring first in processed, then semi-processed and finally in fresh products. In Mexico, the leading chains undertook procurement modernisation in processed goods in the late 1980s and early 1990s, aided by parallel modernisation of supply systems by the major processors; then modernisation of the procurement of semi-fresh products occurred in the mid 1990s, and only at the start of the twenty-first century has the beginnings of modernisation of fresh produce procurement been evident (Reardon et al. 2006a).

There can be substantial variation between sub-categories of products. Berdegué et al. (2005) show that supermarkets in Guatemala moved as early as 2000 to modernise procurement of several large commodities such as tomatoes and some high-value niche products such as lettuce, but they have continued to rely on traditional wholesalers for nearly half of their produce, mainly in the medium- and low-volume categories. Codron et al. (2004) found similar trends in Turkey and Morocco. Digal and Concepcion (2004) illustrate the case in the Philippines where, within the general category of mangoes, chains tend to source processed mangoes centrally (and directly from a large processor such as San Miguel Foods) while for fresh mangoes they may source store by store or zonal depot by zonal depot. Factors such as perishability, availability of a large supplier, transaction costs and seasonality play a role in these decisions. The extent of diffusion differs sharply also among countries, partly related to the degree of competition caused by relative saturation and partly by conditions in the country on the supply side (Wang et al. 2006).

These points are important because they demonstrate on the one hand the extent to which the retail transformation directly affects the wholesale sector, and on the other hand the extent to which the transformation affects processors and farmers and thus the 'upstream' of the agrifood system. If the retailers continued to buy from the traditional wholesale sector, and that sector did not change under the influence of changes in the retail market, then the farmer and processor would not perceive a change in their market conditions arising from the supermarket revolution.

The role of domestic regulation in supermarket diffusion

Domestic regulation of the commercial sector can either promote supermarket diffusion or hinder it. Here we focus on the domestic regulations that have promoted supermarket diffusion and constrained traditional retail development because they appear to be an additional key factor in determining the rapid diffusion of supermarkets in developing regions.

Some governments invest directly in modern retail, explicitly to modernise the food distribution sector as well as generate revenue for government. For example, in China there is investment by the state and by municipal governments in the top three Chinese chains today: Lianhua, Hualian, and Nonggongshang (managed by the municipal government of Shanghai). State-sponsored companies get easy access to credit, cheap real estate and other benefits. This is often a factor in the ability of domestic chains to compete with foreign chains (Hu et al. 2004a). Municipal and state governments sometimes provide incentives for supermarket location in their areas, again as a modernisation and tax revenue generator. Examples include tax incentive policies in South Korea (Lee and Reardon 2005) and Russia (Dries and Reardon 2005).

In many countries there is government regulation of wet markets that by law or in practice constrains their development. The usual reasons given are that wet markets operate in the informal sector and do not pay taxes, can cause street congestion, can be unhygienic and sometimes are considered drags on the modernisation of commerce. Many governments impose strict zoning limits and hygiene regulations on wet markets. The government of China has gone a step further by actively working to stop wet market development (for example, banning new start-ups and requiring existing wet markets to move outside the main territory of the large cities) and in 2003 introduced a policy to convert wet markets to supermarkets.

The Retail-Led Transformation of Agrifood Systems

This chapter has presented the unprecedented speed, scale and scope of the market-led processes driving the supermarket revolution. It shows how foreign-owned chains and a handful of large domestic competitors have come to dominate the domestic retail food markets in increasing numbers of developing countries and to transform traditional procurement systems. It further shows how the processes of consolidation and the nature of supermarket–supplier relations have left a relatively small number of actors in an overwhelmingly powerful position with respect to their suppliers and to governments. We address the impacts and policy responses in Chapter 12.

References

ACNielsen (2002) 'China Dynamics: FMCG Sales Grow 8% in 2001', <www.acnielsen.com>, accessed 14 December 2002.

Alarcon, A. (2003) 'Ecuador Retail Food Sector Report 2003', GAIN Report EC3005 (Washington DC: USDA Foreign Agricultural Service).

Alvarado, I. and K. Charmel (2002) 'The Rapid Rise of Supermarkets in Costa Rica: Impact on Horticultural Markets', *Development Policy Review* 20:4, 473–85.

Anand, V. and V. Nambiar (2004) 'India Food Retail Sector in the Global Scenario' (Hyderabad: Sathguru Management Consultants).

ANTAD (Asociacion Nacional de Tiendas de Autoservicio y Distribuidoras) (2005) 'Tipo de establecimiento donde se compre categoría de producto, 1993–1998 vs 2001–2005' (Mexico City: ANTAD).

ASERCA (2005) 'Coordinación General de Promoción Comercial y Fomento a las Exportaciones', PowerPoint presentation, December (Mexico City: SAGARPA).

Balsevich, F., J. Berdegué and T. Reardon (2006a) 'Supermarkets, New-Generation Wholesalers, Tomato Farmers, and NGOs in Nicaragua', Staff Paper 2006-03 (East Lansing: Department of Agricultural Economics, Michigan State University).

Balsevich, F., P. Schuetz and E. Perez (2006b) 'Cattle Producers' Participation in Market Channels in Central America: Supermarkets, Processors, and Auctions', Staff Paper 2006-01 (East Lansing: Department of Agricultural Economics, Michigan State University).

Berdegué, J.A. F. Balsevich, L. Flores and T. Reardon (2005) 'Central American Supermarkets' Private Standards of Quality and Safety in Procurement of Fresh Fruits and Vegetables', *Food Policy* 30:3, 254–269.

Berdegué, J.A., T. Reardon, F. Balsevich, A. Martínez, R. Medina, M. Aguirre and F. Echánove (2006) 'Supermarkets and Michoacán Guava Farmers in Mexico' Staff Paper 2006-16, April (East Lansing: Department of Agricultural Economics, Michigan State University).

Boselie, D. (2002) 'Business Case Description: TOPS Supply Chain Project, Thailand', KLICT International Agri Supply Chain Development Program (Den Bosch: Agrichain Competence Center).

Burt, T. (2004) 'Global Retailers Expand Markets', *Financial Times*, 22 June, 15.

Cabochan, C.V. (2005) 'Philippines: Modern Retail Trade and Policy Implications', paper presented at the Pacific Economic Cooperation Council's (PECC) Pacific Food System Outlook Annual Meeting, held 11–13 May 2005, Kunming, China.

China Resources Enterprise (CRE) (2002) 'Retailing Strategies and Execution Plan', July 2002. posted on website of China Resources Enterprise Ltd, Hong Kong <www.cre.com.hk>, accessed 6 July.

CIES (2005) 'Wal-Mart Q1 Results, Interest in India', *CIES Food Business Forum*, 13 May, no paging.

CIES Food Business Forum (2002) 'Wu-Mart', *CIES Food Business Forum*, 4 June, no paging.

CIES Food Business Forum (2006a) 'Foreign Retailers Pursue Small-Format Investment in Thailand', *CIES Food Business News*, June, no paging.

CIES Food Business Forum (2006b) 'Freeze on Hypermarket Licences in Malaysia may be Lifted', *CIES News of the Day*, 17 July, no paging.

CIES Food Business Forum (2006c) 'Retailers Faced with Prison/Fines in Thailand', *CIES News of the Day*, 4 October, no paging.

Codron J-M., F. Jacquet, R. Habib and B. Sauphanor (2003) 'Agriculture, Territoire et Environnement dans les Politiques Européennes', *Les Dossiers de l'Environnement de l'INRA* 23, 27–64.

Codron, J-M., Z. Bouhsina, F. Fort, E. Coudel and A. Puech (2004) 'Supermarkets in Low-Income Mediterranean Countries: Impacts on Horticulture Systems', *Development Policy Review* 22:5, 587–602.

de Hernandez, L. (2004) 'Colombia Retail Food Sector Annual', GAIN Report CO4011 (Washington DC: USDA Foreign Agricultural Service).

Digal, L.N. and S.B. Concepcion (2004)'The Case of the Philippines – Regoverning Markets: Securing Small Producer Participation in Restructured National and Regional Agri-Food Systems', <www.regoverningmarkets.org>, accessed 10 June 2004.

Dries, L. and T. Reardon (2005) 'Central and Eastern Europe: Impact of Food Retail Investments on the Food Chain', Report Series no. 6 (London: FAO Investment Center-EBRD Cooperation Program), February.

Dries, L., T. Reardon and J. Swinnen (2004) 'The Rapid Rise of Supermarkets in Central and Eastern Europe: Implications for the Agrifood Sector and Rural Development', *Development Policy Review* 22:5, September, 525–56.

Faiguenbaum, S., J.A. Berdegué and T. Reardon (2002) 'The Rapid Rise of Supermarkets in Chile: Effects on Dairy, Vegetable, and Beef Chains', *Development Policy Review* 20:4, September, 459–71.

Farina, E. (2002) 'Consolidation, Multinationalization, and Competition in Brazil: Impacts on Horticulture and Dairy Product Systems', *Development Policy Review* 20:4, September, 441–57.

Farina, E.M.M.Q., G.E. Gutman, P.J. Lavarello, R. Nunes and T. Reardon (2005) 'Private and Public Milk Standards in Argentina and Brazil', *Food Policy* 30:3, June, 302–15.

Galbraith, J.K. and R.H. Holton (1965) *Marketing Efficiency in Puerto Rico* (Cambridge, MA: Harvard University Press).

Goldman, A. (1974) 'Outreach of Consumers and the Modernization of Urban Food Retailing in Developing Countries', *Journal of Marketing* 38:4, October, 8–16.

Goldman, A., R. Krider and S. Ramaswami (1999) 'The Persistent Competitive Advantage of Traditional Food Retailers in Asia: Wet Markets' Continued Dominance in Hong Kong', *Journal of Macromarketing* 19:2, 126–39.

Gutman, G. (1997) *Transformaciones recientes en la distribución de alimentos en Argentina* (Buenos Aires: Secretaría de Agricultura, Ganadería, Pesca y Alimentación (SAGPyA) and Instituto Interamericano de Cooperación Agrícola (IICA)).

Gutman, G. (2002) 'Impact of the Rapid Rise of Supermarkets on Dairy Products Systems in Argentina', *Development Policy Review* 20:4, September, 409–27.

Hernández, R., T. Reardon and J.A. Berdegué (2007) 'Supermarkets, Wholesalers, and Tomato Growers in Guatemala', *Agricultural Economics* 36:3, 281–90.

Hindu Business Line (2004) 'Metro Cash and Carry to Help Improve Karnataka Farm Supply Chain', 5 October <www.hindubusinessline.com>, accessed 1 March 2005.

Hindu Business Line (2006) 'AT Kearney Ranks India as Top Destination for Retailers', 27 April, <www.hindubusinessline.com>, accessed 15 October 2006.

Holton, R.H. (1953) 'Marketing Structure and Economic Development', *Quarterly Journal of Economics* 67, August, 344–61.

Hu, D., T. Reardon, S. Rozelle, P. Timmer, H. Wang (2004a) 'The Emergence of Supermarkets with Chinese Characteristics: Challenges and Opportunities for China's Agricultural Development', *Development Policy Review* 2:24, September, 557–86.

Hu, D., F. Fuller and T. Reardon (2004b) 'The Impact of the Rapid Development of Supermarkets on the Dairy Industry of China', *Zhongguo Nongcun Jingji (Chinese Rural Economy)* 7:235, 12–18.

Hueth, B., E. Ligon, S. Wolf and S. Wu (1999) 'Incentive Instruments in Fruits and Vegetables Contracts: Input Control, Monitoring, Measurements, and Price Risk', *Review of Agricultural Economics* 21:2, 374–89.

Lee, J-H. and T. Reardon (2005) 'Forward Integration of an Agricultural Cooperative into the Supermarket Sector: The Case of Hanaro Club in Korea', Joint Working Paper (Seoul, Korea: Department of Industrial Economics, Chung-Ang University, and East Lansing: Department of Agricultural Economics, Michigan State University).

Levenstein, H.A. (1988) *Revolution at the Table: The Transformation of the American Diet* (New York: Oxford University Press).

McKinsey Consulting (2001) *India Retail*. Delhi: McKinsey Consulting.

Manalili, N.M. (2005) 'The Changing Map of the Philippine Retail Food Sector: The Impact on Trade and the Structure of Agriculture and the Policy Response', presentation at the Pacific Economic Cooperation Council's Pacific Food System Outlook 2005–6 Annual Meeting in Kun Ming, China, 11–13 May.

Natawidjaja, R.S., T. Perdana, E. Rasmikayati, T. Insan, S. Bahri, T. Reardon and R. Hernández (2006) 'The Effects of Retail and Wholesale Transformation on Horticulture Supply Chains in Indonesia: With Tomato Illustration from West Java', report for the World Bank (Bandung: Center for Agricultural Policy and Agribusiness Studies (CAPAS) Padjadjaran University, and East Lansing: Michigan State University), November.

Neven, D. and T. Reardon (2004) 'The Rise of Kenyan Supermarkets and Evolution of their Horticulture Product Procurement Systems', *Development Policy Review* 22:6, November, 669–99.

Neven, D., H. Katjiuongua, I. Adjosoediro, T. Reardon, P. Chuzu, G. Tembo and M. Ndiyoi (2006) 'Food Sector Transformation and Standards in Zambia: Smallholder Farmer Participation and Growth in the Dairy Sector', Staff Paper 2006-18, May (East Lansing: Michigan State University).

ODEPA (Oficina de Estudios y Políticas Agrarias del Ministerio de Agricultura) (2002) 'Clasificación de las Explotaciones Agrícolas del VI Censo Nacional Agropecuario según Tipo de Productor y Localización Geográfica', Documento de Trabajo No. 5 (Santiago, Chile: ODEPA).

Orellana, D. and E. Vasquez. (2004) 'Guatemala Retail Food Sector Annual, 2004', GAIN Report GT4018 (Washington DC: USDA Foreign Agricultural Service).

Phan, T.G.T. (2004) 'Regoverning Markets: Securing Small Producer Participation in Restructured National and Regional Agrif-food Systems: The Case of Vietnam', report to the Regoverning Markets Project, Ho Chi Minh City, Vietnam: Nong Lam University, September.

Phan, T.G.T. and T. Reardon (2006) 'Avian Influenza's Links with Poultry Market Transformation in Vietnam: Moving from Crisis to Development Strategies' (Ho Chi Minh City, Vietnam: Nong Lam University, and East Lansing: University).

PlanetRetail (2004) 'Consumers Forsake Wet Markets in Asia', *Daily News by M+M PlanetRetail*, 7 June.

PlanetRetail (2006a) 'METRO to Expand Fast in India', *Daily News*, 4 July, no paging.

PlanetRetail (2006b) 'Official Launch of WAL-MART Credit Card in China', *Daily News*, 20 September, no paging.

PlanetRetail (2006c) 'CARREFOUR Brazil Starts Banking Subsidiary', *Daily News*, 22 September, no paging.

PlanetRetail (2006d) 'CARREFOUR Thailand Sells Further Insurance Products'. *Daily News*, 27 September, no paging.

PlanetRetail (2006e) 'CARREFOUR in Talks over Indian Entry', *Daily News*, 3 October, no paging.

PlanetRetail (2006f)'RELIANCE RETAIL to Open for Business this Week', *Daily News*, 30 October, no paging.

PlanetRetail (2006g) 'TRINETHRA to Focus on Supermarkets', *Daily News*, 30 October, no paging.

Rangkuti, F. (2003) 'Indonesia Food Retail Sector Report 2003', GAIN Report ID3028, 12 November (Washington DC: United States Department of Agriculture).

Reardon, T. and J.A. Berdegué (2002) 'The Rapid Rise of Supermarkets in Latin America: Challenges and Opportunities for Development', *Development Policy Review* 20:4, September, 317–34.

Reardon, T. and E.M.M.Q. Farina (2002) 'The Rise of Private Food Quality and Safety Standards: Illustrations from Brazil', *International Food and Agricultural Management Review*, 4, 413–421.

Reardon, T. and L. Flores (2006) 'Viewpoint: "Customized Competitiveness" Strategies for Horticultural Exporters: Central America Focus with Lessons from and for other Regions', *Food Policy* 31:6, 483–503.

Reardon, T. and R. Hopkins (2006) 'The Supermarket Revolution in Developing Countries: Policies to Address Emerging Tensions among Supermarkets, Suppliers, and Traditional Retailers', *European Journal of Development Research* 18:4, 522–45.

Reardon, T. and C.P. Timmer (2007) 'Transformation of Markets for Agricultural Output in Developing Countries Since 1950: How Has Thinking Changed?', in R.E. Evenson and P. Pingali, *Handbook of Agricultural Economics, 3: Agricultural Development: Farmers, Farm Production and Farm Markets* (Amsterdam: Elsevier Press), 2808–55.

Reardon, T., J.A. Berdegué and C. P. Timmer (2005) 'Supermarketization of the Emerging Markets of the Pacific Rim: Development and Trade Implications', *Journal of Food Distribution Research* 36:1, March, 3–12.

Reardon, T., J.A. Berdegué, R. Medina, M. Aguirre, F. Echánove, A. Martínez, R. Cook, N. Tucker and F. Balsevich (2006a) 'Las Tiendas de Autoservicio – y sus Efectos sobre las Cadenas de Comercialización de Productos Hortofrutícolas en México: Implicaciones para los productores y políticas', PowerPoint presentation at the international seminar Supermercados y Desarrollo Agricola en Mexico, Morelia, Michoacan, August.

Reardon, T., J-M. Codron, L. Busch, J. Bingen and C. Harris (2001) 'Global Change in Agrifood Grades and Standards: Agribusiness Strategic Responses in Developing Countries', *International Food and Agribusiness Management Review* 2:3, 195–205.

Reardon, T., P. Pingali and K. Stamoulis (2006b) 'Impacts of Agrifood Market Transformation during Globalization on the Poor's Rural Nonfarm Employment: Lessons for Rural Business Development Programs' plenary paper presented at the meeting of the International Association of Agricultural Economists, in Queensland, Australia, 12–18 August.

Reardon, T., C.P. Timmer, C.B. Barrett and J. Berdegué (2003) 'The Rise of Supermarkets in Africa, Asia, and Latin America', *American Journal of Agricultural Economics* 85:5, December, 1140–6.

Reardon, T., G. Vrabec, D. Karakas and C. Fritsch (2003b) 'The Rapid Rise of Supermarkets in Croatia, with Implications for the Produce Distribution System', report to USAID Under the Raise/Ace Project.

Shwedel, K. (2003) 'Sector agroalimentario en México', presentation at the seminar Conglomerados y Empresas Transnacionales, Economic Commission for Latin America and the Caribbean (CEPAL), Santiago, Chile, 26–7 November.

Singh, S. (2004) 'India Retail Food Sector Report', GAIN Report IN4126 (Washington DC: USDA FAS).

Thailand Development Research Institute (2002) *The Retail Business in Thailand: Impact of the Large Scale Multinational Corporation Retailers* (Bangkok: Thailand Development Research Institute).

Wang, H., X. Dong, S. Rozelle, J. Huang and T. Reardon. (2006) 'Producing and Procuring Horticultural Crops with Chinese Characteristics: A Case Study in the Greater Beijing Area', Staff Paper 2006-05 (East Lansing: Department of Agricultural Economics, Michigan State University).

Weatherspoon, D.D. and T. Reardon (2003) 'The Rise of Supermarkets in Africa: Implications for Agrifood Systems and the Rural Poor', *Development Policy Review* 21:3, May, 333–55.

Wilkin, J., D. Milczarek, A. Malak-Rawlikowska and J. Fałkowski (2006) 'Dairy Sector in Poland', Module 1 and Module 2 Study Report. Regoverning Markets Project www.regoverningmarkets.org, draft, September.

Chapter 3

Regulation, Sovereignty and Accountability in the Food Chain

Megan Waples

Why it is Important to Understand the Regulation of Food Trade

International trade in agriculture and trade regulation strikes at the heart of our most fundamental relationship to the earth and the world around us. Food production and consumption implicate environmental policies and their impacts, social structure and social policies, personal and public health and cultural connections and choices, often in ways that the average consumer is only vaguely aware of. As the international community has aggressively pursued a free trade agenda, the ability of nations and individuals to govern the relationship between themselves and their food has weakened.

This chapter examines at a conceptual level how free trade agreements limit the ability to make choices about regulation of the food chain and how to bring increased accountability and choice back into the system. It focuses primarily on the push to reduce technical or non-tariff barriers to trade through bilateral and multilateral agreements and the impacts of those agreements on the balance of power among citizens, nations and corporations. First the structure and mechanisms by which free trade agreements limit national sovereignty are laid out, highlighting their impact on regulation of food production. The chapter then takes a closer look at the effects of the North American Free Trade Agreement (NAFTA) on the regulation and trade of pesticides in North America. It ends with an examination of the options for increasing citizen power at both the national and international level.

International Free Trade Agreements and the Balance of Sovereignty

International trade agreements bring into sharp focus fundamental questions of power, sovereignty and values. In recent decades negotiations have focused not only on reducing tariffs and subsidies that directly distort trade but also on reducing what are called non-tariff or technical barriers to trade. These, broadly construed, can mean any government action or regulation that may affect foreign goods or investors.

The expanded scope of free trade agreements comes at a high cost; it weakens the ability of national governments to make policy choices about environmental and social issues (Oloka-Onyango 2003; Rittich 2000). Rather than improving trade in order to serve the agendas of the nations involved, each nation is expected to structure its internal agendas to facilitate trade (Steinberg 1997). A core provision of the World Trade Organisation (WTO) accords states 'Each Member shall ensure the conformity of its laws, regulations and administrative procedures with its obligations as provided in the annexed Agreements' (Agreement Establishing the WTO, Art. XVI(4)). In this system trade becomes the goal in itself rather than a means to achieve the overall economic and social goals of a nation. Free trade agreements force a similar shift in the domestic governance of the food chain by attempting to create a system that elevates concerns about trade above environmental, safety and social concerns. By means of harmonisation measures and dispute resolution, trade agreements limit a nation's ability to embrace the precautionary principle or other policy priorities in regulating food production and promoting sustainable agriculture.

Harmonisation and dispute resolution

Under both NAFTA and the WTO agreements nations are required to adopt health, safety and environmental regulations and standards in the 'least trade restrictive' manner possible. Member nations under the agreements are either required or given strong incentives to adopt common measures for environmental, health and safety provisions. For example, the WTO Agreement on the Application of Sanitary and Phytosanitary Measures (SPS Agreement) places additional burdens on nations which do not 'base their sanitary and phytosanitary measures on international standards, guidelines or recommendations' (SPS Agreement, Art. 3(1)). In addition, the agreements state that a member has a right to take SPS measures within its territory that affect trade only if they are 'based on scientific principles and ... not maintained without sufficient scientific evidence' (SPS Agreement, Art. 2(2)). SPS measures may be employed only 'to the extent necessary to protect human, animal or plant life or health' (SPS Agreement, Art. 2(2)). Although the SPS Agreement allows member nations to adopt precautionary measures on a provisional basis where the relevant scientific evidence is insufficient, that ability is limited both in the text of the agreement (which imposes an obligation to review and reassess when more information becomes available: SPS Agreement, Art. 5(7)), and by decisions of the dispute resolution body, as discussed below. The General Agreement on Tariffs and Trade 1994, Article III, also has been interpreted to prohibit nations from treating physically similar goods differently based on the method of production.[1]

These requirements are given teeth in the dispute resolution process. NAFTA, the WTO and other trade agreements allow one nation's regulation to be challenged by other nations, and in the case of NAFTA and other agreements, also by foreign corporations. This dispute resolution process is binding and may force nations to change domestic laws or procedures, face sanctions or pay damages. The law governing the disputes is typically the relevant principles of international law and does not include the national laws of the nations involved. It subjects one nation's exercise of its sovereign power, which may have been completely legitimate under its own constitutional and legal principles, to binding review by a body of three private individuals who are not bound by those principles in a proceeding that is not subject

---

1 For a detailed critical explanation of harmonisation, see Public Citizen (2000).

to the same procedural safeguards as a domestic legal proceeding and that embraces only one question: whether the regulation complied with a trade agreement.[2]

The results of this process have been to narrow the grounds upon which a state may exercise its regulatory authority without facing sanctions or other penalties – an outcome that is particularly problematic with regard to our food chain, as it embodies questions beyond economics relating to safety, environmental and public health, sustainability and ethical and social values.

For example, in 1997 a WTO panel ruled against the European Union (EU) ban on artificial growth hormones used in beef after it was challenged by the US. Although the EU's ban on the sale of beef from cattle treated with six artificial hormones was applied in a non-discriminatory manner to both domestic and imported beef, the US alleged that it violated the SPS agreement. As confirmed by the findings of the WTO Appellate Body in January 1998, the ban was found to violate the WTO agreement because it set a higher standard than that of the Codex Alimentarius (an international standard-setting body) and did not have a sufficient scientific basis. The Appellate ruling stated that the EU could maintain the higher standard only if it was based on a risk assessment done pursuant to WTO-condoned risk assessment rules. The ruling further held that reliance on the 'precautionary principle' did not override the SPS Agreement or provide a justification for deviating from the rest of the agreement's requirements. Therefore, the EU was ordered to either begin imports of US beef containing the hormones or complete a risk assessment based on WTO rules. If it did not do so, or show justification for not doing so by May 1999, the EU would face sanctions by the US. After completing the risk assessment the EU continued to implement a modified version of its ban and the US applied sanctions as a result. Although in this case the EU did not relent and maintained the level of protection it deemed appropriate, it was a costly decision based on a position that is unlikely to be affordable on a regular basis.

In September 2006 another WTO panel found the EU's moratorium on approvals of genetically modified organisms (GMOs) also to be in violation of the WTO agreements. The panel held that the EU's procedures constituted undue delays that violated the agreements, and that individual national bans on GMO products violated the agreements because they were not based on adequate risk assessments. The panel ruled that 'evolving science' and the need for a 'prudent and precautionary approach' could not justify the delays. In addition, although no formal challenge has yet been mounted, the US has indicated its belief that labelling laws that inform consumers of a food's origin or content (such as an EU provision that requires labelling of food containing GMOs) may violate the trade agreements unless the information relates to scientifically established food safety concerns.

As these cases illustrate, through harmonisation and dispute resolution, free trade agreements weaken the ability of nations and their citizens to make policy choices about their food chain, even when those choices are applied in a non-discriminatory fashion to both imports and domestic products. They deter nations

---

2 Critics have identified multiple procedural problems with the dispute resolution processes, including a lack of transparency and exclusion of public participation (Nogales 2002; Lerner 2001; Public Citizen 2000).

from making independent political decisions about the level of protection they wish to embrace and the social policies they wish to promote. The heart of the problem is that our food chain embraces much more than a system of commerce. Regulation of food production involves ethical and political questions such as the treatment of agricultural workers, the obligations of a former colonial power to its former colonies, the importance of farming culture and lifestyle, the preservation of farming communities and landscapes, the treatment of farm animals and the level of risk that producers and consumers of food should face.

Investor disputes and citizen challenges

In addition to weakening nations' regulatory authority through harmonisation and dispute resolution, NAFTA and similar trade agreements provide additional authority to corporations. NAFTA allows private investors to take the government of another nation into an international arbitration process that is both private and binding upon the governmental party. Under the provisions of Chapter 11, when an investor feels its rights under the treaty have been infringed it may take that nation into binding arbitration instead of seeking a remedy in the courts of that country.

Although Chapter 11 was intended to address concerns about government expropriation of assets, the disputes decided have involved not just narrow cases of traditional expropriation but the ability of the parties to enact environmental, health and safety regulations. For example, in the *Metalclad* case a US corporation that planned to open a hazardous waste facility in Mexico challenged a local government decision to deny the construction permits and prevent operation of the landfill by designating the area as a nature preserve. The NAFTA arbitration panel found that the action constituted a 'regulatory expropriation', taking that doctrine far beyond what the national laws of Mexico or the US would support, and required the Mexican government to pay the corporation US$16 million for its 'interference' with the value of the corporation's investment. Mexico challenged the ruling in a Canadian court that reduced the award by US$1 million but upheld the substantive ruling.

Under this system, panels of private arbitrators have the authority to force a government to pay damages to a private party when the panel finds that an environmental, safety or health regulation has resulted in a loss to the investor. These provisions expand the power of multinational corporations to challenge the domestic regulatory authority of a state. Traditionally, the arena of international law was limited to nations; when a citizen or corporation was injured, only the nation could bring a claim by acting on the individual's behalf (Janis 2003). This system was intended to protect state sovereignty and manage disputes in a way that was sensitive to diplomatic issues. Although individuals have increasingly been viewed as subjects with rights in international law, particularly in the field of human rights, the ability to take the government of another nation to binding private arbitration and force the government to pay is a remarkable shift in power and authority, described by one commentator as the 'most extensive set of rights and remedies ever provided to foreign investors in an international agreement' (Nogales 2002).

The investor dispute processes is also in sharp contrast to the citizen enforcement mechanisms of NAFTA. The North American Agreement on Environmental

Cooperation, commonly referred to as the Environmental Side Agreement (ESA), was developed along with an agreement on labour cooperation to assuage the concerns of the public about the possible detrimental impacts of NAFTA. The agreement established a Commission for Environmental Cooperation (CEC) that is charged with – among many other responsibilities – overseeing complaints regarding environmental enforcement by a party (Nogales 2002).

Under the ESA a private person or non-governmental organisation may submit a petition to the Secretariat of the CEC claiming that one of the NAFTA parties is failing to enforce its environmental laws. If the Secretariat determines that the petition has merit it requests a response from the subject party. Once the response is received, the Secretariat may recommend to the Council that a factual record be developed concerning the dispute. The factual record is intended to evaluate the factual and legal basis for the petition. However, the Council is primarily a public body and it must approve development of a record by a two-thirds majority, providing the challenged government an opportunity to sidestep the process if another government agrees or cooperates with it. The Council also decides whether to make the factual record available to the public (Nogales 2002).

While the CEC private-party complaint process gives public interest advocates an international platform on which to act and theoretically binds all parties to follow a well-defined process overseen primarily by professional staff, its power is nowhere near that of a Chapter 11 dispute. There are many opportunities for the CEC to close a matter without the development of a factual record, based on substantive, procedural or political concerns (Nogales 2002). Between 1995 and 2006 the CEC closed 42 cases; in only 11 cases was a factual record developed.[3] More importantly, the process has no final outcome and lacks any enforcement mechanism. While the factual records are intended to evaluate the legal and factual basis of claims, they do not necessarily make 'findings' in the sense of determining whether the government party is in the wrong, much less dictate damages or require the party to change course (Nogales 2002). The citizen enforcement mechanism, without any binding outcome or resolution, simply lacks the power of the investor dispute resolution process.

Pesticides in North America: Harmonisation, Litigation and Arbitration

As nations barter away their ability to set domestic agendas that protect their citizens and their citizens' interests, the power of individual citizens is correspondingly reduced. Unlike corporations that under NAFTA and other treaties have gained new power in international law, citizens have no such voice. This leaves individuals with less power to address their own concerns or injuries related to their food choices. The self-imposed forces of harmonisation and dispute resolution constrain governments from making policy choices about the level of risk or protection that is appropriate in food consumption or production. Because of the conflict over labelling requirements, even the ability of individuals to make such choices for themselves may be put at

---

3 These numbers are drawn from data on the CEC website page on citizen enforcement submissions status, <http://www.cec.org/citizen/status/index.cfm?varlan=English>.

stake. And because they have no corresponding ability to bring binding actions in international law, individuals are limited to national remedies to attempt to address problems that arise. Such remedies are increasingly inadequate in the face of the realities of international commerce.

The North American experience with pesticides is an example of how these dynamics play out. The trade and use of pesticides in North America has popularly been referred to as the Circle of Poisons. Highly toxic pesticides that are banned for use in the US are manufactured there and exported to Central America. They are used by farmers who typically do not receive proper instruction in their application and who do not have access to affordable and appropriate protective gear. The produce grown with those pesticides is then shipped back to the US along with the residues.

Harmonisation to develop a common market for pesticides

Since NAFTA, the pressures fuelling this circle have become more intense. The three nations established the NAFTA Technical Working Group (TWG) on pesticides with the goal of harmonising pesticide regulation in the three countries. The goals of the TWG are to establish work-sharing among the three nations with regard to registering, assessing and regulating pesticides and '[t]o develop a North American market for pesticides while maintaining current high levels of protection' (NAFTA TWG 1998). One study of the TWG's work found that the pesticide industry, and most particularly the patent-holding pesticide producers, has increased its access to the TWG's processes while generic producers, growers and public interest groups have not (Badulescu and Baylis 2006). As a result, the costs of local firms competing with multinational patent-holding producers have increased and a comparative advantage has been created for the multinational producers.

In March 2007 the US and Canada approved the first harmonised pesticide label, allowing easier cross-border movement of that product; 12 more pesticides were in the pipeline for similar label development. (Environmental News Service 2007). In addition, the TWG has begun implementation of an 'Own-Use Import Program' that allows US growers to import certain pesticides from Canada for their own use (Environmental News Service 2007). However, the establishment of common maximum residue levels on produce has made the most progress, driven largely by existing US standards (Badulescu and Baylis 2006). This has led to concerns that Canada is compromising its more protective limits in order to facilitate trade through harmonisation (Patterson 2007). The overall picture under NAFTA is an effort to ease the movement of pesticides between the three nations, both as a product and as a residue.

Increased trade and the circle of poisons

The increased trade has increased the circulation of pesticides in trade with Mexico. Importation and use of pesticides in Mexico jumped dramatically after NAFTA went into effect. According to Coyler (2002), imports of pesticides in the first five years after NAFTA went into effect were almost four times the level of imports in the previous five; imports of insecticides, fungicides and herbicides experienced similar jumps. Meanwhile, with an increased volume of agricultural food trade, the ability to inspect food for pathogens and pesticide residues has declined (see Public Citizen 2007) and, under NAFTA, imported foods cannot be inspected more thoroughly than domestic produce.

Limits on individual justice

The increase in imports of pesticides to Mexico and Central America has heightened concern about pesticide poisonings in the region. Farm workers in particular suffer from both acute and chronic pesticide poisoning. However, workers seeking damages and accountability from US firms producing, exporting and applying the pesticides – many of which have been banned in the US based on findings that they cannot be used safely – face multiple legal challenges. Suits brought in the US are often dismissed on the basis of the doctrine of *forum non conveniens* that allows a court that would otherwise have proper jurisdiction to dismiss the case on the grounds that it would be more conveniently tried elsewhere. These decisions generally hold that the plaintiffs' home country is an adequate and more appropriate forum for the case to be brought, thereby ignoring evidence of the procedural, logistical and political problems that limit the ability of workers to bring suit in their home countries (Waples 2004).

In addition, while most multinational corporations are enterprises involving a complex corporate structure, much of national law is based on a more limited conception of single-entity corporations (Stephens 2002; Blumberg 1993). This means that even when workers can bring a suit successfully in their home country or in the US, they may not be able to obtain a judgment against the parent company and the national subsidiary may not have adequate assets to satisfy any judgments (Blumberg 1993). Moreover, in one case in which Nicaraguan workers obtained a judgment against Dole, Dow Chemical and Shell Oil in Nicaraguan courts, the workers were unable to enforce the judgment against assets in the US because the US court dismissed the claim (*Bloomberg News*, 25 October 2003).[4] Thus, as the pesticide trade increases under the auspices of trade agreements and international law, individuals who are harmed by that trade have limited recourse under the constraints of national legal principles that do not account for the realities of international trade (see Stephens 2002).

Chapter 11 and the CEC

At the international level, the CEC, through the Sound Management of Chemicals Program, has established North American Regional Action Plans (NARAPs) that

---

4 The battle over the Nicaraguan law under which the workers obtained judgment continued into the negotiations on the Central American Free Trade Agreement, as have many of the pesticide issues discussed here. For further information, see Grundberg 2007; Rosenthal 2002.

address persistent and toxic substances of common concern.[5] The NARAPs attempt to reduce the environmental and health impacts of such chemicals through regional cooperation and action. In the NARAP for lindane, a persistent organic pollutant, Canada committed to continue to assess and manage the risks for its sole remaining use as a pharmaceutical, and Mexico agreed to eliminate all agricultural, veterinary and pharmaceutical uses through a phase-out approach. The US, which had no remaining registered agricultural uses, promised to facilitate the development of alternatives for pharmaceutical uses. Agricultural use was eliminated in August 2006. Within the Persistent Organic Pollutants Review Committee lindane comes up for review in May 2009; the US still is seeking exemption for continuing pharmaceutical use. The NARAP also calls for the establishment of a tri-lateral implementation task force to oversee implementation. Yet, while the NARAPs are excellent models of regional cooperation and demonstrate a commitment by the NAFTA parties to address the effects of toxic substances, it is noteworthy the NARAPs are not legally binding. They are entirely voluntary and do not constitute international agreements or establish any enforceable rights in local, national or international law.

In contrast, corporations affected by these agreements do have enforceable rights under NAFTA Chapter 11. In 2001, Crompton Corporation, a manufacturer of lindane, filed a Chapter 11 suit against Canada.[6] Although lindane had been banned for use on canola crops in the US, when Canada moved to implement a similar ban, Crompton alleged that Canada's action broke an earlier agreement with the corporation and filed a notice of intent to arbitrate (*Crompton Corp. v. Canada*, Second Notice of Arbitration, 2005). Crompton subsequently filed two more notices of intent and two notices of arbitration, the second in February 2005. In addition to alleging that Canada had breached the agreement, Crompton alleged that Canada's subsequent actions in cancelling all registrations violated multiple articles of NAFTA. Compton claimed for instance that Canada's ban on lindane breaches its NAFTA obligations because the ban unlawfully favours Canadian producers of substitute products, was not based on credible scientific evidence and did not give consideration to alternative means of addressing the alleged concerns, was not the least trade restrictive measure necessary to accomplish the government's objectives and constituted a taking or expropriation of Crompton's lindane business (*Crompton Corp. v. Canada*, Second Notice of Arbitration, 2005). On those grounds, Crompton seeks to have its registrations reinstated and an award of US$100 million in damages.

Thus far there has been no resolution of Crompton's claims in arbitration. However, the company also requested a review by Canada's Pest Management Regulatory Authority (PMRA), which established a board of three independent scientists to

---

5 As of November 2006, NARAPs have been developed for PCBs, DDT, chlordane, mercury and lindane. Plans for dioxins, furans and hexachorobenzene are under implementation (CEC 2006).

6 Crompton Corporation subsequently changed its name to Chemtura Corporation, and the arbitration is currently proceeding as *Chemtura Corp. v. Government of Canada*. Documents filed in the proceeding are available at <http://www.international.gc.ca/trade-agreements-accords-commerciaux/disp-diff/crompton_archive.aspx?lang=en>, last accessed 15 June 2008.

review the scientific information on which the decision was based as well as more recent information (PMRA 2006). The board submitted a report in August 2005, finding that there were problems with the PMRA's procedures and recommending that the PMRA conduct a follow-up assessment of the occupational exposure risk. The PMRA will consider a study generated by Crompton pursuant to the board's recommendation, evaluate its policy regarding its treatment of uncertainty factors in assessing the risk against vulnerable populations and accounting for differences in toxicological responses between test animals and humans (PMRA 2006).

Although it is unknown at this point how the lindane controversy will be resolved in Canada, the case demonstrates the power of NAFTA's Chapter 11 to force nations to reassess and possibly abandon strongly protective measures to address toxic pollutants in the food chain and also to pay damages. Meanwhile, citizens harmed by pesticides remain restricted to seeking national legal remedies that have proven inadequate.

Increasing Accountability: Standards in Trade and Domestic and International Law

Given the imbalance in power created by the current system of free trade, how can those seeking accountability most effectively act and allow citizens to exercise control over how their food is produced and the concerns that are important to them? One solution, which is both popular and controversial, is to include environmental, health and safety provisions within the agreements themselves, thereby using the agreements to increase rather than decrease levels of protection. A second is to look at ways to empower citizens more directly, strengthening those aspects of national and international law that are developing to allow individuals more concrete rights in establishing and enforcing environmental, social and cultural norms and rights.

Environmental standards in free trade agreements

The idea of including environmental standards in free trade agreement enjoys wide popularity in the US and Europe. The idea is to use trade agreements to raise the floor for protection rather than driving the ceiling down. The suggestion has met with strong resistance from free trade advocates and developing nations on the grounds that it would limit trade and undermine the economic benefits of the agreements, impose substantial costs upon developing countries that do not have regulatory frameworks already in place and put an unfair burden on developing countries that more developed countries did not face during their own development (Steinberg 1997).

The European Union The most success in introducing environmental standards into trade discussions has been seen in situations where there is already a degree of political, economic or cultural integration among the negotiating parties or where the number of parties is limited and the 'greener' country has much more power than the less-green country or countries (Steinberg 1997). The EU has been successful in setting up substantive and protective environmental standards in establishing the single market. The EU treaties require that harmonised standards be based on a 'high level of protection' (Steinberg 1997). In addition, where a harmonised standard is adopted by a qualified majority rather than unanimously, member states are allowed to maintain their own more stringent standards. Based on these provisions, the EU has upwardly harmonised 75 sanitary and phytosanitary measures and 18 other food-law measures, as well as addressing environmental quality issues more broadly. This process has maintained the stricter levels of protection adopted by the greener EU members and simultaneously increased the level of protection throughout the EU. This success has been possible in part because the EU formally places consideration of environmental issues on a par with economic and trade issues, a decision that reflects the high level of cultural, political and economic integration already in place among the founding members.

United States bilateral treaties   In contrast, where there is limited or no cultural or political integration, it is much more difficult to establish any substantive standards or even a common goal. Even where the nation seeking to impose such standards is powerful enough to force the other partner to accept them, the level of achieved protection is lacklustre and tends to be focused on process and procedure rather than on substantive protections.

For example, in response to popular pressure the US made environmental and labour concerns a 'negotiating priority' for its bilateral trade treaties in the Trade Promotion Authority Act (TPA) of 2002. However, the actual provisions called for are largely procedural, requiring only language that ensures that parties to trade agreements do not fail to enforce their environmental laws in a way that affects trade, while recognising that parties retain discretion in making enforcement decisions. The TPA also states that no retaliation may be authorised based on the exercise of these rights.

Shortly prior to and following the TPA, the US signed bilateral agreements with Jordan, Chile, Singapore, Morocco, Bahrain and Australia, in addition to the Central American-Dominican Republic Free Trade Agreement (CAFTA-DR). Each of these agreements includes provisions (1) affirming the right of each party to set domestic levels of protection and committing each party to strive to ensure high levels of protection and continuing improvement; (2) recognising that it is inappropriate to relax environmental laws in an attempt to attract trade and investments, and committing the parties to refrain from doing so; and (3) committing each party to enforce its environmental laws effectively, while recognising that each party retains discretion in this area and is not in violation when it exercises that discretion. In addition, most of the agreements have language either in the preamble or in an 'Objectives' section of the chapter on the environment that recognises the importance of sustainable development and the need to respect parties' differing levels of development.

However, while the Jordan agreement's environmental provisions are in the main text of the agreement and adherence to them is tied to the same dispute resolution process as the provisions on trade, the later agreements require a special and separate consultation process for concerns related to environmental provisions. In these agreements the only matter that can be taken into formal dispute resolution is a failure to enforce environmental laws effectively. In addition, several of the agreements limit the remedies that can be imposed in a dispute resolution over the environment to a fine of US$15 million annually.

None of these agreements establish an organisation like the CEC to address citizen concerns, although each contains provisions for public participation and input into the consultation process. Although the specific requirement and mechanism varies among the agreements, in general the language requires parties to accept public communications and concerns regarding the implementation of the environmental chapter and to share them with the other party or with some institution created by the agreement.

The future The inclusion of substantive environmental standards in free trade agreements has proved to be an elusive goal. Where a shared cultural and political commitment to high levels of environmental protection is lacking it may be possible only to agree to a 'lowest common denominator' type of standard and it may be difficult to allow for continual improvement of standards.

Working with the more common process-based standards, tying compliance to a dispute resolution process that can be triggered by citizens and that has a binding outcome may produce better results. Although the NAFTA citizen submission process is flawed and weak it is notable that it has been used 42 times whereas there have been no disputes initiated under the environmental provisions of the more recent US agreements. Focusing on improving citizen access and power to require nations to enforce their own environmental standards could provide a meaningful counterbalance to the power given to investors and allow levels of accountability comparable to that enjoyed by investment dispute proceedings.

Counterbalancing principles in domestic and international law

Free trade agreements have shifted power away from the domestic political process and towards international trade bodies and corporations. As the possibilities for implementing strongly protective standards through those channels are limited, it is important to consider other ways to bring power and balance back to citizens. Reforming national legal systems to reflect the reality of multinational corporations and international trade and reinforcing other areas of international law that give increased authority to individuals and public interest groups may provide some possibilities for restoring accountability and choice.

Home country jurisdiction As described earlier, one limitation that citizens face is the inability to sue corporations in their home countries for injuries inflicted in foreign countries. Courts in the US, and to a lesser extent in the United Kingdom and other common law nations, frequently rely on the doctrine of *forum non conveniens* to dismiss suits brought by foreign plaintiffs against domestic corporations. As applied in the US the doctrine has a distinct bias against foreign plaintiffs and it has severely limited the ability of those injured by pesticides manufactured in the US to seek accountability. This system is in sharp contrast to the principles of jurisdiction embraced in civil law countries where generally a court having jurisdiction is required to exercise that jurisdiction (Gardela and di Brozolo 2003). Thus in a civil law country a corporate defendant can usually be held accountable in its home forum. This approach was also adopted in the European Council Regulation 44/2001, which establishes a defendant's domicile as having unlimited general jurisdiction over any matter covered by the regulation, with alternate forums for particular subject matters or situations (Waples 2002). International negotiations at the Hague Conference on Private International Law on a draft Convention on Jurisdiction and Foreign Judgments in Civil and Commercial Matters have also sought to eliminate or limit the ability of courts to refuse to hear a case on the basis of *forum non conveniens*. Continuing efforts in international and domestic arenas to limit *forum non conveniens* and ensure that with open borders come open courtrooms would help ensure that workers and consumers that are harmed by the continued use of agrochemicals have a forum where they can seek accountability. Similarly, establishing consistent and clear standards for the recognition and enforcement of judgments from foreign courts is essential to closing the loop between international commerce and domestic laws.

Developing principles of enterprise law   In addition to establishing jurisdiction and access to courts, changes in domestic law governing corporate groups is necessary to come to terms with the realities of multinational corporations. Much of domestic law is based on the principles of entity law that treats corporations as juridical persons separate and distinct from their shareholders (who typically enjoy limited liability) (Blumberg 1993). When this principle is applied to corporate groups that comprise multiple layers of corporate-owned subsidiaries, it becomes difficult to hold one component of a corporate group liable for the actions of another component. This problem has prevented individuals from establishing jurisdiction over or the liability of the parent corporations of foreign subsidiaries. The development of enterprise law instead treats the constituent companies of a corporate group as a single or integrated unit in certain contexts (Blumberg 1993). The continuing efforts to develop the statutory and common law framework for recognising the reality of corporate structures today are key to both regulating the behaviour of corporations and allowing individuals to establish accountability over the group structure.

Developing international human rights and environmental law   Further effort to develop aspects of international law that can balance out the development of trade law is also essential. Although this proposal is too large to cover in depth here, it is important to note the progress already made in these areas. International human rights law continues to develop in directions that accord to individuals the ability to bring international actions against nations and to expand the notion of human rights to include developmental and group rights related to food security and agriculture (Oloka-Onyango 2003; Stephens 2002).

Additional areas essential to promoting sustainable agriculture at the global level include strengthening multilateral treaties covering environmental and labour issues and the development of other voluntary international codes of conduct. These treaties and commitments can establish positive obligations in their own right, and may provide additional principles of international law applicable to dispute resolutions if they are ratified by the parties involved (Palmer 2006; Stephens 2002).

References

Badulescu, D. and K. Baylis (2006) 'Pesticide Regulation Under NAFTA: Harmonization in Process', paper commissioned by the Canadian Agricultural Trade Policy Research Network, <http://www.uoguelph.ca/~catprn/PDF/Commissioned_Paper_Baylis_2006-6.pdf>, last accessed 6 January 2008.

Blumberg, P. (1993) *The Multinational Challenge to Corporation Law* (New York: Oxford University Press).

CBC News (2007) 'Proposal to raise pesticide levels irks Canadian consumers', *CBCNews* [website], (updated 9 May 2007) <http://www.cbc.ca/consumer/story/2007/05/09/pesticide-canada.html>, last accessed 1 November 2007.

Commission for Environmental Cooperation (CEC) (2006) 'The North American Regional Action Plan (NARAP) on Lindane and Other Hexachlorocyclohexane (HCH) Isomers', <http://www.cec.org/files/PDF/POLLUTANTS/LindaneNARAP-Nov06_en.pdf>, last accessed 6 January 2008

Coyler, D. (2002) 'Environmental Impacts of Agricultural Trade Under NAFTA', paper presented at the annual meeting of the Southern Agricultural Economics Association, 2–6 February, <http://ageconsearch.umn.edu/bitstream/123456789/16751/1/cp02co01.pdf>, last accessed 1 November 2007.

Crompton Corp. v. Canada, Second Notice of Arbitration, 10 February 2005, <http://www.international.gc.ca/assets/trade-agreements-accords-commerciaux/pdfs/CromptonCorpdoc3.pdf>, last accessed 15 June 2008.

Environment News Service (2007) 'First NAFTA Harmonized Pesticide Label Approved', 5 March 2007, <http://www.ens-newswire.com/ens/mar2007/2007-03-05-09.asp>, last accessed 1 November 2007.

Gardela, A. and L. di Brozolo (2003) 'Civil Law, Common Law, and Market Integration: The EC Approach to Conflicts of Jurisdiction', *American Journal of Comparative Law* 51, 611.

Grundberg, E. (2007) 'Confronting the Perils of Globalization: Nicaraguan Banana Workers' Struggle for Justice', *Iowa Historical Review* 1, 96 (available online at <http://www.uiowa.edu/~history/Resources/Iowa%20Historical%20Journal%20--%20UG/index.htm>).

Janis, M. (2003) *An Introduction to International Law* (New York: Aspen Publishers, 4th edn).

Lerner, R. (2001) 'International Pressure to Harmonize: The U.S. Civil Justice System in an Era of Global Trade', *Brigham Young University Law Review*, 229.

Nogales, F. (2002) 'The NAFTA Environmental Framework, Chapter 11 Investment Provisions, and the Environment', *Annual Survey of International and Comparative Law*, 97.

North American Free Trade Agreement Technical Working Group (1998) 'A North American Initiative for Pesticides: Operation of the NAFTA Technical Working Group on Pesticides', <http://www.epa.gov/oppfead1/international/naftatwg/2007/general/north-amer-init-1988.pdf>, last accessed 6 January 2008.

Oloka-Onyango, J. (2003) 'Reinforcing Marginalized Rights in an Age of Globaliziation: International Mechanisms, Non-State Actors and the Struggle for Peoples' Rights in Africa', *American University International Law Review* 18, 851.

Palmer, A. (2006) 'The WTO GMO Dispute', paper prepared for members of the GM Amicus Coalition, <http://www.genewatch.org/uploads/f03c6d66a9b354535738483c1c3d49e4/WTO_Biotech_case_dcsummaryfinal_1.pdf>, last accessed 1 November 2007.

Patterson, K. (2007) 'Canada Raising Limits on Pesticide Residues', *Ottowa Citizen* [website] 8 May 2007, <http://www.canada.com/topics/bodyandhealth/story.html?id=2fa3e7f8-9c83-4ea9-ad60-c13b548fe688>, last accessed 1 November 2007.

Pest Management Regulatory Authrority (PMRA) (2006) 'Information Note', 26 April, <http://www.pmra-arla.gc.ca/english/highlights/in20060426-e.html>, last accessed 2 June 2008.

Public Citizen (2007) 'Trade Deficit in Food Safety', <http://www.citizen.org/documents/FoodSafetyReportFINAL.pdf>, last accessed 1 November 2007.

Public Citizen (2000), 'Harmonization Handbook', <http://www.citizen.org/documents/BCKGRNDforpdf.PDF>, last accessed 1 November 2007.

Rittich, K. (2000) 'Transformed Pursuits: The Quest for Equality in Globalized Markets', *Harrison Human Rights Journal* 13, 231.

Rosenthal, E. (2002) 'Free Trade and Pesticides in Central America', *Global Pesticide Campaigner* 12:3, < http://www.panna.org/resources/gpc/gpc_200212.12.3.pdf>, last accessed 1 November 2007.

Steinberg, R. (1997) 'Trade-Environment Negotiations in the EU, NAFTA, and WTO: Regional Trajectories of Rule Development', *American Journal of International Law* 91, 231.

Stephens, B. (2002) 'The Amorality of Profit: Transnational Corporations and Human Rights', *Berkeley Journal of International Law* 20, 45.

Waples, M. (2004) 'The Adequate Alternative Forum Analysis in Forum Non Conveniens', *Connecticut Law Review* 36, 1475.

World Trade Organization Documents:

— Agreement Establishing the World Trade Organization, 15 April 1994, <http://www.wto.org/english/docs_e/legal_e/04-wto.pdf>, last accessed 15 June 2008.

— Agreement on the Application of Sanitary and Phytosanitary Measures, 15 April 1994, <http://www.wto.org/english/docs_e/legal_e/15-sps.pdf>, last accessed 15 June 2008

Chapter 4

Innovation in Policy: The Common Agricultural Policy and Dimensions of Regime Change

Emyr Vaughan Thomas

Introduction

This chapter aims to contribute to a better understanding of just what the key constraints are to achieving innovation at policy level by setting out a framework for viewing change in policy regimes. It is not intended to provide a single theory that can account for regime shift nor to offer a 'how-to' guide for those seeking policy transformation. Rather, it seeks to inspire an appreciation of the pervasiveness of policy regimes and to caution against undue optimism that they might be changed according to a blueprint. At the same time it highlights ways in which change indeed can be brought about.

The first section introduces the Common Agricultural Policy (CAP) of the European Union (EU) as a policy regime and presents an outline framework of five dimensions against which innovation through regime change can be understood. These are examined in turn in the subsequent five sections. Conclusions and reflections form the subject of the final section.

The CAP as Policy Regime

The CAP is the mainframe of policy that determines how agricultural practice is organised. It is also the main source of resistance to the innovations required to progress toward more sustainable agriculture.

There are two broad types of criticism frequently made against the CAP in this regard. First, that it gives rise to detrimental effects on the environment, including damage to biodiversity, soil and water quality. While recent reforms have increased the scope for CAP money to support organic cultivation, agri-environmental and rural development activities, the bulk of the expenditure remains directed at supporting conventional intensive agriculture. Secondly, the CAP is criticised for exploiting many developing countries. The high internal prices paid to EU producers, coupled with rapid adoption of new technologies and higher yields, have led to chronic overproduction of some agricultural products. Surpluses that reduce world prices, together with restricted access to EU markets for certain temperate products grown in Europe, exacerbate the poverty of many less developed countries.

The CAP spans a large number of states and involves a complex system of coordination by means of committees and national administrations. To try to capture this complexity I employ the term 'policy regime'. In the international relations literature regimes are defined as sets of:

> implicit or explicit principles, norms, rules and decision-making procedures around which actors' expectations converge. Principles are beliefs of fact causation and rectitude. Norms are standards of behaviour defined in terms of rights and obligations. Rules are specific prescriptions or proscriptions for action. Decision-making procedures are prevailing practices for making and implementing collective choices (Krasner 1983, 2).

The above definition applies directly to the CAP. It includes principles about causation in this field of policy intervention. Further, it has norms, rules and a complex set of decision-making procedures to secure collective action.

The next sections analyse the CAP as a policy regime. The following issues are examined in turn:

- Changes that arise from the internal domain, that is, the institutions and processes that belong to the core of decision-making and operational dynamics within the policy regime.
- Shifts arising from actions and activities within what is hereafter termed the intermediate domain. This wide 'space' lies between the institutions of the policy regime and the external world.
- Changes emanating from the domain that is wholly external to the policy regime.
- Discourse: the term covers the concepts and categorisations that are employed to make sense of the world and give meaning to it and that orient action. If a new discourse originates in any one domain it may traverse policy regime boundaries to varying degrees.
- Orders of regime-change. Regime-shift is not constituted in a single, uniform change but a process that can be seen to have qualitatively different degrees. This has consequences for how we conceive of regime-shift and innovation.

The Internal Domain: Institutional Processes

Some shifts in a policy regime emanate from the decision-making processes within its own formal institutions. One reason that the CAP regime survives is because of the particular sets of institutions involved in the setting of policy and the structure of the decision framework in which they operate.

The central institution of CAP decision making is the Council of Agriculture Ministers (CAM) where agriculture ministers formally enact any CAP reform. Thus all factors involved in the CAP reform process can be traced back to the Council. Formally, the European Commission controls the agenda of the CAM. It enjoys the sole right to propose legislation. For the CAM to agree something different from an initial Commission proposal requires unanimity or the consent of the Commission. Hence it might be said that the European Commission creates the possibility of a regime shift by its ability to control the agenda. The agenda shapes the final policy outcome even if the power of enactment resides in the CAM.

Yet at the same time it must be recognised that the European Commission has to undertake a political assessment of what the CAM is likely to agree. It is thus sometimes argued that the importance of institutions in engineering regime shift should not be exaggerated because a great deal of policy is debated within policy communities that extend far beyond the EU institutions designated as responsible. However, it should be recognised also that the existence of policy communities is often a product of these same EU institutions. Sometimes it is the latter that set the agenda of the policy community and dominate the way that different views within it are integrated.

CAP reforms start with the Commission and end with the CAM. These two institutions determine the characteristics of the reform process and the reform outcomes. The processes that trigger individual reforms of the CAP are generally long (nearly two years for 1992 and 1999). The internal organisation of the Commission provides part of the explanation for why the reform of the CAP tends to take a long time. The Directorate-General (DG) for Economics and the Directorate-General for Budgets have wrestled (so far unsuccessfully) with DG Agriculture for control of the CAP agenda. A horizontal separation within DG Agriculture has hindered the internal development of reform because reform proposals had to be conceived in small groups sitting well away from the main policy or administrative channels of DG Agriculture. In addition, the staff of the Agriculture Commissioner's Cabinet have played an important part in each of the reforms of the 1980s and 1990s.

Whilst these details serve to remind us of the importance of the institutional dimension in eliciting regime shift, it is important to also highlight its scope for resisting such a shift. An institutional system that is supported by fragmented political structures will be slow to embrace change. Reform to a policy requires a group or party able to acquire authority within the political system. Fragmented political structures such as the EU yield comparatively fewer opportunities to generate such authority since they are composed of many competing decision-making centres that act to stifle coordination (Atkinson and Coleman 1989). Such a configuration breeds an incrementalist style of policy making in which decision makers act on limited knowledge, respond to political pressures, engage in limited successive comparisons and make small tentative adjustments to existing policies.

A further internal process that may contribute to a shift within a policy regime is the process of implementation. Implementation always involves, to varying degrees, a departure from the ideals enshrined in a policy decree (see Hogwood and Gunn 1993). But implementation sometimes can yield opportunities for creativity that serve to promote a shift in the overall direction of a policy regime. A good example of this is the significant new discretion permitted to Member States (MS) in the current CAP reform process that gives scope for MS to 'modulate' direct payments to farmers. Modulation breaks the link between support payments and production (so-called 'decoupling'). Since January 2005 farmers in the United Kingdom (UK) have received a decoupled Single Farm Payment (SFP), that is, a payment unrelated to their current production. In return they are required to keep their land in 'good agricultural and environmental condition'.

Another example of the discretion allowed to MS is that of working out how the SFP is calculated. One approach links it to historical entitlement. Another is to calculate it as an 'area payment', spreading the available funds so that all land receives a payment per hectare (either a simple flat rate or differentiated to take into account land quality so that poorer farming land might receive a higher payment). A hybrid of these approaches offers a further possibility. As a result of political devolution, the four countries of the UK have been able to take different approaches to the implementation of the SFP. Wales and Scotland have chosen the historic payment approach. England and Northern Ireland have both adopted different forms of hybrid systems.

The example of Wales shows something of the contextual considerations that have had to be incorporated into the design of an SFP system. Wales chose a qualified historic option largely because both the area and hybrid models would have involved too great a degree of redistribution between farms. From an environmental standpoint, historic payments appear to benefit those farmers who have stocked their animals most intensively in the past. Without some qualification of the historic calculations those farmers who have de-intensified their farming to join agri-environment schemes thus would lose out. That aside, many environmentalists in Wales recognise that area payments would shift resources to larger farms – something that would itself lead to a more industrialised form of agriculture – so they have supported a basic historic approach while calling for suitable modifications. What this illustrates is that the experience that national and regional administrations in the MS are acquiring in implementing the SFP will become one route by which the grip of production-related support as a basic policy principle within the CAP regime is weakened.

A further example of implementation yielding opportunities for creativity that serves to promote a shift in the overall direction of a policy regime is associated with that part of the 1999 reform that allows MS to reduce compensation payments to farm businesses by up to 20 per cent. The resources saved through this modulation may be used within MS as additional Community co-financing for Rural Development Regulation (RDR) 'accompanying measures', namely agri-environmental and forestry measures and early retirement schemes for farmers and farm workers. The need for this discretion arose from the fact that no new resources to implement the RDR were provided at the EU level. Hence the money had to be found from within existing allocations.

The UK has applied modulation since 2001, starting with a flat rate of 2.5 per cent and increasing this gradually over time. In 2002 the UK Policy Commission on the Future of Farming and Food recommended the rate be increased to 10 per cent and that the receipts from the increase, plus associated UK matching funds, be used to finance a new agri-environment scheme, Entry Level Stewardship, for which all farmers would be eligible. Entry Level Stewardship was introduced in 2005.

In choosing to apply modulation the UK has embraced the creative scope available through policy implementation to reinforce the trend toward a redirection of CAP resources to socially and environmentally beneficial ends. Such creativity creates a tension between the discretion permitted through implementation and the coherence of the internal domain of the policy regime. In order to maintain the regime's integrity the parameters of implementation have to be set centrally. Without this restraint the CAP effectively would become the prerogative of the Member States and would cease to exist as an EU-wide regime.

The Intermediate Domain: Interests, Advocacy and Innovations

The intermediate domain lies between the institutions of the policy regime and the external world. It includes those who participate in a policy community (whose members share at least some commonality of interest) as well as those who are concerned about a policy issue such as the CAP but do not share the same interests as the majority within the agriculture policy community. For example, some environmentalists reject the special status accorded to farming in the CAP. As such they are outside the agriculture policy community but can still be said to belong to the intermediate domain within the CAP policy regime. It should be noted also that the intermediate domain includes both the actions motivated by economic interests and also actions motivated by beliefs and values.

The activity of interest groups provides an important stimulus for regime-shift. Tracy (1989) and Milward (1992), for instance, trace the construction of a common agricultural policy in terms of the political influence of national farm groups. Others such as Olson (1965), Becker (1983) and Brooks (1996) emphasise the role of the farm lobby as a well-organised grouping that is readily able to exert political influence.

CAP interest groups generally are active at the level of two lobbying arenas: national and European. Interest groups lobby in the national arena for MS' votes in the CAM. At the European level they lobby the Commission directly through their membership of umbrella organisations, the most important of which is the Comité des Organisations Professionelles Agricoles (COPA). Distinct strategies are employed in these two lobbying arenas, as discussed in Grant (1993) and Averyt (1977). The literature suggests that up until at least the late 1990s COPA was widely perceived to be influential in the CAP policy regime because it secured membership on committees capable of taking decisions of major political consequence. Grant (1997) illustrates how COPA's influence far exceeds that of the agribusiness lobby despite the fact that the latter is economically far more significant. The principal reason for the latter's relative weakness has been its heterogeneity. This in itself makes it difficult for it to link to a policy community where consensus on the means and ends of policy are important. The formation of the agribusiness umbrella organisation, CropLife, is designed in part to overcome this perceived lack of influence.

The more influential interest groups operate by securing a place within a formal policy community (Miller and Demir 2007). According to Richardson and Jordan (1979) and Mazey and Richardson (1993) such policy communities consist of a small number of state institutions and interest groups in which the members interact frequently and across all aspects of policy. They share a high degree of consensus on the means and ends of policy in the particular area covered by the community and regard their influence as maximised by their membership. Many other scholars employ the term 'policy network' for what is broadly the same thing (although an attempt at a degree of differentiation is made in Dowding 1995, 140 and Greer 2005, 29).

The concept of a policy community can help us appreciate how some beneficiaries of policy are able to resist change. Cohesive policy communities are particularly resistant to change because of two key factors. First, their members agree about the key principles and ends of policy. Secondly, their consensus on policy principles enables them to advance a compelling technical case that renders the impression that those outside the network are without the requisite knowledge to make an informed judgement.

The existence of a cohesive policy community is one significant factor in explaining why the MacSharry reform of 1992 was such a minor regime shift. COPA repeatedly affirmed that prices and not direct income support should remain the principal component of farmers' income. There was complete agreement within the policy network that the European Community should protect farmers from market forces and ensure that they had a reasonable income so that the actual shift in the CAP in 1992 related only to a disagreement over which policy instruments to employ for this purpose. The arrival of new member states with the 2004 enlargement of the EU seems to have changed the dynamic of close agreement among members of the formerly cohesive policy community, both closing and opening opportunities for regime change in the future.

A further key contribution to shifts within a policy regime is made by the activity of policy entrepreneurs (Baumgartner and Jones 1993; Kingdon 1995; Mintrom and Vergari 1996; Mintrom 1997; Baumgartner and Jones 2002, 250 ff.). Policy entrepreneurs act to bring new policy ideas into the public arena by identifying unsatisfied needs and innovative ways of fulfilling them. They bear the reputational risks and early financial costs involved in experimenting with untried approaches. They define policy problems in a way that attracts the attention of decision makers and they are able to assemble networks of individuals or organisations to undertake change.

These four features can be said to characterise the role of the Countryside Commission, a UK government advisory body, in developing a pioneer approach to the conservation of marshland. The Broads Grazing Marsh Scheme (BGMS) was put together by the Commission at short notice to persuade a group of farmers to continue to farm one of the last remaining stretches of grazing marsh in eastern England in a manner friendly to conservation. Previous UK schemes had involved conservation payments only in cases where individual farmers had to be persuaded to refrain from damaging important conservation assets. The BGMS was innovative in that it offered a flat-rate payment to all farmers within the designated area. Moreover, the UK agriculture department (then, Ministry of Agriculture, Fisheries and Food) agreed that conventional production grants would not operate within the designated area.

By 1985 the BGMS had become sufficiently popular with farmers for the UK government to successfully campaign in Brussels for its adoption as part of the 1985 Regulation on improving agriculture structures (Regulation 797/85). This enabled the Community to 'contribute towards the introduction or continued use of agricultural practices compatible with the requirements of conserving the natural habitat and ensuring an adequate income for farmers' (Article 19). In the ensuing years the UK proceeded to establish an Environmentally Sensitive Areas scheme and other agri-environment programmes. The CAP reform of 1992 made agri-environment programmes under Regulation 2078/92 operational in all MS.

In short, the Countryside Commission exemplified all four dimensions of a policy entrepreneur. It identified a means to fulfil the need to maintain traditional farming practices and the conservation benefits they yielded. It risked its reputation and some financial investments in experimenting with untried approaches. It defined policy problems in a way that attracted the attention of decision makers by focusing on outputs rather than processes, thereby offering a means of achieving in a particular geographical domain a decisive decoupling of environmental support and agricultural objectives. And it assembled organisations into a network to undertake change.

The intermediate domain also includes those whose interest departs very significantly from the current mainstream within a policy community. The Advocacy Coalition Framework (ACF) as set out by Sabatier (1988) and Weible and Sabatier (2007) focuses on advocacy collations, comprising 'people from a variety of positions (elected and agency officials, interest group leaders, researchers, and so on) who share a belief system – for example, a set of basic values, causal assumptions, and problem perceptions – and who show a non-trivial degree of coordinated activity over time' (Sabatier 1988, 130). Coalitions seek to achieve the realisation of their shared beliefs, often at variance with others in this policy domain. This sharing of beliefs is a key feature that differentiates them from interest groups that coalesce around shared interests rather than beliefs.

Advocacy coalitions seek to affect policy subsystems, the network of individuals from a variety of organisations who have an interest in policy in a particular domain. Within a sub-system there is generally a dominant coalition and one or more minority coalitions. Each coalition operates under its own belief system. Change occurs when some external perturbation or event has an impact on the sub-system and presents advantages to minority coalitions able to take advantage of policy learning and increased resources.

One example of an advocacy coalition is the Land Use Policy Group (LUPG).[1] This represents the statutory conservation, countryside and environment agencies in the UK. These agencies are funded by government but are one step removed from the decision-making process carried out by the central government departments. The LUPG seeks to influence government and the EU to develop conservation-minded policies for agriculture and rural areas. It has operated since the early 1990s as a strong advocate for the wider application of agri-environment schemes within the CAP framework. On occasion it has worked with non-governmental lobbyists in other countries and with the Institute for European Environmental Policy, a think tank active in promoting the development of increasingly effective EU-level environmental policies.

---

1 The LUPG comprises Natural England, Countryside Council for Wales, Environment Agency, Joint Nature Conservation Committee, Scottish Natural Heritage and Department of Environment and Heritage Northern Ireland.

LUPG's role can be illustrated by reference to efforts to influence the types of practice recognised in the new standards for Good Agricultural and Environmental Condition (GAEC) that farmers have to meet in order to receive the new Single Payment introduced in the 2003 CAP reform. The relevant EU Regulation sets a framework for defining GAEC but MS must define their own standards within this framework. The LUPG sought to secure widespread agreement on the scope and definition of the GAEC standards for minimum levels of maintenance of semi-natural grazed habitats and unused agricultural land as well as standards for landscape features. In September 2007 the LUPG organised the presentation of four papers to a major conference in Brussels that included participation of key staff from the European Commission; one of the papers was a keynote speech by the EU Commissioner for Agriculture, Mariann Fischer Boel. This enabled the LUPG to publicise its refined aim: 'to promote sustainable rural land management and to safeguard both natural and cultural heritage. Over the next 10–15 years we see land management expanding beyond traditional farming and forestry to cover the provision of a growing range of environmental goods and services, including dealing with climate change' (LUPG 2007).

The LUPG's intention was to use the conference to highlight how 'traditional' environmental interests such as biodiversity management, soil and water conservation, access and cultural issues are recognised as critical to helping to deal with climate change and building robust rural economies. At the same time it sought to put forward a novel defence of EU funding for the rural areas as the geographic spaces that provide important environmental goods and services. By appealing to the recent policy priority given to climate change, it attempted to justify the importance of rural policy by tactically linking land use policy to this issue.

Pressures from the External Domain

According to the theory of punctuated equilibrium advanced by Baumgartner and Jones (1993), public policy is always made up of long periods of stability interrupted by spurts of change when policy monopolies are broken up. The key factors responsible are the: 'changing allocation of attention by national political leaders, the media, and the public, and by the ability of policymakers to appeal to different institutional venues for decision making by raising new understanding of old issues' (Baumgartner and Jones 1993, 59).

On this view, we can expect policy regimes to be liable to frequent shifts of focus. This view may serve also to explain why the CAP has historically been more resistant to external incursions than most policy regimes. Until the 1990s top politicians were not ready to focus on its faults, and voters were not unduly aware of its effects. Downs (1957) neatly described the rationally ignorant voter in a situation where the benefits of government interventions are concentrated but their costs are widely spread. The more diffuse the incidence of the costs of the policy intervention, the less incentive there is for the individual voter to learn about the issue.

A policy regime may be shifted by external factors that disrupt the policy community. Such change generally involves extensive media coverage, the mobilisation of counter-groups and the intervention of the highest levels of government. A dramatic example is provided the destruction of over four million head of livestock between March and September 2001 and the closing of the UK countryside in order to eradicate foot-and-mouth disease. This created an economic and political environment for deeper-rooted reform. The narrowly focused Ministry of Agriculture, Fisheries and Food was restructured into the Department for Environment, Food and Rural Affairs (DEFRA). A new minister was appointed with determination to reform the CAP and transform farming practices the better to meet the demands of sustainable production and development.

Perhaps the most significant case of political leaders 'breaking into' the policy monopoly of the CAP was in 1987 when governments belonging to the Organisation for Economic Co-operation and Development (OECD) committed itself to a concerted reduction in agricultural support and the inclusion of agriculture in the Uruguay round of multilateral trade negotiation. A commitment was made to a common strategy for improved market access, replacement of price support with 'decoupled' income payments and the phased elimination of export subsidies in the 1993 signing of the Uruguay Round Agriculture Agreement (URAA). This external constraint led to the 1999 CAP reform, together with the 2003 mid-term review that introduced a significant degree of decoupling into the CAP regime.

Budgetary crises provide further examples of external pressures imploding on a policy regime:

> What makes a budgetary crisis so threatening ... is that it turns the policy process into a zero sum game where agriculture's demand for new resources is seen as coming at the expense of other programmes. No other crisis is likely to create the same kind of outside interest. (Moyer and Josling 1990, 19)

In previous CAP reforms budgetary crisis has always been a prominent factor in shifting the regime. For example, by the 1980s the European Community was set to spend about 70 per cent of its entire budget on market support although this had not enabled average farm incomes to increase. The crisis in March 1984 resulted in a package of changes that included the introduction of dairy quotas and a commitment to future limitations on price guarantees. In recent years the accession of additional Central and Eastern European countries to the EU has brought about a wider realisation that the traditional CAP is far too costly to be sustained and that the 1999 reform and 2003 mid-term review were an incomplete remedy. The political agreement that agricultural expenditure up to 2013 would not increase in real terms means that the original MS have had to agree to incremental subsidy cuts in order to finance payment to the 2004 entrants to the EU.

The emergence of new policy drivers also can act as external pressures on a policy regime. Climate change (see IPCC 2007) and the European Commission's proposed target that biofuels form 10 per cent of transport fuel by 2020, for instance, are both likely to affect the future direction of the CAP and influence land use decisions on a European scale.

Discourse and Socioeconomic Arrangements

Sometimes a shift in a policy regime is the result of changes in 'discourse'. Hajer defines discourse as 'a specific ensemble of ideas, concepts, and categorizations that are produced, reproduced, and transformed in a particular set of practices and through which meaning is given to physical and social realities' (1995, 44). On this view, regime shift can occur only if a new discourse can dominate public discussion and policy rhetoric and penetrate the routines of policy practice through institutionalisation within laws, regulations and routines.

An example of an evolving new discourse is found in the approach pioneered by the Countryside Commission in England. In *Paying for a Beautiful Countryside* (1993) the Countryside Commission set out the idea of paying for a product rather than subsidising particular farming methods held to be beneficial to the environment. It employed the discourse of '"countryside products" which farmers and land managers may choose to provide in response to payment schemes, and which the agencies who run these schemes are effectively buying on behalf of the public' (Countryside Commission 1993, 9). This marked the emergence of market-based principles in agri-environmental policy whereby farmers can be recompensed financially for the production of a range of goods such as maintenance of particular habitats or the construction of landscape features such as hedgerows and traditional boundaries. By now this discourse has become established within the CAP.

The discourse on countryside products sowed the seed for the discourse on multifunctionality and the new policy paradigm associated with this. According to this discourse farming does not merely provide tradable commodities. It also produces a number of positive externalities and collective goods (jobs, culture, landscape, environment and so on) that are valued by society and need to be publicly supported. In the words of the then European Commissioner for Agriculture, Franz Fischler:

> If asked to define the 'European Model' of agriculture in a nutshell, I would stress the multifunctional role that EU agriculture plays, and its underlying objectives, which are: the promotion of a competitive agricultural sector and of production methods that protect the environment and supply quality products, the support of rural communities, and simplicity and subsidiarity in agricultural policy. (Fischler 2002)

The European Commission appealed to multifunctionality to defend the CAP against the criticism of public financial support for this sector made at World Trade negotiations. In the conclusions of the Berlin European Council in March 1999 that sealed the agreement on the CAP reform and the wider Agenda 2000 package, the idea of multifunctionality was set out as both an objective and, implicitly, as enshrining all the goods that are deemed valuable by the key stakeholders:

> The European Council welcomes the agreement reached by the Agriculture Council at its March session on an equitable and worthwhile reform of the Common Agricultural Policy. The content of this reform will ensure that agriculture is multifunctional, sustainable, competitive and spread throughout Europe, including regions with specific problems, that it is capable of maintaining the countryside, conserving nature and making a key contribution to the vitality of rural life, and that it responds to consumer concerns and

demands as regards food quality and safety, environmental protection and the safeguarding of animal welfare. (European Council 1999, paragraph 20)

The final listing of functions is an affirmation of the goods that the policy seeks to realise. The term 'multifunctional' has become a dynamic orienting principle used in the policy-change process to reform agriculture policy.

From the perspective of the discipline of political economy, discourses are initiated and shaped to legitimise and sustain existing policies and institutional arrangements. This limits how far regime shift is possible (Gramsci 1980). The economic liberalisation in Australia illustrates how a particular discourse is anchored in particular socioeconomic groups. Australia is a member of the Cairns Group of nations that espouse free trade and demand significant reform of the CAP. The country's geographic position has exposed Australia to pressure from transnational corporations for Australia to accommodate itself to the new realities of globalisation (McMichael and Lawrence 2001). Unlike the EU, Australia lacks a significant small and medium farm constituency that is differentiated politically and ideologically from large farm or agri-business interests who would have a stake in more interventionist domestic policies.

Paradigms and Orders of Regime Shift

'Shifting' a policy regime involves different orders of change. A first-order shift involves only adjustments to existing structures, as occurred in the CAP from its inception up to the early 1990s. Second-order changes, such as the 1992 MacSharry reform, involve changes to policy instruments such as the compulsory adoption of agri-environmental programmes by MS under Regulation 2078/92.

It is third-order shifts that involve a genuine 're-imagining', that is, a change in the objectives of the policy regime and in the underlying policy paradigm. It is useful to illustrate third-order change in more detail. In 1996 the European Conference on Rural Development was convened in Cork by the European Commission with the aim of securing new objectives for the CAP. The Cork Declaration saw agriculture as one among many activities in rural areas. Rural development policy henceforth would be designed in an integrated, multidisciplinary and multisectoral way, 'encompassing agricultural adjustment and development, economic diversification, management of natural resources, enhancement of environmental functions, promotion of culture, tourism and recreation' (European Conference on Rural Development 1996).

The Declaration marked the emergence of a new paradigm in which rural areas, not just farms, became the site for policy intervention. The 1999 reform and the 2003 mid-term review partially adopted this paradigm in the establishment of a Rural Development Regulation, modulation and the introduction of the SFP. The so-called 'Lisbon Strategy' relaunched by the Commission in February 2005 has become a major EU policy priority. It seeks to promote higher economic growth, job creation and greater competitiveness in world markets through higher value added and a more flexible economy: 'The Lisbon Strategy focuses, among other things, on improving education and training, research and development and the promotion of innovation and sustainability. These are exactly the results the Rural Development tool-box can deliver' (D-G Agriculture 2006). The EU Agriculture Commissioner has announced recently that 'within ... the Lisbon Agenda for jobs and growth, it is our policy to draw out unused potential in all parts of the Union. The CAP must continue to do its part' (Fischer Boel 2007). Rural areas are now viewed as spaces that contribute to economic growth rather than, as under the traditional CAP, areas worthy of Community support.

Conclusion and Reflections

The following have been highlighted as conducive to understanding regime-shift:

- Factors in the internal domain, the institutional structures of decision making. These include the creative opportunities available through policy implementation.
- Factors operating in the intermediate domain. These include the actions of interest groups, the degree of cohesion in a policy community, the creative activity of policy entrepreneurs and the opportunities available for advocacy coalitions to gain ascendancy.
- Factors emanating from the external domain. These include public concern, budgetary pressures and the intervention of high-level political leaders changing the policy objectives and even the pattern of organisation within the policy field.
- The role of discourse as an orienting dimension that serves to move policy regimes towards adopting a new policy paradigm or to constrain change by reinforcing existing social and economic arrangements.
- Order of change in a policy regime. Regime shift is not 'all or nothing', but can be understood in terms of three distinct orders of change, with third-order changes involving a new and innovative policy paradigm.

These factors rarely act alone. Sometimes they interweave in very complex ways. Appreciation of this point allows us to see why they offer a framework for understanding rather than a theory of regime shift. Everything depends on the manner in which the factors come together and the particular context in which this occurs. Innovation in policy regimes cannot be forced but the analysis provided here shows the ample scope for preparing and nurturing processes of change over time.

References

Atkinson, M.M. and Coleman, W.D. (1989), 'Strong States and Weak States: Sectoral Policy Networks in Advanced Capitalist Economies', *British Journal of Political Science* 19:1, 47–67.
Averyt, W.F. (1977), *Agropolitics in the European Community: Interest Groups and the CAP* (New York: Praeger).
Baumgartner, F.R. and Jones, B.D. (1993), *Agendas and Instability in American Politics* (Chicago: University of Chicago Press).

Baumgartner, F.R. and Jones, B.D. (2002), *Policy Dynamics* (Chicago: University of Chicago Press).

Becker, G.S. (1983), 'A Theory of Competition Among Pressure Groups for Political Influence', *Quarterly Journal of Economics* 98:3, 371–400.

Brooks, J. (1996), 'Agricultural Policies in OECD Countries: What Can We Learn from Political Economy Models?', *Journal of Agricultural Economics* 47:2, 366–89.

Countryside Commission (1993), *Paying for a Beautiful Countryside: Securing Environmental Benefits and Value for Money from Incentive Schemes*, booklet CAP 413 (Wallingford: Countryside Commission).

D-G Agriculture (2006), 'The Common Agricultural Policy and the Lisbon Agenda', European Commission Directorate-General for Agriculture [website] <http://ec.europa.eu/agriculture/lisbon/index_en.htm>, accessed 3 November 2007.

Dowding, K. (1995), 'Model or Metaphor? A Critical Review of the Policy Network Approach', *Political Studies* 43:1, 136–58.

Downs, A. (1957), *An Economic Theory of Democracy* (New York: Harper and Row).

European Conference on Rural Development (1996), 'The Cork Declaration: A Living Countryside' (published online 9 November 1996) <http://europa.eu.int/comm/agriculture/rur/cork_en.htm>, accessed 4 November 2007.

European Council (1999), 'Presidency Conclusions Berlin European Council, 24 and 25 March 1999 (published online 26 March 1999) <http://ec.europa.eu/regional_policy/sources/docoffic/official/regulation/pdf/berlin_en.pdf>, accessed 16 June 2008.

Falconer, K. and Ward, N. (2000), 'Using Modulation to Green the CAP: The UK Case', *Land Use Policy* 17:4, 269–77.

Fischer Boel, M. (2007), 'The Future of the CAP: Supporting Sustainable Farming', speech delivered at the conference organised by Birdlife International on 'CAP Vision', Brussels, 3 October 2007 (Brussels: European Commission).

Fischler, F. (2002), 'Development and Fisheries European Agricultural Model in the Global Economy', speech by the Agriculture Commissioner at the Second International Conference on Globalisation, University of Leuven, 26 November 2002, Speech/02/590 (published online 26 November 2002) <http://europa.eu.int/rapid/pressReleasesAction.do?reference=SPEECH/02/590&format=HTML&aged=0&language=EN&guiLanguage=en>, accessed 4 November 2007.

Gramsci, A. (1980), *Selections from the Prison Notebooks of Antonio Gramsci*, edited and translated by G. Hoare and G.N. Smith (New York: International Publishers).

Grant, W. (1993), 'Pressure Groups and the European Community: An Overview', in S. Mazey and J.J. Richardson (eds), *Lobbying in the European Community* (Oxford: Oxford University Press).

Grant, W. (1997), *The Common Agricultural Policy* (London: Macmillan).

Greer, A. (2005), *Agricultural Policy in Europe* (Manchester: Manchester University Press).

Hajer, M.A. (1995), *The Politics of Environmental Discourse: Ecological Modernization and the Policy Process* (Oxford: Oxford University Press).

Hill, M. (ed.) (1993), *The Policy Process: A Reader* (Hemel Hempstead: Harvester Wheatsheaf).

Hogwood, B.W. and Gunn, L.A. (1993), 'Why "Perfect Implementation" is Unattainable', in M. Hill (ed.), *The Policy Process: A Reader* (Hemel Hempstead: Harvester Wheatsheaf).

IPCC (2007), *Climate Change 2007 – The Physical Science Basis*, contribution of Working Group I to the Fourth Assessment Report of the IPCC (Geneva: Intergovernmental Panel on Climate Change).

Kingdon, J.W. (1995), *Agendas, Alternatives and Public Choices* (second edition, Boston: Little, Brown).

Krasner, S. (1983), *International Regimes* (Ithaca, NY: Cornell University Press).

LUPG (2007), 'Future Policies for Rural Europe: 2013 and Beyond', Land Use Policy Group [webpage] <www.lupg.org.uk>, accessed 3 November 2007.

McMichael, P. and Lawrence, G. (2001), 'Globalising Agriculture: Structures of Constraint for Australian Farming', in S. Lockie and L. Bourke (eds), *Rurality Bites: The Social and Environmental Transformation of Rural Australia* (London: Pluto Press).

Mazey, S. and Richardson, J.J. (eds) (1993), *Lobbying in the European Community* (Oxford: Oxford University Press).

Miller, H.T. and Demir, T. (2007), 'Policy Communities', in M.S. Sidney, F. Fischer and G. Miller (eds), *Handbook of Public Policy Analysis: Theory, Politics and Methods* (New York: CRC Press).

Milward, A. (1992), *The European Rescue of the Nation State* (London: Routledge).

Mintrom, M. and Vergari, S. (1996), 'Advocacy Coalitions, Policy Entrepreneurs and Policy Change', *Policy Studies Journal* 24:3, 420–34.

Mintrom, M. (1997), 'Policy Entrepreneurs and the Diffusion of Innovation', *American Journal of Political Science* 41:3, 738–70.

Moyer, W. and Josling, T. (1990), *Agricultural Policy Reform: Politics and Process in the EC and the USA* (New York: Harvester Wheatsheaf).

Olson, M. (1965), *The Logic of Collective Action* (Cambridge, MA: Harvard University Press).

Richardson, J.J. and Jordan, A.G. (1979), *Governing Under Pressure: The Policy Process in a Post-Parliamentary Democracy* (Oxford: Martin Robertson).

Sabatier, P.A. (1988), 'An Advocacy Coalition Framework of Policy Change and the Role of Policy-Orientated Learning', *Policy Sciences* 21:1, 129–68.

Sidney, M.S., Fischer, F. and Miller, G. (eds) (2007), *Handbook of Public Policy Analysis: Theory, Politics and Methods* (New York: CRC Press).

Tracy, M. (1989), *Government and Agriculture in Western Europe 1880–1988* (London: Granada).

Weible, C.M. and Sabatier, P.A. (2007), 'A Guide to the Advocacy Coalition Framework', in M.S. Sidney, F. Fischer and G. Miller (eds), *Handbook of Public Policy Analysis: Theory, Politics and Methods* (New York: CRC Press).

Chapter 5

The Swedish Foodshed: Re-imagining Our Support Area

Susanne Johansson

When we eat an apple it may make no difference to us where it comes from as long as it looks like an apple and tastes like an apple. However, it will have had very different impacts on the environment and on other people's lives depending on whether it came from Argentina, France or our own back yard, even if the apples from these three sources look just the same and cost the same in the supermarket. What we choose to eat and where our food comes from are major determinants of how natural resources are used – and misused – as a result of variations in the environmental and social impacts of different foods.

What people eat and how we get our food has changed drastically over time. More than 10 000 years ago, humans subsisted on a diet drawn from a large variety of plants and animals and were reliant on what could be found in nature through hunting and gathering, without the help of tractors, fertilisers, harvesters or any of the other external inputs used in modern agriculture. Early humans were reliant on a large area of land such as savannah and forest, about 80 hectares per person (Buringh 1989) (see Figure 5.1). Since these hunting and gathering days, humans have gradually domesticated animal and plant species and become more and more dependent on a specific area for their food supply. This area has decreased over time with the invention of efficient tools and production systems, use of fertilisers and various crop protection techniques. There has been not only a decrease in appropriated agricultural area but also an increased use of mostly non-renewable external inputs. There has been a major increase in the use of commercial energy and at the same time an equally notable decrease in human labour requirements.

Major changes have occurred in the past 100 years. Since the end of the eighteenth century, a significant switch has taken place from human and animal power to machine power, fuelled by fossil energy. This is the main reason for the considerable increase in economic productivity in the world economy and in agricultural production. Today the world's population largely depends on 30 plant species, with four crops (wheat, rice, maize and potatoes) contributing more tonnage to total world consumption than the next 26 species combined. Over 95 per cent of the global food supply now originates from agricultural land. The average available arable land area per person has declined to about 0.25 hectares. At the same time, future food supply is being jeopardised principally because of over-use of natural resources and degrading ecosystems, a growing global population, increased temperatures and

Figure 5.1 Contrasting dependency on land for food. Early humans were reliant for their food on what could be found on about 80 hectares per person of natural land, with the sun as the only energy source; today we rely on the produce of 0.4 hectares of arable land per person, external inputs and fossil fuels as the major energy sources

Design: Fredrik Stendahl

changes in freshwater supply related to climate change and because consumption patterns are becoming more and more resource intensive.

At the beginning of the twentieth century most food was still produced locally and prepared in domestic kitchens. However, current food consumption is supported through the work of a global food system, fuelled by the forces of the free market and cheap fossil fuels. Food undergoes numerous transformations and transportations before it is purchased in the supermarket. One key factor influencing land use patterns and use of ecosystem services is the international trade in food. The current trend is for an increasingly global food system that is so transnational that the only way it is governed is by the invisible hand of the market, although the way this currently operates is not in everyone's interests. While consumers everywhere enjoy these foods, which are often cheaper to import than to produce domestically, it must be borne in mind that there is no such thing as a free lunch; there are hidden costs involved with imported foods today. For instance, the social costs of producing the food in a country with lower wages than in the country where it is consumed, the environmental costs of producing food in a country with lower environmental standards and the indirect costs of long-distance transport on climate change are not reflected in the current purchase price.

Food supply under current conditions may be approaching its limits. At a global level, available agricultural land per capita is decreasing as the global population grows. Since almost all food is so obviously derived from land it perhaps has been too easy to evaluate future food security by means of area-based studies that consider only the use and loss of agricultural land. While it is true that external resources can be used to increase yields in agricultural production and decrease agricultural land use, the true efficiency of these improvements can be understood only by accounting for the land area and environmental support that provide these external resources. Earlier studies have shown that analysing only the agricultural area can give a false impression that societies are living within their limits and being efficient in their food production.

The well-being of both present and future human populations is imperilled by the rapid changes in ecological life-support systems and degradation of these support areas. The ability of ecosystems to supply services and goods is frequently taken for granted, often because many of them are free of charge and invisible. As a consequence, many ecosystems have been overused and degraded, thereby decreasing their ability to function fully. It is therefore important to make visible the use of ecosystem support.

Many experts are concerned about the ability of the planet to feed a growing population with fewer available resources and degrading ecosystems. Consumers, policy makers and researchers increasingly are concerned about where food is produced and how it is transported. How can consumers, food producers and markets identify their role within this global food system, which is so hard to appreciate, and act responsibly and effectively for change? This chapter introduces two terms that have been coined to facilitate critical thought on the origins of our food: the foodshed concept and the foodprint approach. Food consumption in Sweden is used as an example to illustrate these two approaches.

Food Consumption in Sweden

The typical Swedish diet includes a high proportion of dairy and cereal products as well as meat and meat products. These are the main sources of energy and protein. Swedish consumption of various dairy products, such as milk, cheese, butter, yoghurt and other fermented milk products is among the highest in the EU. Most of the dairy products consumed in Sweden are produced domestically but we should question how 'Swedish' these foods really are since much of the protein for animal feeds is imported, for example in the form of soybeans from Brazil. Meat consumption in Sweden is among the lowest in Europe although it has increased by over 50 per cent in the last 50 years. Fruit and vegetable consumption has more than doubled over the same period and a larger proportion of fruit and vegetables are now imported.

Swedish consumers enjoy many imported products that either cannot be produced within the country at all or only during the summer period. A global food system has allowed them to ignore the constraints that seasons of the year and climate once placed on the diet of a country situated so far north; today they consume most bananas per capita in Europe, while per capita coffee consumption comes second in the world, with neighbouring Finland in first place.

The Foodshed Approach Helps People Understand Where Their Food is Coming From

A foodshed, analogous to a watershed, is an area that is defined by a structure of supply. More concretely, foodshed analysis means answering the question: where is our food coming from and how is it getting to us? The analogy of the foodshed to a watershed suggests the need to protect a source, here agricultural production and the producer. Common sense and past experience have demonstrated the wisdom of conserving a watershed area to protect a freshwater resource (Getz 1991). A process is currently underway in Sweden and elsewhere to extend similar concepts to the food supply system as understanding grows of the need to protect natural resources such as arable land, ecosystem services and freshwater for future food security.

The foodshed is easy to understand as a metaphor or concept but foodshed analysis is not yet a standardised methodology. It currently offers a useful way of thinking about where our food is coming from. However, even if it is not yet as 'mappable' as a watershed, it may still be measurable, as suggested by Getz (1991), by monitoring a border over which food passes and documenting the amounts involved. Such a border can be national, regional or even the boundary of a community or a single household. The foodshed thus provides a framework for thought as well as for action by measuring the flow and direction of these tributaries and documenting the many quantitative and qualitative transformations that food undergoes as it moves towards consumption. The foodshed approach is food systems thinking. It is applicable to the study of single foods or whole diets at a local or national level. Two questions that can be answered by engaging with foodshed analysis are: is a country's food consumption sustainable? Where is the food I eat produced, and by whom?

The Swedish Foodshed

When trying to visualise the foodshed of Sweden we obtain a rudimentary map that resembles an octopus with long tentacles extending out from a food market to remote tropical banana plantations in Ecuador and to vast soybean fields in Brazil, as well as to rye fields in the north of Sweden supplying a typical breakfast food, Wasa crispbread, and to the apple groves of Kivik in the south and the greenhouses on the islands of Lake Mälaren in the centre of the country (see Figure 5.2).

Unfortunately, establishing the exact origins of imported foods has become impossible since Sweden joined the EU. There has been no record of country of origin for imported food since 1995; only the last country of port is registered. This is generally not the country where the food was produced. This difficulty applies especially to foodstuffs such as tropical fruits, coffee and soybean products that arrive by ship at large ports in the EU and are then sent on to Sweden by truck. Food import statistics thus cannot be used to derive information on the country where

The Swedish Foodshed: Re-imagining Our Support Area 59

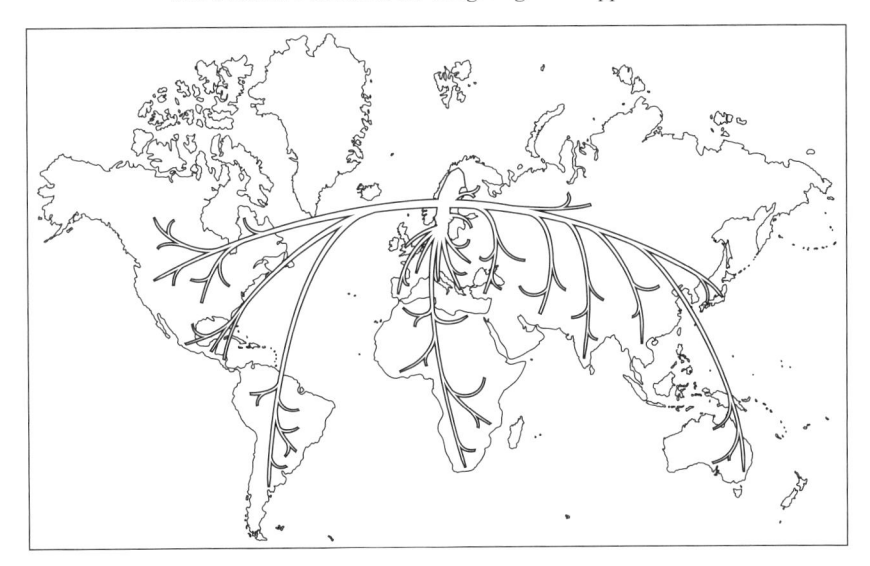

Figure 5.2 **The Swedish foodshed, with food flows extending from remote agricultural land areas to consumers in Sweden from a 'global everywhere'**

Design: Fredrik Stendahl

the food was produced. Sweden's major import partners for agricultural products and food in 2000 were Denmark, the Netherlands, Norway and Germany, but many of these imports were produced in other countries and these four countries were responsible for only about half the import value. The main import partners outside Europe for the same year were USA, Brazil, Costa Rica, Colombia, Panama and Thailand. If we are to be able to critically analyse our foodshed in future, trade statistics need to become much more transparent.

How large is the Swedish foodshed? How large an area is Sweden dependent on for its food consumption today? Is Sweden using more than its fair share? To explore these questions we turn to the concept of the foodprint.

The Foodprint Makes Visible the Big Picture

Because people consume the products and services of nature, every person's food supply has an impact on the planet. This is not a problem as long as the load exerted by human activities stays within the global regeneration capacity, but often it does not.

Footprinting is a way to translate human activities into the environmental area supporting these activities. If the footprint exceeds a certain size, for example the national land area, it might be interpreted as 'not being equitable' or that stored resources are being used faster than they can be replenished. The term for the footprint of food consumption, that is, the area that supports a population with food, is the 'foodprint' (Johansson 2005). In the following section various ways of estimating the footprint of Swedish food consumption are calculated and explained.

Agricultural land use

The most obvious spatial demand that people make for their food consumption is the agricultural land area on which crops are grown for human consumption and animal feed. When estimates are made of our potential to feed a growing population the available agricultural land area per person is usually calculated.

The agricultural land area appropriated per capita depends on agricultural practices and the amount of external inputs used but also on the consumption pattern of the population, that is, how much of certain foods are consumed, since different foods have different area requirements. The current agricultural land use can be calculated by dividing the reported data on the tonnage produced of basic agricultural commodities and processed foods by their respective domestic yield figures to determine the size of the land area necessary to grow the crops. Processed foods can be converted to their raw materials by the use of standard conversion factors. For example, imported apple juice first must be converted into apple equivalents in order to calculate the area required to grow the apples. The agricultural land area used for the imported food is then added to domestic agricultural land and the area for exported foods is subtracted.

The global availability of agricultural land is roughly as follows. About one-third of the Earth's surface is covered by land and two-thirds is covered by water. Of the land area, a little more than a third is agricultural land and of that agricultural land almost a third is arable and two-thirds is pasture. The arable land comprises soils of sufficient quality for tillage and sowing and over 90 per cent of the food consumed globally originates from this arable land. The rest comes mainly from pasture and a small fraction from marine sources. Pasture is only suitable for grazing; it is often too arid, stony or steep and insufficiently fertile to be financially viable for cultivation.

The global agricultural land area is a variable but limited resource. It is a resource that is under threat of increasing degradation, in particular the 11 per cent of the land surface that is currently used as arable land. With a growing global population and rising incomes, the demand on arable land and on the ecosystems that support agriculture will increase.

Environmental support area and ecosystem services

Earlier studies have shown that by considering only the agricultural area a false impression is given that societies are living within their limits and are efficient in food production. As Swedish society has moved from low-input to high-input, high-yield agriculture, replacing local ecological goods and services with technologies and transport systems based on fossil fuels, about 20 per cent of Swedish agricultural land has been taken out of production during the past 40 years.

Considering the agricultural land alone when carrying out a foodshed analysis is like mapping a watershed by calculating only the surfaces of rivers and lakes, disregarding the fact that the water originates from a larger system of clouds that release rain onto land, mountains and vegetation that collect the water into smaller creeks and then into rivers, wetlands and lakes. The area that is not water surface area can be thought of as the support area for the bodies of water in a watershed. Most watershed hydrologists understand the vital importance of the surrounding area for the existence of a river. However, food policy researchers and agronomists have not yet developed a comparable sophistication. They typically simply consider agricultural land use when addressing current and future food production. Yet, for example, in an apple orchard the apple trees are not the only resources needed to grow apples. An apple grower uses other resources such as fertilisers, machinery and tools to pick the apples, human labour, fuels to run the machines and transportation. These inputs demand the use of resources external to the orchard. Moreover, the production of these external inputs is also dependent on a support area, such as the ecosystems for sequestering the carbon dioxide from burning fossil fuels and in the manufacture of fertilisers and agrochemicals. The apple tree also is dependent on ecosystem services such as rainfall, pollinating insects and wind, increased soil fertility by a variety of soil organisms and so on. These additional areas for ecosystem services are called support areas.

Ecological footprinting Various footprinting methods have been developed to determine whether human loading is within the global regeneration capacity. The most well-known approach may be the 'ecological footprint', developed by Wackernagel and Rees (1996), which translates energy and resource use in a society into biologically productive areas. In an ecological footprint the following six major components of biologically productive space are commonly calculated:

- fossil energy land, meaning the spatial impact of fossil fuel use, corresponding to the area needed for newly planted forest to sequester fossil carbon (and not the area needed to produce new energy)
- arable land
- pasture land
- forest for production, for instance of wood and paper
- built-up area
- sea space.

The addition of these six major component areas, plus an (arbitrary) additional 12 per cent of the total area set aside for biodiversity, results in the ecological footprint.

Emergy footprinting However, there is more than meets the eye in an ecological footprint. Many goods and services supporting the food system are not included in the ecological footprint estimate. A more holistic method is needed to illustrate the foodprint, one that has the ability to account for all the work necessary to produce food, that is, the work carried out both by nature and by humans and including the past creation of fossil fuel. An estimation of ecosystem support and environmental load involves more than simply estimating the sequestration of carbon dioxide and a habitat for biodiversity. Sustaining a carrying capacity for a population and its food consumption activities requires balancing the use of the environment as a source of resources and its use as a sink for wastes.

The concept of carrying capacity is used by some analysts in the estimation of such balances. It relates resource use to environmental support. According to Brown and Ulgiati (1998), carrying capacity is the ability of a local environment to provide necessary resources for a population, or an economic endeavour, on a renewable basis.

Yet scholars disagree about what and how to calculate carrying capacity, in part because of uncertainties about where to draw the energy boundary. Ultimately, the energy driving all processes on the planet comes from the sun, the Earth's deep heat and from tidal energy. Many natural processes and ecosystem services, such as wind, rain, photosynthesis, soil formation and the concentration of metals are the products of aeons of these driving forces. Solar energy is converted into useful energy by plants, and animals and humans obtain their energy by eating plants and animals. The human food supply thus uses energies of various qualities, including solar energy, fossil fuels, biofuels and wind.

Another approach to estimating the demand on global energy processes required by a human activity such as food consumption is that of emergy analysis (Odum 1996). Emergy is defined as the amount of energy required to make something, that is, it is the 'memory of energy' that is degraded in transformation processes according to the laws of thermodynamics. The more work done to produce something, the more energy is transformed and the higher the emergy value of the product. Emergy thus is a measure of the environmental work – both past and present – necessary to provide a given resource. It is also a measure of the global processes required to produce something, expressed in units of a form of energy of consistent quality, most often solar energy. The method is based on the science of systems ecology, grounded in thermodynamics and general systems theory. Since all driving processes (the sun, Earth's deep heat and tidal energy) supporting the biosphere are incorporated in the scientific underpinnings of the method, an emergy evaluation includes all processes and resources involved in supporting a system. A fuller explanation of the concepts, principles and applications of emergy analysis can be found in Odum (1996).

In emergy terms the long-term carrying capacity of an area is limited by the flux of renewable emergy that is characteristic of that area. The direct and indirect land use based on emergy is similar to the concept of 'ecological footprint' in that it relates resource use to an area. The difference is that when the land use estimation is based on emergy, resources that are not directly tied to an areal demand (such as farm buildings, machinery and other infrastructure) can be included and consistently converted to the amount of environmental support needed to generate them (Brown and Ulgiati, 1998). This means that an areal demand based on emergy use gives a more far-reaching comparison of the actual area needed for different activities. It also means that the area can be very large for a system that uses resources produced over a long time period and/or large external area, as in the case of fossil fuel. An emergy footprint develops the foodshed approach further by tracking the total resource network converged and transformed within the food system, using solar emergy as a common basis of accounting.

The Swedish Foodprint

Agricultural land use for food consumed in Sweden

Consumers in Sweden claim an agricultural area of 0.4 hectares arable land per capita. This corresponds to a total of 3.7 million hectares of arable land for the country's 9 million inhabitants (see Figure 5.3). The agricultural land area within Sweden is about 2.7 million hectares, which means that roughly a third of the agricultural area appropriated lies outside its national borders. Sweden is therefore responsible through trade for an impact on agricultural land in other parts of the globe. Since the average available arable land area per capita on a global scale is only 0.25 hectares, and the average Swedish diet requires 0.4 hectares today, Sweden is claiming more than its 'fair share' of global available arable land (Johansson 2005).

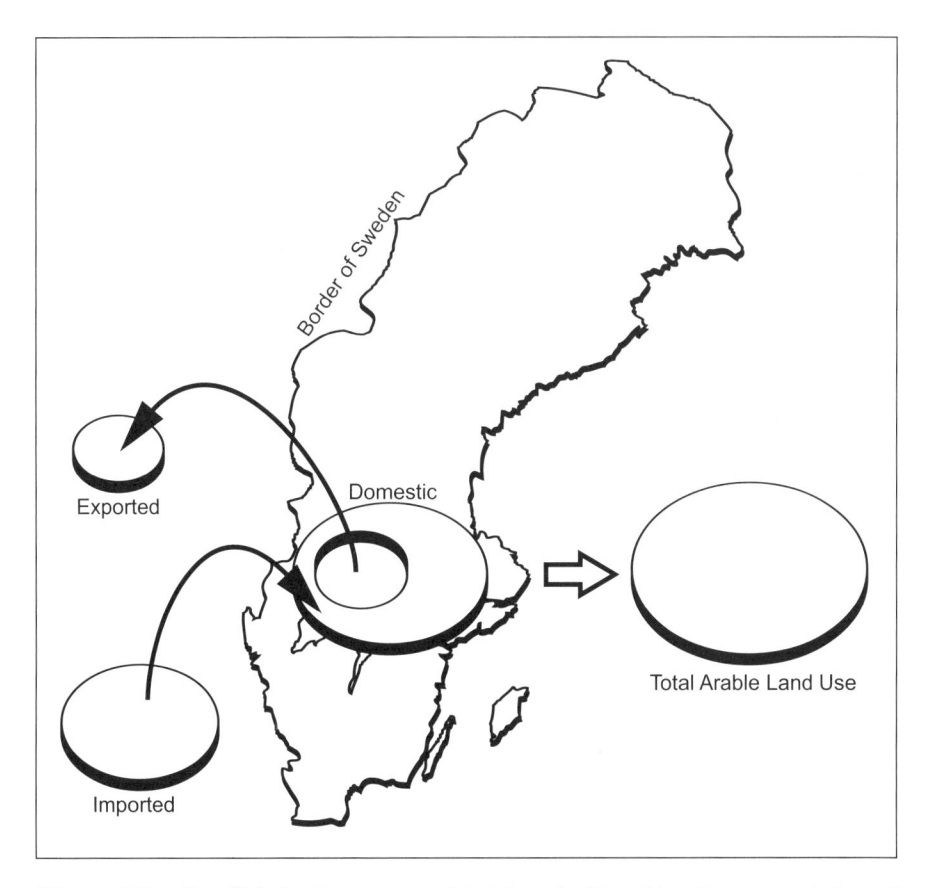

Figure 5.3 Swedish food consumers' total agricultural land use, consisting of domestic agricultural land, including the land used for production of imported foods but excluding the land used for exported foods

Design: Fredrik Stendahl

The environmental area required to support Swedish food consumption

The ecological footprint for food consumption in Sweden is calculated to be 0.8 to 1.6 hectares per capita, that is, an area two to four times larger than the average agricultural area. Most of this is 'fossil energy land' needed for forests to absorb the carbon dioxide emitted in the production, processing and transport of the food consumed (Johansson 2005).

The 'emergy support area' required by the Swedish food system of 1996 in its entirety has been estimated to be more than 140 million hectares. As a consequence, the emergy footprint was more than 40 times the direct agricultural area needed to support food consumption in Sweden (see Figure 5.4). Almost a quarter of the emergy footprint supported the direct agricultural production, that is, a footprint ten times the direct agricultural area. Food distribution in markets and supermarkets needed the largest emergy support area, accounting for 40 per cent of the total emergy footprint. The part of the food system in which consumers play a larger role, that is, transport back and forth to the supermarket, cooking and so on, appropriated the rest of the emergy footprint (Johansson 2005). The results of this foodprint exercise provide evidence that the area needed to support Swedish food consumption is extensive, to say the least. The emergy support area is 3.6 times the land area of Sweden.

Interpreting the results What do these figures mean? What is this area? When studying a system such as agriculture, which uses a high degree of external input, the emergy support area necessarily becomes large since it takes a large area to

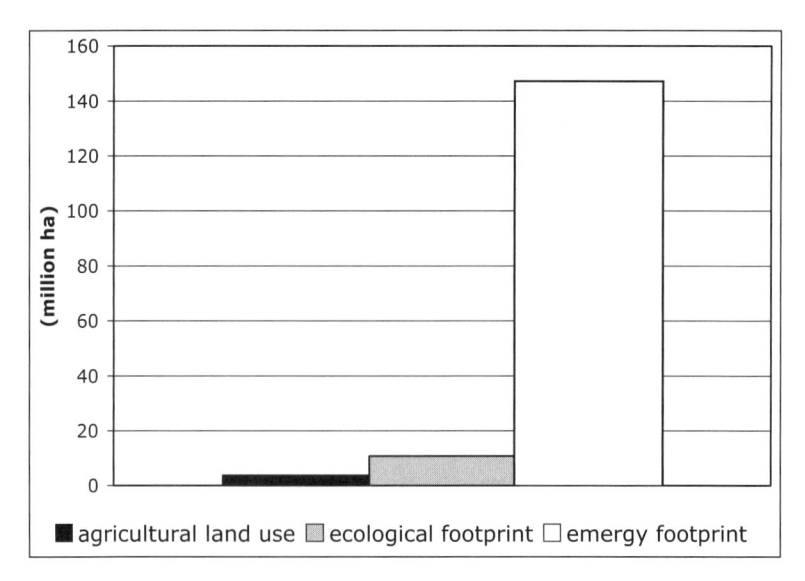

Figure 5.4   Different ways of estimating the foodprint for Sweden: agricultural land use (3.7 million hectares), ecological footprint (10.7 million hectares) and emergy footprint (147 million hectares)

Source: Johansson 2005

concentrate the solar energy required. When a system uses fossil fuels and quantities of metal ore that are built into the material technology of the system, it is using resources produced over an extensive period of millions of years. The emergy support area thus also exerts a 'historical' claim: the resources used by Swedish food consumption in one year take many more years to produce.

Calculating a foodprint for a household, school, community or a whole nation such as Sweden can shed light on the effect that food consumption has elsewhere. It may prevent 'out of sight – out of mind' behaviour and help make visible the extent of the impacts that consumption choices have. The ecological footprint is often described as an efficient pedagogical tool for this purpose. Areas can be easier for consumers to interpret than effects expressed as volumes, calories or monetary values. However, because Swedish consumers use resources and ecosystem services from all over the world and affect far-off places and distant peoples with their waste and environmental impacts, it may be that they do not relate to these areas: food comes from a global everywhere but not anywhere in particular. The exact location of food production is not specified, and taking action to make changes can seem difficult for the individual. Therefore, combining the foodprint with a foodshed analysis, where there is an investigation of food's origins, can deliver information that is more meaningful to the consumer.

Discussion

The global food system has allowed Sweden to distance itself from the problems associated with food production in faraway places. Until recently, food production relied on knowledge that was local and had a familiar ecological context. Education for domestic food storage and preparation is no longer common. The food industry and global markets have obfuscated food production boundaries and diluted the role of local institutions. Economies have drawn workers away from rural areas, extending families and consumers beyond their communities, and diminishing the need for local knowledge. Reconnecting production and consumption could be an important step towards food system sustainability. Progress towards sustainable food supply necessarily will move supply chains to make calculations of their environmental and overall production capacities. Other actions will include reducing intermediate sector demands, transport distances and use of indirect services. Institutions that manage foodsheds, local labour and ecological knowledge will increase in importance.

A more sustainable foodshed could start in our kitchens. What we eat is a major determinant of how human and natural resources are used and misused. Diets for better health are being designed and discussed continuously in society and in healthcare programmes. On an almost daily basis we are given recommendations on what to eat to stay healthy or lose weight. Diets for a sustainable environment and a fairer distribution of global resources are discussed less often. Nevertheless, diet matters for environmental sustainability; any change in diet also changes resource use. Dietary choices and consumption patterns may be more influential on resource use than population growth in the future. With the choices we make in the supermarket, we have an impact on the lives and environments of other people.

The study explored in this chapter has investigated the food system supporting food consumption in Sweden by means of a foodshed approach. The support area for the Swedish food system was made visible in a foodprint. The results showed that this area was much greater than it originally appeared. The areas indirectly required were in fact shown to be larger than the agricultural land used within Sweden and elsewhere in direct production of the food consumed, because of the system's dependence on external inputs. In order to develop sustainable and fair food systems Swedish society must move towards measuring the environmental work invested in the food consumed.

References

Brown, M.T. and Ulgiati, S. (1998) 'Emergy Evaluation of the Environment: Quantitative Perspectives on Ecological Footprints', in Ulgiati, S., Brown, M.T., Giampietro, M., Herendeen, R.A. and Mayumi, K. (eds), *Advances in Energy Studies. Energy Flows in Ecology and Economy* (Musis: Rome, Italy), 223–240.

Buringh, P. (1989) 'Availability of Agricultural Land for Crop and Livestock Production' in D. Pimentel and C.W. Hall (eds) *Food and Natural Resources* (London: Academic Press Limited), 69–83.

Getz, A. (1991) 'Urban Foodsheds' *The Permaculture Activist*, 24, 26–7.

Johansson, S. (2005) *The Swedish Foodprint: An Agroecological Study of Food Consumption* (Uppsala: Department of Ecology and Crop Production Science, Swedish University of Agricultural Sciences).

Odum, H.T. (1996) *Environmental Accounting – Emergy and Environmental Decision Making* (New York: John Wiley).

Wackernagel, M. and Rees, W. (1996) *Our Ecological Footprint: Reducing Human Impact on the Earth* (Gabriola Island, BC: New Society Publishers).

Chapter 6

Growing Sustainable Communities: Understanding the Social-Economic Footprints of Organic Family Farms

Matthew Reed, Allan Butler and Matt Lobley

The robustness and quality of life offered by rural communities have long been topics of debate and controversy. For many commentators, rural livelihoods and businesses are wrapped in a warm nostalgic glow in a belief that the past and the rural walk hand-in-hand and that the present is always worse. Others present the rural as a form of bleak reality in which farm life and rural work epitomise hard labour, low rewards, social isolation and a resounding marginality to contemporary life. In the debate between advocates of organic farming and those in favour of non-organic farming many of these controversies are rehearsed. The proponents view organic farms as working with nature, nurturing not just the soil but also those who work it and from which spring vital and vibrant communities (Pugliese 2001). Those in favour of non-organic farming see 'organic' as exploiting at best a niche market, an indulgence of middle-class people playing out fantasies of a rural idyll whilst the poor and hungry actually are fed by applying the fruits of science and technology (Coleman 2000).

In one form or another these differences have rumbled on since the beginning of the organic farming movement nearly 70 years ago. The questions raised by the protagonists have become ever more pressing as rural communities fragment, the pressure on ecosystems increases and the demands for high-quality food continues to grow. If one type of farming could be demonstrated to nurture communities that are strong and vital as well as ensuring environmental security then policy makers and citizens might be able to help those farming communities create a sustainable future. In the UK case such a future would involve family farms because British farming remains dominated by family farms and the 'familyness' of these businesses shapes them in a particular way. In order to understand the social role of farms in this context we have to understand the social lives of those who operate them and their families. We thus choose to refer in this chapter to the 'social-economic' footprint of family farm businesses.

Neither side in the debate has been able to table definitive evidence to support their opinions. The debate has remained a clash of ideologies and philosophies rather than a discussion of the different qualities of farm businesses and what they bring to communities. An understanding of farms as the complex mixture of the families that own and work them, the businesses that often are part of a global trading system and the ecological specifics of place would require a synthesis of economics and social science as well as a way of comparing organic and non-organic farms. This chapter is about the 'Impacts Project' that sought to achieve such a synthesis. It tells in part the story of how this was achieved and the intellectual foundations on which it was based, but most of the chapter is about what this research project discovered (Lobley et al. 2005).

It would be unrealistic to expect one project to provide all the answers or answers that would be accepted by all. Yet this research has been able to suggest what questions need careful consideration and that the answers might have more nuances than a simple distinction between organic and other farms would indicate. It suggests that the behaviour of families who live on farms needs to be considered: how do they make their living? how do they interact with others? where do they come from? At the same time, consideration has to be given to how a hill-farm is assessed against an arable, dairy or a mixed enterprise or even a large against a small farm. Even posing the question in this form raises opposition from those perhaps fearful of the answer.

Intellectual Roots

The Impacts Project grew out of long-term collaboration among a group of researchers working at the universities of Exeter and Plymouth in the UK. Over several years they developed a body of research and theoretical insights that allowed a comparison to be made of organic and non-organic farms. In this section we review the work that contributed to this approach and the insights that fed into this way of viewing the activities of farm businesses.[1]

Ruth Gasson and Andrew Errington's (1993) analysis of the operation of the farm family business in the UK provided a point of departure for developing our analysis: 'The family farmer has sought and in large measure achieved political legitimacy by seeking to distance himself from "capitalism" at the ideological level, whilst fully embracing it at the economic level' (Gasson and Errington 1993, 3). They argue that family farm businesses are characterised by six attributes: the family must be resident on the farm; family members must provide the capital for the business; the main actors in the farm business must all be related by kin ties or by marriage; the business must be managed and not just owned by the family; the family do the farm work; and the farm assets and control are transferred to the next generation of the same family. In this characterisation the business and family are intertwined in a way that is highly unusual in contemporary society in so far as the business may be guided not just by the aim of making an operating profit in the current year but of securing a livelihood for the next generation of the family. Because many of the businesses are inherited they may have low levels of debt, making them very robust in economic downturns. The final effect of the passage across generations is that the same family may have been resident in one area for hundreds of years. In an

---

1 A wide range of academic work was reviewed and analysed; for a full set of references see Lobley et al. (2005), Lobley, Butler and Reed (2008).

economy where the average business lasts for seven years, farm businesses have both a different history and a different trajectory.

Errington with his then students, Lucy Harrison and Paul Courtney, studied local economic multipliers with particular regard to rural and small market towns (Harrison-Mayfield et al. 1998). They were interested in how businesses traded within a locality and how much of the economic benefit of their activities remained within the immediate locality. Money retained within a local community often confers a very direct series of benefits as it moves through the economy creating and sustaining the livelihoods of local people, while money that leaves a community very quickly does little to sustain the economy of the area further. In developing tools to measure these effects the research team began to find ways of comparing different types of business. Although firmly rooted in economics this work had obvious links to economic sociology as well as to considerations of the role of the farm within its broader natural, social and cultural environment. We drew on their work in developing the social-economic footprint concept discussed below. It also shaped the discussion of the footprint metaphor as being about a particular shape or configuration of activities rather than their size or geographical spread alone.[2]

Two other projects were influential in shaping our work and both involved the authors of this chapter. The 'Rural Restructuring' project investigated whether structural changes in the agricultural industry would gradually ease family farm businesses out of the industry (Lobley et al. 2002). Using an extensive survey of farmers in England, the project concluded that the shape of farm businesses was becoming increasingly complex as farmers engaged in a wider range of enterprises, but that their commitment to farming remained strong. The 'Farmers on the Edge' project resurveyed 100 family farms in the county of Devon who had been the subject of a study 20 years before. These families had experienced numerous changes to the society around them and the industry they worked in; they also had been at the centre of the foot-and-mouth livestock disease outbreak of 2001. Serious questions were being asked at the time of the study about their ability to continue farming and how they might manage to do so. The study concluded that these businesses were highly robust because of their grounding in a family but that both the families and the farms had suffered considerably in the preceding years (Reed et al. 2002). The detail of these two projects provided significant insights not just into the immediate questions posed but also in how to investigate family farms in contemporary society.

The Farmers on the Edge project threw into stark contrast the importance of the social life of farmers and of their families. This issue can be explored by using the related concepts of social capital and embeddedness. By social capital we mean the resources that people can draw on by belonging to a group or network of kin, friends and associates. Some people's social life is formed around a small tight core group of friends and family; others have many associates but few long friendships or families. It is often presented as common sense that the first is the best for communities and the second as typical of rootless cosmopolitan life. The leading theorist of social capital, Robert Putnam, distinguishes between 'bonding' and 'bridging social capital'

---

2   The local economic trading patterns of organic and non-organic farms are discussed in greater length in Lobley et al (2005).

(Putnam 2001). Bonding with other people is important and a key social skill, that is, being able to get along with people day in and day out and being part of the group, yet with too much bonding the group becomes exclusive and rigid. Bridging means being able to reach out to others, to communicate beyond one's immediate group and to form new contacts and groups, yet with too much bridging social networks cannot hold together. Putnam uses the metaphor that bonding is the 'superglue' and bridging the lubricant of social life, both constructive in their proper place and in balance. We found these concepts useful for exploring social life; measuring and describing them is more of a challenge.

The second concept, embeddedness, is related to social capital. Mark Granovetter observed the importance of being involved in a place and in the social interactions of that place (Granovetter 1985). While we mostly think of embeddedness in terms of social life, the concept is also important in economic life. To be known and to know people over a period of time creates situations of trust where people are prepared to conduct business, lend money or share information and opportunities in a way they might not with strangers. There are risks in becoming too embedded for it might mean that it is difficult to change roles, that attempts to change create social friction and can stop new ideas from being taken up. It is easy to say anecdotally that someone is part of a community – embedded – but measuring or describing this phenomenon is more difficult. Yet in order to understand social life as it laps over into the economic activities of a farming family it is necessary that these social attributes can be measured between families and groups as well as described in theoretical terms.

The Social-economic Footprint

The Impacts Project investigated by means of a postal questionnaire and case study interviews over 300 organic and 300 non-organic farms in England. It gathered a range of data about the farmers, their biographies, the businesses they run and the lives they lead in their communities. The main explanatory tool we used to demonstrate the differences between these businesses is a form of radar diagram that allows comparisons to be made between different types of farm simultaneously (see Figure 6.1).[3] As we explain the results of survey we detail why each measurement was chosen and what it means. When all the metrics are taken together we refer to the result as the social-economic footprint (SEF). In this analysis the footprint is not spatially grounded since social and economic relationships are not defined to any single location and the shape of the footprint is as important as its size.

The measurements

The various measurements we made can be subdivided into two major groups: the first describes farmers' social capital by means of four variables. 'Community

---

3   Whereas conventional radar diagrams have axes that are related to each other through a single fixed scale, the radar diagrams constructed in this project have independent axes that enable different scales to be adopted for each metric.

activity/membership' measures the participation of respondents in their community and civic life; literally, by how many groups, clubs and societies they take part in. The average in the survey was 2.38, the highest 10. The 'informal network ratio' is the quotient of informal relationships (family and friends) and formal business relationships (accountants, veterinarians and bank managers) that comprise the farmers' social network. Here a value of zero indicates wholly formal networks; a value of one signifies equality between informal and formal relationships; and values greater than one point to more informally arranged business networks. By means of these two measurements we are looking into the social capital of the farmers. Our hypothesis is that those taking part in many clubs and societies will have a wider range of friends and associates, that they will be more likely to hear new ideas and have the contacts who will spread these. These measurements are describing not just the extent of the social life of the farmer but also the form of that activity.

The next set of measurements capture 'family embeddedness' and 'birth embeddedness', respectively measurements of how close the family members live to each other and their proximity to their place of birth.[4] When taken together these two measurements represent how embedded farm businesses are in their community. Those who have inherited a family farm will live in the place where they were born, with their immediate family near by, whilst those who have entered farming by choice rather than birth will have a more scattered score. It is assumed that people who have lived in an area all of their lives with their family close by might be very bonded within their communities as well as embedded. They will probably enjoy high levels of trust with and knowledge about people in their network but membership of this group might be very limited.

As we have discussed, farm businesses couple the management of nature with a business enterprise. The next three metrics compare the management and performance of different businesses. By measuring the 'salaries of those employed on the farms' we provide a way of comparing the success of different businesses and their employees. Rather than measuring the scale of the business in terms of turnover or profit we then recorded the farm's 'turnover per hectare', thereby allowing large and small farms to be compared. The measure of 'short or direct marketing routes' indicates that the farmer sells produce to the end consumer rather than through longer or more convoluted routes or to multiple retailers. A similar logic is followed in measuring the 'number of workers employed per hectare', which combines seasonal, casual and part-time workers with the full timers. We refer to the combined figure as full-time equivalent (FTE) workers. In these ways we can compare the economic activities of farm businesses of different types and scales.

The results of the survey

When we examine Figure 6.1 we can see that organic farmers are generally more active in joining organisations and groups and so in the most general terms can be said to have a wider social circle. This indication is reinforced by the relative

---

[4] The metrics for the embeddedness measures are between zero (no embeddedness) to six (total embeddedness).

importance for organic farmers of informal over formal networks. These findings are of importance because successive studies suggest that those with a wider social circle and who are less embedded in communities are more likely to be involved in innovation, to be receptive to new ideas and to implement them. Richard Florida (2002) has measured and mapped these phenomena in urban areas and we suggest that our findings indicate that a similar process is taking place in rural Devon. Our findings on embeddedness also suggest that a number of organic farmers are new entrants to the industry. They live away from where they were born and from their family and are less likely to be bound by the social norms of a place-based community.

As is quickly apparent in Figure 6.1, the market for farm labour is fairly even, representing the only point of convergence in the whole figure. The value of sales per hectare for the organic farms is greater, for both indirect and direct sales. Yet for direct sales the top of the scale is £5000 per hectare and for indirect sales it is £3000, demonstrating that there is added value for the farm business in direct retailing. The line for the non-organic farmers is level on both these measures – there is less value for them in selling directly. Although these figures do not reveal levels of profitability, they suggest a greater opportunity for profitability and that organic farmers are receiving more for their produce. In turn the organic farmers are employing more people per hectare.

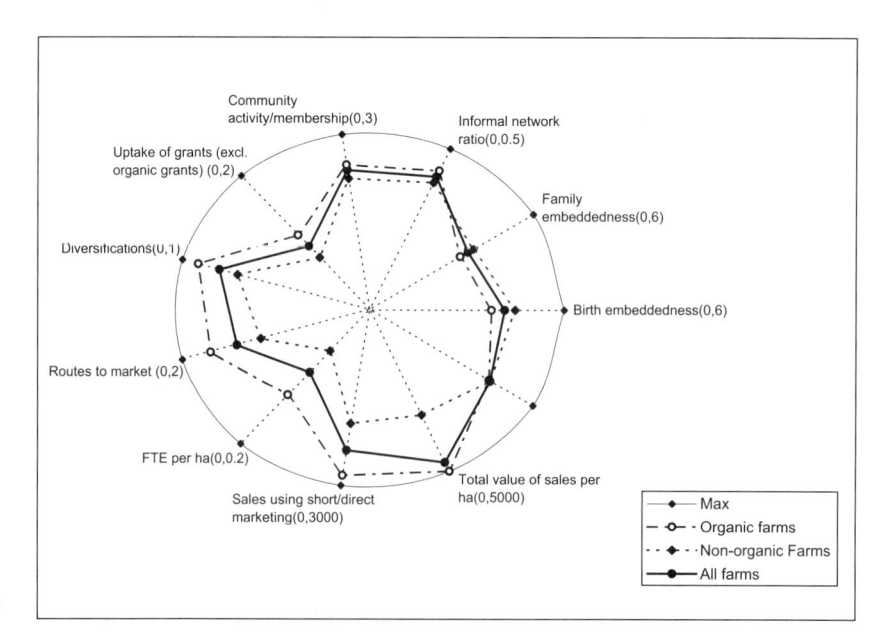

Figure 6.1 The social-economic footprints of different farms compared
Source: Lobley et al. (2005)
Note: For each indicator the values in the parenthesis indicate their minimum and maximum values.

These findings speak directly to some of the most controversial aspects of organic farming – the price of organic produce and the use of labour. For many years progress in food and farming was seen by many in terms of a continuing and sustained fall in food prices and in the number of people employed in agriculture. In terms of the sustainability of rural areas neither trend is particularly desirable. Cheap food prices tend to mean that there is less money in circulation in rural areas, making sustaining a vibrant farm-based community more difficult. A reduction in the number of people employed on-farm means that it is difficult to create sustainable communities. Such communities become dominated by those with few economic links to each other, such as commuters and the retired, and therefore also with weaker social links to the area (Midmore and Whittaker 2000). More money in local circulation does not mean that it is evenly or justly distributed and more employment does not mean that local people are being employed (Morison et al. 2005). All we can say is that local businesses earning money and employing people are an important foundation for sustainable communities. On this basis the organic farms are doing much better than their non-organic peers.

The three measurements of the economic scope of farm businesses measured the diversity of their activities and their involvement with the state. The first of these, the number of routes that the produce of the farm takes to market, shows that those farms producing only one product – such as milk – and which sell it to only one customer – the milk cooperative – have a very narrow footprint. Those selling a range of products such as meat, milk, vegetables, cereals through a range of retailers and processors have a wider footprint. Many farms run a range of enterprises, some related to the agricultural industry such as contracting, others complementary enterprises such as bed and breakfast or livery services and others unrelated to farming, such as information technology consultancies or alternative health practices. Many of these enterprises draw either explicitly or implicitly on the output or landscape that is produced through the farming arm of the business, yet diversification changes the configuration of the farm's economic footprint. The final measurement in this set relates to the uptake of government schemes. Farms are entitled under EU legislation to a range of support measures but different farms and farmers engage with them in a different ways.

Figure 6.1 shows that organic farms have a much broader scope of activities than their non-organic counterparts, sending their goods to a wider range of markets and running a greater diversity of businesses from their farms. This finding can be interpreted in a number of different ways. Some would argue that it shows that organic farmers are struggling to make ends meet through organic farming and so need to cross-subsidise their activities through other businesses. This would imply further, according to some, that the organic market is not a serious market, that it is crowded by part-timers or dabblers or that organic farmers are poor business people. Alternatively, it could be that because organic systems demand a varied farming system organic farmers have a range of produce to sell. The range helps them establish businesses independent of the supermarkets. Another of the important development effects of diversified farm businesses is that they offer a wider range of employment opportunities that are not so reliant on the fortunes of the agricultural industry. Organic farms with their wider footprints offer a better scope

74   *Creating Food Futures*

for employment and are engaged with the wider agricultural industry in a different manner to their peers.

State subsidy support for farming activities has been and remains for many deeply controversial. Many advocates of the free market see it as 'feather-bedding', cushioning the farming industry from the rigours of economic discipline. Others concerned with global equity see state subsidies in rich countries as denying the poor in developing countries the opportunity to trade their way to development because each European cow attracts a per capita income higher than the income of many of the world's poor. If we leave aside the schemes directed to supporting organic and conventional production, our perspective in this matter is that engagement with state programmes indicates farm businesses that are responding to the wider policy signals of the society they are part of. If farmers take the opportunity for grants to improve wildlife, they not only benefit financially by providing this public good but are also engaged in a dialogue with the wider community. Organic farmers are taking up government support but, as we will discuss below, they are doing so from a wider range of sources than others, responding to a more diverse set of policies. This means that organic farms are positioning themselves to be more responsive to public demands as mediated by rural policy support. It signals that a dialogue of sorts is occurring between the farm industry and the wider community over securing public goods such as the wildlife or animal welfare. This may not be welcome news for those who for whatever reason are opposed to such measures.

When we turn to Figure 6.2 we can see that the choice of marketing channels marks a difference between farms. Hidden in the averages visualised in the figure

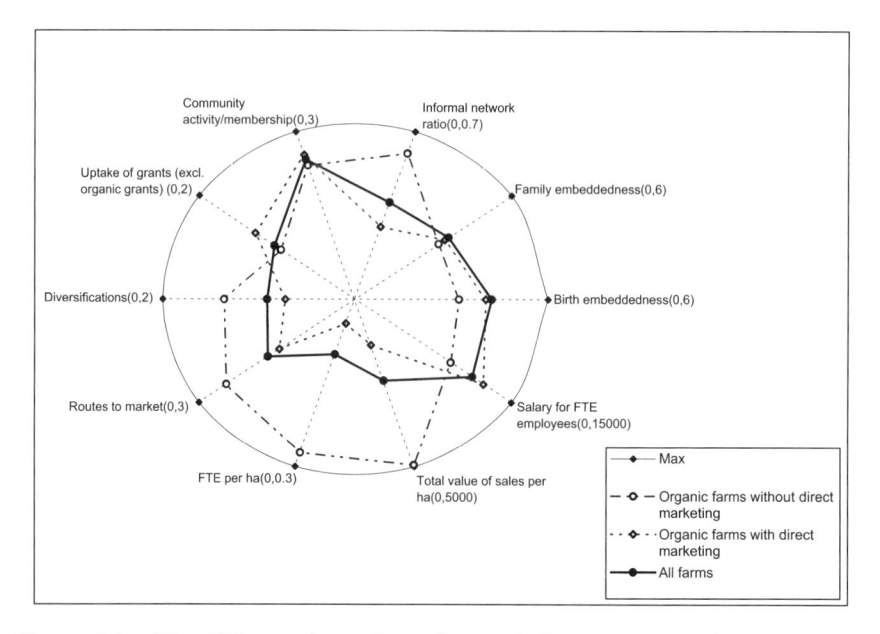

Figure 6.2   The different footprints of organic farms compared
Source: Lobley et al. (2005)

are a subgroup of organic producers who are distinct; in fact their radical difference skews the picture of the average organic farm. Their produce, raw or processed, is sold directly to consumers or through very short marketing chains and the farm retains control over the value of the produce. This group are younger, more outward looking in their opinions, less likely to have been born into farming, more highly educated and frequently have had careers outside agriculture. These characteristics mean that as business operators they have access to different sets of information flows and a wider range of generic business skills that are applied to developing their organic businesses in innovative directions.

By examining Figure 6.2 in more detail, we can see that the subgroup of organic farms that sell directly to consumers have a much more extensive social-economic footprint. Their networks tend to be less formal and with more friends and family members providing support and information to their businesses networks. As 46 per cent of this subgroup are new entrants into farming, it is not surprising that they are less embedded in their community than the average organic farmer who does not sell directly to consumers. They have entered farming with a vision to farm organically and, given their previous non-agricultural experiences, they are able to develop new forms of marketing, such as reaching consumers through the use of the internet. This in turn is reflected in the management and performance metrics of their footprint: their salaries tend to be lower but the value added and the labour per hectare are of far greater significance.

The processing of produce is one of the ways that organic farms selling directly to the consumer capture additional value and provide additional rural employment. The development of trading enterprises is another way. For instance, ten times as many organic farms that sell directly have on-farm trading enterprises than organic farms that sell through longer, more indirect marketing routes. These enterprises range from farm-gate kiosks through to sophisticated shops supplying a range of food products. There is also considerable evidence that they have a growing involvement in the processing of food on their farm, thereby shortening the food chain further. These same businesses also increasingly are using the internet as a means of communicating with their customers, and through box schemes these customers are making a lasting commitment to the producers.

The presence of processing and trading enterprises is reflected in the footprint in terms of 'economies of scope'. Direct selling, using a range of marketing routes, frequently creates synergies with other farm businesses. Alliances are formed that are often informal and do not involve contracts but are based on trust between farmers and other growers and produce outlets. Produce that cannot be sold directly or locally is sold through local wholesale markets or is traded to organic cooperatives, thereby broadening the range of market routes used. The development of farm-based processing and trading enterprises also explains the increased diversification that occurs on farms that sell directly as compared to organic farms that do not. The development of processing and trading enterprises also accounts for their greater uptake of government grant payments.

Discussion

We do not want to argue that organic farms are 'good' and non-organic farms 'bad' in terms of their social-economic footprint or rural development in general (Guthman 2004). In fact, if we break down our findings by farm type, we see that organic dairy farms, for instance, are hard to differentiate from non-organic dairy farms. Both types of dairy farm have very narrow footprints, contributing little to the rest of the community, selling to only one source and being in many ways very demanding on the environment. Yet it is these farms that are under most commercial pressure from the supermarkets and frequently it is these farms that have families with dependent children. In the past, the regular income generated by dairying has made it very attractive to those with a growing family. So a simple association of a particular farming system with a particular outcome is not justified; understanding the context in which it operates is essential. The context has to be built from its social, economic and cultural elements and the limits of any one household's family or business options understood (Elder et al. 2000).

What we can see from the Impacts Project is that a determined, ideologically driven and highly educated group of farmers are carving out a new role in British agriculture. It is a paradox that much of what they are doing in terms of diversification of business activities, direct retailing to the end consumer and responding to market and policy opportunities is not related to organic farming as a production system. Their role speaks of their openness to communication, innovation and change that the measurements of social capital indicate. As we discuss below, this finding does not necessarily provide easy suggestions as to the future direction of policy.

The characteristics displayed by this subgroup of innovators cannot define an entire industry and indeed they may not be conducive to establishing sustainable communities if we conceive 'sustainable' as implying continuity of pre-existing social-economic relations. The innovations and experimentation of the organic direct suppliers is consciously transformative. They are not looking to preserve the rural communities that currently exist; they are looking to create new dynamism in their communities. In so doing this group may be seen as engaging in a political act. Their energy is not directed to explicit changes in policy or to parliamentary elections. It is aimed at changing food and farming, recognising that such a change might displace those who have farmed for several generations, engender a new level of environmental sustainability and alter the character of many existing rural communities.

Further Reflections

The research reported here presents a complex picture. Although we can conclude that some organic farms are offering a far better return for the public money invested in them in terms of rural development, compared to most non-organic farms, we cannot generalise this finding to all organic farms. This may not be a comfortable conclusion. Many of the farms that are at the forefront of creating positive social-economic returns do not necessarily respond to efforts to direct change by means of policy incentives in the agricultural sector. The organic status of a farming system is only one component in creating a farm business that maximises returns to the rest of the rural economy. At the moment these characteristics are closely tied to a farm's organic status but they are not codified within organic practices or food chains.

A number of options for broadening the returns to rural communities could be considered by policy makers, supermarkets and citizens. Policies and purchasing choices could be targeted towards farms that supply locally, are diversified and employ a range of people. Start-up or venture capital, business advice, support services such as local abattoirs or food processing units could be directed to these ends. Local and regional government and local development projects could initiate such schemes, without waiting for central government to act.

Organic farming encompasses a wide range of practices; not all of these are associated with the strongest or most positive rural development impacts. The Soil Association and Organic Farmers and Growers certification agencies set many of the standards for British organic agriculture and they could make considerable changes that incorporated rural development goals. For instance, the development of a higher-level trading network in which farmers are bound to sell through local markets or direct to the end consumer, coupled to obligations to honour fair trade and good employment practices, could be used to reward such farms through the marketplace. Such a development has been resisted for fear of confusing consumers yet those purchasing organic goods are already differentiating between organic foods whose labels signal distinctive social-economic footprints.

Many farmers, especially those in commodity sectors under price pressure such as dairying, argue that there is no direct supply option for them. Our interviews reveal that while they might acknowledge that they do not contribute as much to the local community they feel they have little alternative; they do not control their market but are controlled by it. Consumers might make a parallel point: that they do not get the opportunity to buy diversified products or from a range of trading networks. Either they cannot physically gain access to them or the price excludes them. Our study shows there is a limit to the autonomy of the producer and consumer even when they are working together towards a common end. In many ways this returns us to our initial questions about the configuration of the contemporary food system. It is clear from our research that considerable losses and gains can be created for rural areas by changing the configuration of contemporary farm businesses. The question remains open as which path citizens want to take.

Acknowledgements

Our thanks to Defra for their intellectual and funding support for the Impacts Project (RE0117), on behalf of all at the Centre for Rural Research, Paul Courtney, Martin Warren and the late Andrew Errington.

References

Coleman, D. (2000) 'Comparative Economics of Farming Systems', Tinker, P. (ed.) (2000) *Shades of Green – A Review of UK Farming Systems* (Stoneleigh: Royal Agricultural Society of England).

Elder, G., Conger, R., King, V., Matthews, L., Mekos, D., Russel, T. and Shanahan, M. (2000) *Children of the Land. Adversity and Success in Rural America* (Chicago: University of Chicago Press).

Florida, R. (2002) 'The Economic Geography of Talent' *Annals of the Association of American Geographers* 92:4, 743–55.

Gasson, R. and Errington, A. (1993) *The Farm Family Business* (Wallingford: CABI).

Granovetter, M. (1985) 'Economic Action and Social Structure: The Problem of Embeddness' *American Journal of Sociology* 91 November, 481–510.

Guthman, J., (2004) *Agrarian Dreams. The Paradox of Organic Farming in California* (Berkeley: University of California Press).

Harrison-Mayfield, L., Dwyer, J. and Brookes, G. (1998) 'The Socio-Economic Effects of the CSS' *Journal of Agricultural Economics* 49:2, 157–70.

Lobley, M., Errington, A., McGeorge, A., Millard, N. and Potter, C. (2002) *Implications of Changes in the Structure of Agricultural Business* (Newton Abbot: University of Plymouth).

Lobley, M., Reed, M. and Butler, A. (2005) *The Impact of Organic Farming on the Rural Economy in England* (London: Defra).

Lobley, M., Butler, A. and Reed, M. (2008) 'The Contribution of Organic Farming to Rural Development' *Land Use Planning* (in review).

Midmore, P. and Whittaker, J. (2000) 'Economics for Sustainable Rural Systems' *Ecological Economics* 35, 173–89.

Morison, J., Hine, R. and Pretty, J. (2005) 'Survey and Analysis of Labour on Organic Farms in the UK and Republic of Ireland' *Journal of Agricultural Sustainability* 3:1, 24 43.

Pugliese, P. (2001) 'Organic Farming and Sustainable Rural Development. A Multifaceted and Promising Convergence' *Sociologia Ruralis* 41:1, 112–31.

Putnam, D. (2001) *Bowling Alone* (London: Penguin).

Reed, M., Lobley, M., Winter, M. and Chandler, J. (2002) *Family Farmers on the Edge: Adaptability and Change in Farm Households* (Exeter: Countryside Agency).

PART II
Case Studies: Innovations in Stakeholder and Organisational Relationships

Chapter 7

Balancing Business and Empowerment in Fair Fruit Chains: The Experience of Solidaridad

Irene Guijt and Edith van Walsum

Establishing value chains for fairly traded and organic produce requires social innovations at many levels and in diverse quarters. To succeed, two questions need to be addressed: who pays for social innovation and who benefits? In this chapter[1], we explore the tug-of-war between business imperatives on the one hand, and the empowerment and anti-poverty ideals that are embedded within fair trade and organic produce chains on the other hand. Our observations are grounded in the case of Solidaridad, a Dutch non-governmental organisation (NGO), which has pioneered fair trade since the mid-1980s.

Solidaridad has taken a variety of groundbreaking initiatives to promote the development of 'fair' and 'clean' chains. From the outset, its strategy has been to find significant markets in the North to ensure substantial demand for fair trade items. The underlying idea is that only if fair trade becomes mainstream at the consumer end can enduring and substantial change occur along the entire food chain, which is necessary if sustained improvement in the working conditions and livelihoods of producers is to be achieved. To realise its aims, Solidaridad has spawned a wide range of governance, certifying, supervision, marketing and mainstreaming institutions that operate as a web of independent but interrelated institutional innovations. For example, Fair Trade Labelling Organisations International (FLO) is an offshoot of Solidaridad's efforts to create independent certifiers. Solidaridad's focus on these and other institutional innovations has proved vital to the functioning of this novel, value-driven type of trade.

Solidaridad launched the Max Havelaar Coffee trademark in 1986, creating a mechanism that enabled producers to get a fair price for their coffee. This made it possible for coffee retailers to work on corporate social responsibility and gave consumers a choice to buy fair trade coffee in supermarkets. Solidaridad's pioneering work in establishing a fair coffee chain started in Mexico and expanded to other countries in several continents.

In 1996, Solidaridad initiated the Oké label for fair trade bananas. This involved establishing AgroFair, an independent trading company, which has seen an explosive

---

1 We are grateful for critical comments by Jeroen Douglas, Cathy Farnworth and an anonymous reviewer that helped in the final editing.

growth of banana imports especially since unfair licensing systems (Roozen and van Hof 2001) were abolished in January 2006. The 'tropical fruit basket' concept was created in 2003 to include mangoes, pineapples, oranges, mandarins, lemons and other fruit ingredients. Solidaridad has gradually incorporated the environmental and health costs of production, thus expanding its fruit label from Oké to Eko-Oké (the Dutch indication for Organic and Fair Trade). Since 2000, Solidaridad has also been working on the development of fair and organic textile, biomass and soybean chains. Each commodity chain offers unique challenges and opportunities.

Initially Solidaridad was primarily funded through private donations via its church-based constituency, but today funding is more diverse and has facilitated expansion of the early coffee experience into the other commodities and areas described above. Current funding sources include the Dutch government aid agency for fair trade bananas from Peru (see Case Study 1) and the European Union for the West Africa experience (see Case Study 2).

As a pioneer and innovator, Solidaridad is no stranger to steep learning curves. In this chapter, we outline some key strategic choices, tensions and dilemmas with which Solidaridad has been confronted in its efforts to mainstream fair trade. These reflections are based on an evaluation that we undertook in mid-2006 for Solidaridad's Dutch-funded 'Mainstreaming of Fair Trade' programme (van Walsum and Guijt, 2006). Although derived from that evaluation, the observations in this chapter do not constitute an assessment of Solidaridad's work, but rather an exploration of where the key strategic challenges and tensions lie when trying to mainstream fair trade in such a way that there is a balance between business and empowerment.

We start by discussing Solidaridad's theory of change regarding the mainstreaming of fair trade. We introduce the idea of strategic choices – about commodity, programme partners and participants, intervention mechanisms and modalities, and geographical areas of intervention – as central in determining the impact of Solidaridad's work to date. The concept of strategic choice is illustrated with two case studies from Peru and West Africa. We then turn to three critical questions: what is being mainstreamed and for which purpose? What is being sustained – specific enterprise, the chain, or the concept of fair trade? And what is fair in fair trade – and for whom? We conclude with observations about the importance of understanding 'success' in this pioneering phase and the value of learning processes in institutional innovation.

Solidaridad and its Theory of Change

Every individual and organisation takes action based on its 'theory of change' – the overarching assumptions and philosophies that influence one's vision and understanding and shape one's views on how change occurs in society. Being clear about one's theory of change is essential, particularly in a pioneering process, as it enables a critical review of assumptions that have not yet stood the test of time.

Solidaridad's 'theory of change' has always been based on the conviction that poverty reduction must occur through changes in the terms of trade and that fair trade can only make a significant and enduring impact if it becomes a commercial norm. Three concepts guide its work: piloting, upscaling and mainstreaming, for each of which there are different expectations and strategies. Piloting refers to the testing of new products, chains and organisations; its work with cotton in Peru is one example (van Walsum and Guijt 2006). Upscaling refers to the consolidation of successful pilots into independent and commercially viable organisations or initiatives that enable a financially interesting volume of goods to be produced and marketed. Finally, of core interest to this chapter, is mainstreaming, which we define as the process of society embracing an innovation. In the case of fair trade, this becomes evident through a steady and economically interesting demand of supply from consumers.

The pilot phase began in the 1970s. During this period, environmentally and socially improved production and distribution chains were established. Product distribution was organised mainly through shops run by charities supporting the third world, such as the Dutch Wereldwinkels (http://nieuw.wereldwinkels.nl/) and the British Association for Fair Trade Shops (http://www.bafts.org.uk/buy_location.asp). The upscaling phase started in the mid-1980s and was characterised by the establishment of certifying agencies and the initial breakthrough to regular distribution in supermarkets.

The third and current phase, which began in the 1990s, is characterised by a breakthrough into the mainstream economy. This has demanded a two-track strategy. First, it has been critical to maintain activities in the alternative distribution chains, where the highest fair trade standards are upheld and the highest premiums and prices are paid to the producers. Through these outlets, producers can sell relatively small quantities but with high returns. This track is related to the Fair Trade brand. Second, Solidaridad has sought to increase absolute volumes traded by engaging with companies on the basis of corporate social responsibility. This has been possible in the case of coffee through Utz Kapeh, a worldwide certification programme that has several advantages for producers, but does not guarantee a minimum price independent of market developments.

In the current mainstreaming phase, new business models and alliances play a central role. The marketing of fairly traded products occurs through ever more diverse channels, and thus there is greater emphasis on product quality and branding. Solidaridad sees itself as a catalyst, contributing to a societal climate in Europe, and the Netherlands in particular, that is more favourable to concepts like responsible entrepreneurship and the Triple P (People-Planet-Profit). It develops innovative models that facilitate this breakthrough to the mainstream economy. A substantial part of its funding for this piloting function is provided by the Netherlands Ministry of Foreign Affairs under a programme called Mainstreaming of Fair Trade (Solidaridad 2003).

A number of assumptions underpin Solidaridad's theory of change. Some assumptions are explicit and others implicit. Explicit has been the organisation's conviction that it is essential to tackle the entire chain at once in order to create the push–pull effect of producer–consumer dynamics. It is also clear about the need to focus on creating a viable business, first and foremost, in order to ensure there is 'trade' to share fairly with poor producers.

Implicit assumptions in Solidaridad's theory of change are supported to varying degrees by staff at Solidaridad and related organisations. We found little evidence of their being made explicit and challenged. These implicit assumptions strongly influence the strategic choices that have been and are being made. Examples of implicit assumptions in Solidaridad's work include:

- accepting market standards and demands as non-negotiable
- seeing the need for a pivotal organisation that acts as broker along the commodity chain and buffer in the initial difficult start-up period
- recognising the importance of allowing evolution in the engagement with, and capacity building of, producer organisations
- seeing the need to set precedents that convince the mainstream and not to ask others to embark on something that one has not tried oneself
- investing, or ensuring investment, in producer organisations
- identifying quality assurance schemes that are appropriate for each segment commodity/chain (FLO, ISO 8000 and so on).

We do not comment on the validity of such assumptions here. Many will stand the test of time. However, we advocate more explicit articulation in order to understand better the circumstances under which mainstreaming of fair trade has most chance of success.

One implicit assumption that we argue is questionable pertains to gender. Solidaridad believes that women's involvement in fair trade automatically implies a strengthening of their position. It assumes that gender issues are dealt with because fair trade generates formal labour opportunities for women and because FLO regulations on gender are followed. However, there is no deeper understanding and critical reflection of gender equality that guides the organisation's theory of change.

Also implicit is the idea of what we term 'strategic choices', and the juggling of goals that this entails. The mainstreaming of fair trade entails a continuous and complex balancing act between (perceived) consumer needs and producer realities, and between business requirements and the empowerment of farmers. Tackling such tensions in a creative and informed manner is core to the future of the entire mainstreaming effort. At the heart of this confrontation lie the strategic choices that Solidaridad has had and still has to make, and the interconnections between these choices – with regard to commodity, to programme partners and participants, to intervention mechanisms and modalities, and to geographical areas of intervention. We have selected two case studies to illustrate the strategic choices made and dilemmas faced by Solidaridad and its partners.

Fair Trade and Organic Fruit: Examples from Peru and West Africa

Bananas in Peru

Solidaridad's work in Piúra, northern Peru, started in 2001 in collaboration with AgroFair. They bought an existing banana export company and turned it into a co-owned subsidiary company. Through this company, Biorganika, and producer organisations, Solidaridad seeks to ensure that 'producers and workers enjoy increased incomes, decent work places, and a cleaner environment by means of sustainable organic banana production and a fair trade exporting company in Piúra, Peru' (Solidaridad, 2003). The first bananas were sold by Biorganika in 2002, and in 2006 it started incorporating producer organisations as shareholders. The producer organisations are the Valle de Chira Association (VCA) and the harvesters' association, with a third (producer) organisation about to join. FLO is another key actor in the banana chain and wields considerable decision-making power, as the discussion below makes clear.[2]

The export of fair trade organic bananas from Peru might appear to be an odd choice, given that bananas are not a traditional export product. Indeed, exports only commenced in 2000. Since all banana operators, including Dole and Biocosta, have just entered the country, start-up challenges have been considerable. They include limited logistical facilities and infrastructure, low volumes and relatively high operational costs, no local producer organisations with experience in the banana trade, not to mention the additional novelty of fair trade standards.

However, the natural environment has kept bananas' main disease, *Sigatoka negra*, at bay, providing a distinct advantage for organic production. Year-round water from nearby dams and a nearby port offer other advantages. Furthermore, the national banana market is disadvantageous to producers because of strong price fluctuations as a consequence of overproduction in the summer months. Banana harvesters lack the security of timely payment and any form of social security. Thus the fair trade option provides easily measurable advantages to producers and harvesters and to the Peruvian banana sector in general. The emerging fair trade organic export market has already taken some of the glut out of the local market, so prices fluctuate less strongly, and conventional banana producers receive higher prices.

Having presented the context, we now explore three types of strategic choices that have been necessary: that of programme participants, organisational partners, and the empowerment strategy.

Choice of programme participants   Once the choice of commodity was clear, Solidaridad had to decide with which producers to work. Were there other significant social groups that required attention? And what were the implications of the choices it made?

The export programme of Biorganika with Solidaridad has enabled some 200 banana smallholder families, for the first time ever, to obtain access to lucrative export markets. Three-quarters of these families own less than one hectare and more than 50 per cent of the producers do not have access to basic services such as potable water. Increased income marks a significant improvement in well-being for these families.

---

2   FLO was established in 1997 and is an association of around 20 labelling initiatives that promotes and markets the fair trade certification standard in their countries. It provides fair trade certification to producer organisations; this is mandatory if their produce is to have access to fair trade markets and related prices and premiums. Certification is given following adherence to a fixed set of standards.

However, Biorganika has chosen to operate in an area where farmers have smaller acreages than, for example, in Dole's area. This has organisational implications as it increases the number of farmers with which Biorganika must interact in order to break even financially. The positive choice to work with small producers places heavy demands on both its own organisational capacities and those of producer organisations.

With respect to considering the needs of other significant social groups, Solidaridad discovered that it had difficulties with the fair trade certifying agency, FLO. FLO only recognises two types of producer, either independent producers whose organisations are certified or plantation workers (FLO 2006). FLO standards do not address the needs and rights of agricultural workers such as banana harvesters if they are subcontracted by independent producers. In Peru, this means that FLO's standards do not benefit the banana harvesters/packers, who are distinctly worse off than producers, being landless, only partially employed, and dependent on producers for wage setting. Biorganika has, therefore, engaged with harvesters as a separate group, who now have their own association. Biorganika has a dedicated staff member on its payroll to accommodate the harvesters' needs, and has all harvesters on its payroll as staff, thus giving them access to national social security.

Another problematic issue is that of gender equality. Neither Solidaridad, nor Biorganika, nor VCA have policies on gender equality, or an equality-oriented perspective on fair trade. Gender is not recognised as an issue and is not built into the programme, hence leading by default to a programme of work in which men far outnumber women. Women are only members of the growers' association if their husbands have left or passed away and thus are not involved in discussions and decision making. Women are not present in the chain, apart from a very few who are harvesters. The implications of this in terms of 'fair trade for whom' are significant.

Choice of partners and mechanisms A second area of strategic choice relates to the configuration of organisations that is needed to create a viable fair chain and then dealing with the assumptions and capacities that they bring into the system.

Solidaridad's main vehicle for fair trade in Piúra, Biorganika, considered itself for the first two years a 'top-down' model, arguing that this was needed to create order and trust in a chaotic and partially corrupt business environment. Thus Solidaridad implanted a model that links AgroFair and its benefits directly to producers. Following this period of establishment, a joint operation co-managed by smallholders and Biorganika is now taking place. Gradual transfer of Biorganika shares to the beneficiaries is planned for 2007, 2008 and 2009. In this day and age of participatory development, 'top-down' mechanisms may be viewed with suspicion. However, in order to benefit smallholders over the long term, Biorganika and Solidaridad considered it essential for a company to perform well financially and thus adhered to core business procedures.

Where Biorganika deviates from a 'standard' business operation is in its decision to play a more expanded brokering role. In addition to ensuring the export market for bananas, it implements various capacity development measures that it sees as critical for mainstreaming fair trade. It has hired two social development team members. One is dedicated to improving working conditions for the harvesters, and the second works with the producer organisation to develop capacity to meet the requirements of organic certification. Biorganika ensures that producers receive appropriate inputs, pays an extra price on top of FLO's minimum price and social premium, deals with quality claims and provides the additional accounting needed to ensure transparent and timely payments to producers and harvesters.

The VCA is another key partner for Solidaridad. As a young organisation established in 2002, it is not surprisingly still struggling to reach the maturity and strength of internal democracy to make optimal use of fair trade's potential. The VCA also lacks expertise in handling the detailed commercial transactions currently being undertaken by Biorganika. It is likely that the high level of social premiums obtained on bananas, which totalled over US$400 000 in May 2006, has distorted the VCA's understanding of what it really takes to coordinate operations worth US$3 million. For example, at the time of the review (van Walsum and Guijt 2006), Biorganika was buffering the VCA from losses related to quality claims as part of the pilot phase, recognising that these could cripple the immature association. However, FLO insisted that this responsibility, and the very high level of costs, be transferred to the VCA, along with responsibility for conducting other commercial transactions.

FLO is the third critical partner for the success of the banana initiative. The VCA has opted into its certification system in order to access the prices and premiums that FLO offers. However, FLO stipulates that producers must be in charge of all post-harvest activities until the delivery of palletised boxes of bananas to the exporter (that is, Biorganika). While appearing to be a logical requirement, this may not be feasible. At the time of the review, the VCA had not yet manifested sufficient capacity to meet the levels of logistical organisation, quality management, fairness towards workers, efficiency, financial accounting skills, transparency and democratic decision making that is required.

FLO's requirement appears to be based on the assumption that in all situations a democratic and mature producer organisation exists. However, the VCA is not yet a participatory democratic organisation, although formally appearing to work as a representational democracy. FLO's adherence to its definition in a context where the underlying assumption is not valid is likely to lead to extra costs in the chain that could swallow up the fair trade premium and jeopardise the sustainability of the initiative in the long term.

Biorganika and Solidaridad thus face strategic choices in relation to VCA and FLO. Should Biorganika continue to provide a buffer for the problems that are very likely to emerge – quality claims, accounting problems, potential loss of certification – and yet continue to accommodate all the harvesters' needs? Can Solidaridad pursue innovation in the fair trade arena by engaging with FLO to push for a broader definition and transitional model, with clear indicators and objectives guiding the payment of increasing levels of social premium?

Choices for building capacity towards empowerment When and how does empowerment figure as a conscious strategy in the evolution of a fair trade partnership? And what is the role of capacity building in this process?

Since fair trade organic bananas represent an innovative endeavour in the Peruvian context, establishing a new way of doing business has required several reconfigurations of the relationship between Biorganika and VCA to keep up with changing understandings about what is needed and with evolving capacities. Flexibility on the part of Biorganika has been paramount in the difficult transition period of an innovative venture. It is important to acknowledge this when assessing the speed and efficiency with which mainstreaming of fair trade is occurring. It has had to upgrade its own capacities to deal with new challenges, bringing in new staff in the process.

Producer participation in the banana chain still represents a significant hurdle; capacity issues figure strongly in this. The current board of VCA has not supported Biorganika's attempts to help build the capacity of producers as much as it could. It has been reluctant to invest in developing joint transition plans towards becoming shareholders of Biorganika as well as meeting the farm gate price-related requirements of FLO.

A critical question for the mainstreaming of fair trade is who is supposed to arrange the organisational strengthening that is the bedrock of empowerment in a transition phase. As Biorganika says, 'We are not interested in business at whatever cost. But we can also not work with weak producer organisations' (van Walsum and Guijt 2006). So far, the company has been footing the bill and taking on the responsibility of organisational development. It has been unable to share the load, as there appear to be few NGOs active in the region that could help support producer organisation development. As Jack Garcia-Barandiaran, manager of Biorganika, says, the company is stereotypical. It imposes rules, works with passive producers and determines market strategy. This is perhaps a reasonable approach when developing new fair trade value chains, as long as it is accompanied by measures to empower producer organisations so that they can in due course actively access markets themselves. This is a concern that Biorganika takes seriously and is trying to address within its financial margins. Nonetheless, without a clearer definition of 'empowerment', and how an empowerment process can be facilitated, an empowering approach to accessing markets – and ensuring resilience in the marketplace – will be difficult to realise. Equally critical is the question of who pays for the empowerment process.

The West African Fair Fruit project

While Ghana and Burkina Faso continue to face widespread rural poverty, both are also the scene of encouraging developments in the fruit export sector (World Bank, 2001). Ghana made important strides in developing its exports of pineapple and banana during the 1990s. It became the third exporter of pineapples to Europe within four years. Though a small player in the African banana export market, Ghana is so far the only African country to export organic and fair trade bananas. Burkina Faso has a growing export market for mango. Mango production is naturally organic in the country, and is mainly grown by small and medium farmers. The fruit export sector is gaining increasing recognition and support from the private sector, funding agencies and research institutions. Multinational companies are tending towards greater geographical diversification and are keen to establish themselves in West

Africa. Solidaridad's strategic choice to engage in the fair fruit trade in Ghana and Burkina Faso, therefore, has been the right choice at the right time.

Solidaridad initiated the West African Fair Fruit project (WAFF) in 2003, with funding from the European Union. WAFF's objectives are twofold: to promote new and sustainable sources of income and employment for rural poor people in Ghana and Burkina Faso, and to establish a farmer-owned service company to promote fair trade and organic fruit production and exports.

In Ghana the WAFF project works with Farmapine Ltd, a production cooperative of 360 small to medium-size pineapple farmers, and with VREL, a banana plantation that employs 600 labourers. Both manage their own packaging and transport to Europe. In Burkina Faso WAFF has established a company, Fruiteq, which manages the selection, packaging and transport of mangoes to Europe. Two newly formed mango producer cooperatives supply their fruits to Fruiteq. At the time of our evaluation, the legal holder of WAFF was a Ghanaian NGO. This was, however, a formality. In practice, the project is run by a small team steered by AgroFair. Solidaridad continues to play a guiding role in the background, as shareholder in AgroFair.

WAFF has made many strategic choices. First, we consider the issue of consumer preferences and consequences for small producers. Second, we explore the question of gender equality. Third, we discuss the role of middlemen in the fair fruit chain.

Consumer preferences and farmer realities   Northern markets and the assumed taste and needs of mainstream consumers dictate choices elsewhere in the commodity chain, for instance which variety of pineapple a farmer should grow. Ghanaian smallholders have long grown the Smooth Cayenne pineapple variety, which has sold well locally and internationally. However, a new kid on the block, the MD2 variety, has become increasingly popular internationally. This variety is renowned for its very sweet taste and its broad, angular shoulders – it looks like the 'ultimate' pineapple. MD2 has been marketed aggressively by international fruit companies and now dominates the international pineapple market.

The business rationale for growing MD2 appears obvious, as the price paid per box is three times that for Smooth Cayenne. Therefore, WAFF has encouraged farmers to grow MD2 pineapples. It imported MD2 planting material from Cuba, which it then multiplied and distributed among farmers.

However, small producers face problems with MD2 as its production costs are twice as high as those of Smooth Cayenne, because of the high costs of the inputs required, and production and storage are technically more demanding. Without access to credit, they find it hard to make the shift to the new variety. Furthermore, MD2's popularity has ruined the market for Smooth Cayenne. Our review in May 2006 (van Walsum and Guijt 2006) indicated that many small pineapple producers face financial crisis as a result of the collapsing market for Smooth Cayenne. This also affected Farmapine Ltd as farmers were unable to repay loans taken from Farmapine. As a result, a situation of spiralling mutual indebtedness has arisen between Farmapine and farmers.

Underlying the immediate concern to find a solution to the situation is a more fundamental question. Does the wish to mainstream fair trade imply that 'mainstream choices' must always be made regarding markets and assumed consumer preferences? Or should fair trade companies seek opportunities for marketing innovations, for instance, by making the case for 'Smooth Cayenne, a vintage pineapple variety'? (J-M. Voisard, personal communication).

Thus far, AgroFair has no intention to promote anything but MD2, as alternatives do not fit with its focus on mainstream markets, and additional marketing costs would arise. However, this then raises the question: what then is the difference between 'fair' and 'conventional' trade, if there is no space for challenging consumer preferences that are socially counterproductive? This is a relevant question that merits attention, not just by AgroFair but by the larger fair trade constituency.

In the current situation, two issues require immediate attention. First, the financial crisis of Farmapine will need to be resolved (and was being looked at seriously at the time of our review). Second, to be fair to small producers, WAFF should help them deal with the obstacles they face in adopting the MD2 variety. This could include providing adequate credit arrangements and hands-on agronomic expertise. More generally, fair trade organisations, including Solidaridad, need to develop greater clarity about the level of collateral damage that is acceptable as a result of market-related choices and innovations.

Making the choice for gender equality   If fair trade is to benefit women on a par with men, choices have to be made for gender equality. Logical as this may sound, in the WAFF project we saw no deliberate choices aimed at promoting gender equality. While WAFF partners ensure that FLO norms regarding working conditions of men and women are followed, for instance that toilets and washing facilities are provided for women, other aspects of women's participation in WAFF-related enterprises do not appear to be the product of intentional design.

Labour opportunities merit a critical look. Currently, women's involvement in production reflects the common division of labour in the area. Whereas men do the plucking – 'an arduous task', women are considered experts in packing – 'needs precision and patience'. But which women, and which men, gain or lose from the changing divisions of labour associated with the shift from local to export marketing; and what is needed to compensate for any adverse effects on gender relations? For instance, in the case of mango production and marketing in Burkina Faso, some women have gained from new employment opportunities at the packing station. However, other women appear to have lost as a result of reduced marketing opportunities. Mangoes that women used to sell locally are now marketed internationally, but the role of women in the international marketing chain is much smaller than in the local market. What is the balance between gains and losses in this case, and what are likely future developments? These questions have not been addressed by the project or its partners.

Women's involvement in decision making is another issue. The premium committee formed at the VREL banana plantation has two women members. This shows that the need for women's participation is formally recognised. However, these women have little say in determining how the fair trade premiums are spent. They lack the assertiveness or power to express their views and to influence the decision-making process. It had not occurred to VREL staff to stimulate and support women to play a more active role.

Summing up, women participate in WAFF as part of the labour force but not as active decision makers. This is, we believe, a result of WAFF's lack of a gender strategy and in its not making a deliberate choice to involve women. WAFF limits itself to meeting the minimum demands. Formal gender equality, as expressed in fair trade norms, is respected. But there is little concern for and awareness about substantive gender equality[3] – the actual influence or control of women, and what they stand to gain or lose when certain decisions are made.

Choices in evolving partnerships FLO standards seek to ensure transparent arrangements that avoid producer exploitation, for example by eliminating middlemen. However, it is questionable that eliminating middlemen would, under no circumstances, add fairness and transparency to the system. In some areas, their removal could negatively affect product quality and reduce the system's overall performance. Middlemen do not always earn excessively, and should indeed be understood in some cases as effective agents dealing with important questions of risk, hidden action, hidden characteristics, enforcement of contracts and rent seeking behaviour (Fafchamps 2001, quoted by H.W. van der Waal in personal communication). For this reason, Fruiteq, the Burkina-based mango export company, has been trying to negotiate between FLO norms and local institutional realities.

The picking system in Burkina Faso's mango export chain has three key local actors: producers, buyers/exporters and middlemen – the pisteurs. Pisteurs are independent entrepreneurs in charge of harvesting, selecting and transporting mangoes from farms to the packing station. They supervise groups of between 20 to 100 harvesters. Pisteurs thus have crucial know-how of the selection and harvesting process, making them an important link in the export chain. But they are not always transparent about quality criteria and prices offered by the buyers (Délégation d'Intercooperation Sahel 2003). Producers have little understanding of the entrepreneurial role of the pisteurs and the risks they take with fresh produce.

Fruiteq has introduced small but important innovations in this system. It recognises the pisteurs' critical role in harvesting but seeks greater transparency and cooperation between chain partners. It has therefore negotiated transparent agreements with pisteurs and producer groups regarding prices and payment systems, so that each party understands the money flows and the amount they are due. Fruiteq is now investing in uniting producers and pisteurs in a single association. It is envisaged that this partnership will improve quality throughout the chain and allow partners to become EurepGAP certified. Partners could eventually become co-owners of Fruiteq

---

3 Formal gender equality refers to the formal aspect of gender relations, such as the percentage of women members in a committee. Substantive gender equality refers to the factual balance of power, for example, can women exercise real influence in a committee? Formal equality may help improve women's living conditions and contribute to substantive equality, or it may be a mere formality. However, women are truly empowered when there is substantive gender equality. The notion of substantive vs. formal gender equality is central in the international women's rights movement.

with the employees and management of the packing station (H.W. van der Waal, personal communication).

This innovative and 'localised' approach contrasts with FLO's position that middlemen ought to be excluded from fair trade systems. A thorough discussion with FLO will be needed and choices have to be made, by both Fruiteq and FLO, on whether the modified pisteur system can be considered an appropriate and 'fair' institutional mechanism in the West African context.

Who Pays for Social Innovation and Who Benefits?

The Peruvian and West African cases are distinct in scale, complexity, age, challenges and institutional arrangements. However, the issues surrounding strategic choices and how to respond to each new twist and turn in the evolution of the process have led us to identify three considerations for those engaged in furthering fair trade and organic commodity chains.

Mainstreaming of what and for which goal?

There is a clear linkage between organising the supply side among primary producers and processing/export companies, and the demand side among retailers and consumers. What happens and is prioritised on the demand side has major implications for choices elsewhere in the chain. Fundamental, therefore, are reflections on who and what drive the process of mainstreaming fair trade. Solidaridad starts by trying to mainstream demand. Once a demand-driven model works out well and supply pilots have revealed results, supply can be upscaled. Is it the need to mainstream the demand side that dictates the rhythm and direction or is it mainstreaming at the producer and processing end? This question directly addresses the challenge of balancing empowerment with business and the many daily decisions that are made along the commodity chain.

A related issue considers the current dominance of the South to North flow of produce. Can fair trade chains be created that feed local or regional markets? Countries such as India and Brazil have massive and growing well-to-do urban middle classes. The scope for developing local niche markets for high-quality products is considerable. Other third world countries are likely to follow in the years to come.

Is fair trade fair to everyone?

One issue that has received very little attention in the fair trade discourse to date concerns gender equality. Fair trade implies that producers and workers in the chain – men and women alike, producers and harvesters alike – are entitled to their 'fair share'. Within this concept there should be no place for exclusion or marginalisation of women. Just as fair trade requires a proactive strategy towards marginalised farmers or harvesters, it also requires a proactive strategy towards women: women as leaders and decision makers, not just as labourers.

However, while fair trade standards include gender-specific criteria, this does not mean that the organisations in fair trade commodity chains operate with a clear gender-aware vision or theory of change. We noted an absence of gender vision in the work in Peru and West Africa, with women present as silent members of cooperatives or committees, or referred to as 'benefiting within the context of the family'. In both situations we observed that formal norms for gender equality, as expressed in Fair Trade standards, are being respected. But the notion of substantive gender equality – women's actual influence or control, what do they gain and lose – receives little attention. It has not been internalised as an issue of concern.[4] The situation elsewhere in the world of fair trade is unlikely to be different, if the absence of documented experiences and silence on this issue in the fair trade sector is indicative.

Opportunities to address gender inequalities are being missed. Women deserve better under the auspices of fair trade. If women are sidelined and gender is not considered within the mainstreaming process of fair trade, one could argue that fair trade objectives will never be reached. Furthermore, failures to tap into women's potential amounts to inefficiencies that are likely to obstruct sustainability of overall efforts.

Sustainability of what – fair trade enterprises, chains or concepts?

Currently, Solidaridad is focusing its efforts on ensuring that individual enterprises such as Biorganika, WAFF and Fruiteq can become and remain commercially sustainable. The second order challenge is to ensure sustainable fruit chains that can weather the rise and fall of individual enterprises. The long-term issue, of course, is whether the concept of fair and clean trade will become the new commercial norm. Organisations such as Solidaridad need to keep their eyes on all three levels simultaneously to ensure that mainstreaming succeeds.

While enterprises may survive if the owners/managers uphold the fair trade concept and maintain profits, ensuring that the chain and concept is sustainable requires a much wider ownership of fair trade principles and practices. Solidaridad has been touting the concept of 'Made-By', an umbrella label set up within the cotton chain to link consumers of clothing in the North with those by whom the product was made (van Walsum and Guijt 2006; <www.made-by.nl>). The notion of 'owned by' is equally important within fair trade. Interviews with stakeholders in Peru and West Africa indicated limited awareness about what fair trade represents. Ensuring ownership by all stakeholders in a chain is the next challenge for Solidaridad.

To achieve a sustainable impact, a considerable scaling-up of Solidaridad's current pioneering efforts is required. Collaboration, capacity building and concerted stakeholder action will be central in this process. Multi-stakeholder processes can become leveraging mechanisms to scale-up impact, but only if Solidaridad and similar

---

4   Solidaridad's position is that fair trade brings many producers from an informal to a formal economy, that new jobs are created, especially for women; hence women are benefiting most from this change. While this is certainly often the case, a broader understanding is needed of the impact of fair trade on gender equality in formal and substantive terms.

organisations understand how to use such mechanisms consciously and strategically. Learning from other multi-stakeholder processes constitutes an important first step.

Conclusion: Understanding Success and Valuing Learning

Solidaridad's experience with coffee and banana show that it takes about ten years before a fair trade chain matures. It is essential to keep this time frame in mind when assessing the success of Solidaridad's efforts. Judging success too early in any pioneering effort, including the work of Solidaridad, may lead to the mistaken conclusion that interventions are inefficient. However, when viewed from a longer time perspective, apparently high initial investments may very well be necessary to kick-start the transformation of the terms of trade. This is the nature of innovation in a dynamic setting and when taking on the entire chain from harvesters to consumers. Flexibility and sufficient freedom to grasp unexpected opportunities or create new ones are critical, alongside clarity of partnerships and respective roles and a focus on alleviating crucial bottlenecks.

Nevertheless, an important question about empowerment needs to be asked. If empowerment is about creating work for men and women, then the work to date is more than promising. If, however, empowerment refers to the political consciousness and informed choice that marked the early origins of Solidaridad's work on fair trade, then we suggest that organisational strengthening and farmer empowerment be given further support at this stage.

Learning by doing is central to the mainstreaming of fair trade. There are no precedents – they must be created. This requires experimentation and leaps of faith by partners, including funding agencies, along the entire chain. Innovations will be needed and will emerge from ongoing critical analysis of success factors and obstacles by all parties, which can help them to re-strategise at crucial moments and sustain the motivation. Partners that hold on to outdated perspectives will fall by the wayside. Having a comprehensive story and evidence of success will greatly facilitate the upscaling of current efforts. Mistakes will be made but do not need to be repeated.

Let us return to our central question: Who pays for social innovation and who benefits in the context of fair trade? Our review of the work of Solidaridad and its partners in Peru and West Africa has revealed that major efforts have been made towards social innovation, with clear benefits for poor producers and labourers. The process of mainstreaming fair trade is in full swing. Yet the road ahead is likely to be lengthy and arduous. Imbalances continue to exist between Northern supermarket demands and producer realities in the South; existing gender imbalances at the producer end tend to be perpetuated; and crucial producer organisation development is complex and costly, with a lack of clarity about who should foot the bill. It is vital to understand and appreciate the underlying tug-of-war between business imperatives and empowerment. Unless choices are explicit and questioned, the very real possibility exists that costs and benefits of social innovation will be unequally shared and lead to unsustainable outcomes at the expense of the most vulnerable categories among the very people who were intended to benefit. An inclusive social learning perspective will be essential in assessing and monitoring the entire process towards the mainstreaming of fair trade, and in managing the fine balance between 'business' and 'empowerment'.

References

Délégation d'Intercooperation Sahel (2003) *Potentialités et problématiques pour le développement des filières liées à l'arboriculture fruitière dans le sud Mali. Le cas des mangues.* Mali: Délégation d'Intercooperation Sahel.

Fafchamps, M. (2001) 'Networks, Communities and Markets in Sub-Saharan Africa: Implications for Firm Growth and Investment', *Journal of African Economies* 10: 109–42.

Fairtrade Labelling Organizations International (FLO) (2006) 'Standards', <http://www.fairtrade.net/sites/standards/general.htl>, accessed 19 July 2007.

Roozen, N. and F. van der Hoff (2001) *FairTrade. Het verhaal achter Max Havelaar koffie, Oké bananen en Kuyichi jeans.* Amsterdam: Van Gennep.

Solidaridad (2003) *Mainstreaming of Fair Trade. TMF Programme Proposal.* Netherlands: Solidaridad.

van Walsum, E. and I. Guijt (2006) *Mid Term Evaluation: Mainstreaming of Fair Trade Programme, Solidaridad (funded through TMF between 2003 and 2006)*, internal document. Utrecht: Solidaridad.

World Bank (2001) *Ghana's International Competitiveness. Opportunities and Challenges Facing Non-Traditional Exports*, World Bank Report no. 22421 – GH, 21 June. Washington, DC: World Bank.

Chapter 8

The FoodTrust of Prince Edward Island, Canada

Woody Wilson

Prince Edward Island, Canada is a finite resource that has almost reached its production capacity. There is no more land for expansion. A productivity gain at the expense of environmental degradation is not an option. There is an agreement between fishing, farming and the community to share this resource, keeping it pristine and continuing to develop the infrastructure as a major tourist destination. Tourism and eco-tourism in particular is becoming a major contributor to the Island's gross domestic product.

The island cannot compete on size against its competition in North America. It has to compete on quality. The challenge is to find a reward in the market for this. This means eschewing the commodity model and focusing on differentiation strategies. The FoodTrust initiative is an example of a process that seeks to promote high-quality foods from sustainable production systems and to create an equitable partnership in the value chain between the producer, the retailer and the consumer. To achieve this objective, a branded approach has been implemented.

This started as a place-based initiative, seeking to exploit the locality and uniqueness of Prince Edward Island. While an important attribute, it was quickly established through consumer focus group discussions in selected target markets in North America that local identity programs work best in their own environments. This was no solution for the island, given its small population of 140 000 people. Exceptions such as Champagne and Parma ham, which seem to contradict this hypothesis, are apparent, but closer examination reveals that these regional brands also have the attribute of unique quality and differentiation. They are not truly place-based when seen from a branding perspective. FoodTrust recognized this, and the importance of high-quality foods from sustainable production systems in its mission statement became apparent. Thus the brand proposition was conceived.

The results have been encouraging. By defining and meeting a consumer need in addition to the emotional appeal of the less tangible but equally important social and environmental dynamics of preserving a beautiful island and its unique way of life, such credibility has been achieved that FoodTrust is commercially marketing its produce in conventional distribution channels across North America. In combining the above elements a unique brand has been created. Marketers studying the model presented in this chapter will find ways to replicate this in their own markets.

Setting the Scene

The Dawson Farm

David Dawson and his brother Paul farm potatoes at Augustine Cove near the famed Confederation Bridge connecting Prince Edward Island with Atlantic Canada across the Gulf of St Lawrence. The family traditionally based their produce business on a supply agreement with an independent grocery retailer in the Maritimes. In the early 1990s, this group was bought out by one of the national retail chains, produce supply was integrated into national procurement and the Dawson family business dried up overnight. David and Paul were stuck with a warehouse full of potatoes and nowhere to sell them.

This harsh lesson led the Dawsons to seek ways to diversify so that they would never encounter the same problem again. They sought and found foodservice accounts and spread their supply across several retailers and distributors. They increased their packing-house capacity. Further diversification involved contracting their facility to smaller farmers in the surrounding area to help spread some of the risk and reduce cash flow requirements. These measures were all aimed at increasing efficiency by using economies of scale. Even this was not enough and price competition continued to squeeze margins.

This is a familiar story that is being played out in agricultural communities across the globe. As populations concentrate with increasing urbanization, so too must the food supply chain consolidate to meet the demand. These needs are currently being met at the expense of environmental equity. Urban sprawl and pollution, coupled with environmental degradation from the pressures of large-scale monocultural agricultural production manifest themselves in growing environmental pressure in a system that is becoming increasingly unsustainable in the long term.

For David and Paul, they were more than prepared to consider the branding option that FoodTrust was developing. They participated in the early workshops to try and find a solution to their problems. For them and a growing number of farmers, FoodTrust of Prince Edward Island represents a way forward to a viable and sustainable future in agricultural production.

The commoditization of North American agriculture

Canada's farming sector has changed significantly since the number of farms peaked at 732 832 in 1941;[1] the 2001 census states there were 246 923.[2] This decline of almost half a million family farms has given way to highly effective industrialized farms that are cropping more and more land. Over the 20-year period from 1981 to 2001 the land in crops increased by 5 429 339 hectares to a total of 36 395 151 hectares in crops.[3] As the farms become larger there is an ever-increasing need to

---

    1   Census Stat Fact, 2002. Number of Census Farms. Saskatchewan Agriculture, Food and Rural Revitalization.
    2   Statistics Canada, 2002. *The Daily*, May 15 edition.
    3   Statistics Canada, 2004. Census of Agriculture, Agricultural Land Use.

find new markets. Canada now exports about half of the food it produces and imports about half the food it consumes.[4]

The inescapable fact is that there has been a massive global expansion in agricultural output and trade in first world economies since the end of the Second World War. As farms have consolidated and grown bigger, food has never been cheaper to purchase. For the first world it is truly a commodity to be acquired as cheaply as possible.

Concentration of the distributive trade

The last four decades have seen a massive shift in margin from the producer to the distributive trade across all commodity groups. By way of example, Figure 8.1 on pork pricing shows that pork prices have remained fairly static since 1970, but the value captured at the retail level has increased dramatically, while the producer margin has declined.

Much is written about concentration in the retail trade; most scenarios predict that three to five retailers will emerge as the global players of the future. Whether the retail trade has consolidated to accommodate today's high volume of agricultural output or vice versa is a moot point – the result has been a disconnection between the consumer and the producer. Food supply is increasingly oriented towards more efficiencies through economies of scale. Price competition among retailers has forced continual margin pressure on the supply chain and efforts are focused on streamlining overheads in order to survive. This has been achieved through consolidation and logistic integration to capitalize on the mechanization and massive increase in yield per acre that advanced agricultural production methods provide.

The North American consumer

Never has the standard of living in first world society been this high. But also, never has society been more stressed. The most precious commodity in the world today is time. Consumers are time pressured to a degree never before imagined. The increase in the standard of living has come at a terrible price. Compared to the nuclear family of the 1960s with a single breadwinner, a single car, one TV set and a washing machine, today's household has to sustain more than two cars, microwaves, home computer networks and theatre systems, ride-on lawn mowers, snow blowers, and a host of other gadgets designed to make life more convenient and save time. From 1982 to 2001 the per capita debt doubled[5] and 47 percent of Canadian households are spending more than their pre-tax income.[6] Consumer debt is now at the point where consumers are carrying three credit cards on average. While enjoying a high standard of living, servicing the resultant debt load is putting pressure on society. Trends in drug and alcohol abuse, suicide and divorce rates underlie a social system

---

4   Statistics Canada, 2006. *The Daily*, June 5 edition.
5   Statistics Canada, 2005. *The Daily*, March 22 edition.
6   Cheat, Tom. 2006. CBC News Online, 'Buy Now, Pay Later: Canadians and Debt', in-depth report, September 12.

Price Spreads - Pork

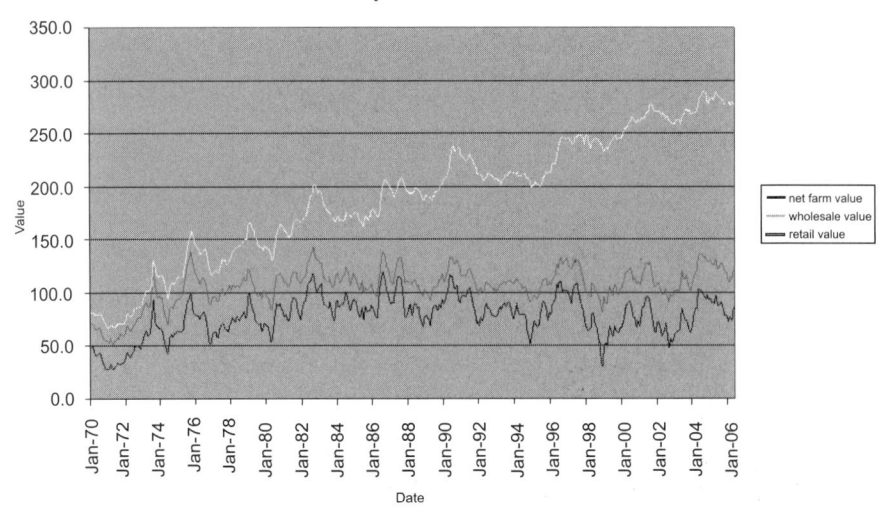

[Chart showing net farm value, wholesale value, and retail value from Jan-70 to Jan-06, with values ranging from 0.0 to 350.0]

Figure 8.1   Pork pricing

that too is becoming increasingly unsustainable. In 2003, Canadians owed $49.8 billion to VISA and MasterCard.[7]

Households themselves have undergone fundamental change with nearly 38 percent being single homes or one-parent households. There is a consequent lack of nurturing to be found in modern urban society and consumers are increasingly stressed. Seventy percent of Canadian households eat a meal outside the home at least once a week while 22 percent have four or more meals outside the home during a week.[8] This means a significant number of today's meals are consumed outside home, largely due to time pressure. Spending of money for private consumption varies greatly from country to country for food, with high-income countries such as the United States and Canada spending 8.7 percent and 10.5 percent respectively, while South Africa and Tanzania spend 30.3 percent and 71 percent.[9] Food itself has become a commodity. Almost half the food purchased is thrown away and the glut in supply has meant that food is no longer valued in a society that is increasingly being criticized for being obese and overweight. Consumerism itself has led to increased levels of stress and there is a counter anti-global culture that is becoming more and more vocal at G8 summits.

---

7   CBC Marketplace. 2005. CBC News Online, 'By the Numbers: Credit Stats and Facts', broadcast, February 27.

8   Health Canada, 2003. Consumer Perspectives on Healthy Eating – Summary of Quantitative Research.

9   Meade, Birgit and Rosen, Stacey. 1996. Income and Diet Differences Greatly Affect Food Spending Around the Globe. United States Department of Agriculture, Economic Research.

Ironically, future demographic trend analyses suggest a return to the nuclear family of the past, albeit now being driven by economic considerations. Multigenerational households are on the rise and are forecast to reach about 25 percent by the year 2020. Perhaps the system is trying to heal itself. In the interim, consumers seek to escape the pressures of modern living by adopting a time-out mentality, taking vacations and the summer exodus to cottage country. Movies, theaters, sports and entertainment provide relief too. People also turn to brands for comfort, and shopping has become the second largest pastime in North America. It is here that an opportunity exists to reconnect the producer with the consumer.

Environmental impacts of food production

There is increasing consumer concern at how food is produced and where it comes from. Health issues such as *E. coli* contamination, pesticide residues, BSE, avian influenza and foot-and-mouth disease are strongly associated by consumers with agricultural systems that have production efficiencies rather than their well-being at heart. Given the concentration of production capacity in the hands of fewer producers, little problems can become large ones very quickly.

Agricultural run-off is responsible for contaminated water supplies and damage to marine ecosystems and aquatic life. Increased off-farm inputs cannot indefinitely sustain an untenable production system. Lack of proper soil-nutrient management decreases carbon retention in the soil, which contributes to the greenhouse effect. Concentrated monocultural production over large areas of land increases pesticide use as the natural ecosystem balance is disturbed. Modern food production is completely reliant on the oil economy, from supplying the energy to produce fertilizer, plant and harvest the crops to processing, transporting and refrigerating. The average farm in the United States consumes three calories of non-renewable energy resources to produce one calorie of food.[10] As the environmental equity is being spent so the entire system becomes increasingly unsustainable.

Prince Edward Island is no exception to this trend. The number of registered farms dropped from 10 137 in 1950 to 1845 by 2001.[11] However, the size of each farm has in fact increased from 44 hectares to 142 hectares of land utilized per farm over the same period. This has resulted in increased environmental pressures on a finite resource.

Potatoes are a major crop on Prince Edward Island and production there accounts for almost 26 percent of Canadian potato production. It is less than 5 percent of North American, and well below 1 percent of world, production. An increase in acreage in the mid-1990s to support an expansion in French-fry processing capacity led to an increase in environmental pressures. Marginal land, brought into production to

---

10 Horrigan, Leo, Lawrence, R., and Walker, P. 2002. 'How Sustainable Agriculture Can Address the Environmental and Human Environmental Health Perspectives Health Harms of Industrial Agriculture', *Environmental Health Perspectives* 110: 5.

11 Prince Edward Island Department of Treasury, 2006. Prince Edward Island, 32nd Annual Statistical Review.

accommodate the increased demand, led to an escalation in agricultural pesticide run-offs and incidents of fish kills.

Practices such as integrated pest management, strip cropping, crop rotations, nutrient management and buffer zones were followed to ameliorate some of the above issues, but in a system where the producer is not rewarded for doing the right thing there is little incentive to follow these practices. If one is increasingly trapped on a commodity treadmill, economic survival dictates short-term measures at the expense of long-term environmental equity. This is not sustainable and there is a growing concern in the agricultural community; steps are taken to address these issues.

The Branded Approach

Branding offers a chance to reconnect with the consumer, an opportunity to be rewarded for doing the right thing. Branding is a means of differentiating oneself from the commodity model. Branding, however, is far more than simply putting a trade name on a package. Branding is all about trust. In fact, the origins of branding can be traced to early artisans applying their mark to their produce and developing a reputation in their community for integrity, diligence in their work and attention to quality. These early traders learned the importance of the value that customer goodwill associates with a name they could trust.

Today's marketers apply the same time-honored principles on a global scale in offering consistent quality and reliability through their standardized processes. People learn to trust a brand name through association with consecutive positive experiences. The entire value chain to the consumer is part of the branding process. Any weak link in the supply chain can destroy a brand. A lack of attention to quality at the production end or a lack of proper stock rotation by the distributive trade can result in dissatisfied consumers and reduced brand equity. The path is fraught with potential problem areas. Aligned partnerships and common objectives among all participants in the value chain will result in branding initiatives that succeed. Recognizing this, FoodTrust seeks out distribution partners with similar values to ensure a seamless delivery of the brand to the consumer.

The branding process

There are three different types of brands. At a primary level there are product brands. Detergents and toothpastes are prime examples of these. They rely on their efficacy for their franchise. These brands need to continually reinvent themselves and find new propositions for consumers to buy them. One has only to look at the toothpaste wars, where manufacturers play on the problems associated with plaque and tartar, to the latest fad in whitening tooth enamel. Each innovation made, however, is soon matched by the competition and a new product-plus has to be developed to retain market share.

This is a game that only the really big consumer companies can afford to play. Consider the competitiveness in the razor-blade market between Gillette and Schick.

How many more blades a face is expected to accommodate is anyone's guess. One result of this approach, though, is the exclusion of the smaller player, leaving the market available to two or three competitors at the most. Private label programs by retailers have traditionally focused on taking up any slack in the market by offering a price alternative to the market leaders. This parasitical arrangement has worked to establish formidable barriers to entry for new competitors and concentrate the market and the distributive trade in the hands of a few major players. Product brand relationships with consumers are therefore generally not an option for smaller producers in developing a branded approach to the market unless there are vast resources available to keep competitive through high R&D investment and continual renewal of the product, packaging and communication with the consumer.

The second type of brand is the personality-based brand. Here the product is marketed through positive image association with a popular person, character or even place. Sanca coffee in the 1970s had a powerful franchise with the character of Juan Valdez, a coffee grower and spokesman for the brand. Pepsi used rock stars and other celebrities as icons of the new generation as a platform to promote their cola. The Martha Stewart Living brand is a contemporary example of a personality brand. The problem with personality brands is that they do not generally last. Personalities eventually fade from the spotlight. Any negative imagery can quickly bring about a brand's downfall. Generally, only fashion or trendy products with short life cycles benefit from personality brands. For long-term sustainability there is a third form of branding relationship with consumers, brands based on values.

Values-based branding

A values-based brand connects with the consumer at an emotional level. Comfort foods like Campbell's tomato soup or Kraft dinners are not about the intrinsic product. In reality, there are tastier and healthier options available, but consumers have adopted these brands as tried and trusted favorites. Tim Hortons coffee is a Canadian icon, even though the strength and flavor intensity of their coffee is lower than Starbucks, for example. Despite this, Canadians consume Tim's coffee through the emotional attachment they have with the brand. A cup of coffee bought at a Tim Hortons drive-through on the way to work offers succor from the stress of congested traffic jams and the daily commute.

Coca-Cola, the greatest of all the values-based brands, is about a slice of life rather than quenching a thirst. The Coke moment is a reward and an indulgence for the consumer. The consumption of Coke is a celebration of life and a time out from the pressures of modern-day living. Incidentally, it also offers relief from thirst, a mild caffeine kick and a calorie rush.

Values-based brands are the ones that endure. Some have made the journey from product brands; however, all have a larger-than-life image in the mind of the consumer. Understanding the drivers to developing values-based relationships with consumers is the key to sustainable branding. Psychographic market segmentation, an understanding of consumer relationships, usage and consumption attitudes with brands, brand rationale and tonality all come into play in developing a brand proposition within a defined target group of consumers.

At a product level a brand must satisfy a consumer need. At a values-based level, a brand must be in empathy with the way a consumer feels about the product. Values-based brands are created through connecting consumers' needs with their emotions in a way that satisfies both. Qualitative research into consumer dispositions toward products and a thorough understanding of the consumption moment is important in identifying these needs. A values-based brand has to be positioned according to the consumers' experience or interaction with it and not from a product intrinsic or production viewpoint.

FoodTrust Identity and Organization

The FoodTrust brand was created out of an audit of the attributes and properties that consumers associate with Prince Edward Island. As a place, the island is known for its rich red soil and pastoral landscape. Farms must remain small by law. Its clean pristine environment is cleansed by cold winters. Its uniqueness and isolation ensure a protected environment. Warm summer days alternate with cool, salty ocean breezes at night, making for ideal growing conditions. Legislation was enacted to keep a farming community by not allowing corporations to own more than 3000 acres (7410 hectares) of land or individual farmers more than 1000 acres (2470 hectares). Consequently the island is probably the last region in North America where more people live in the country than in the city. The people of Prince Edward Island are known for their warmth and hospitality. Here a strong sense of community prevails and people look out for each other. It is a community that has been time tested through generations. Here people take pride in their work and believe that doing the job right is as important as getting the job done. Within such a small community people are hard working and honest. Traditional values prevail. A strong sense of place, family and community values make up the character of Prince Edward Islanders.

This was summed up and an initial brand positioning statement was created and subjected to qualitative consumer research: 'For generations, people have trusted Prince Edward Islanders to grow and harvest food that nurtures the body and the soul.' The research confirmed the hypothesis as credible and it remained to find a way to elaborate it in the marketplace. Three alternatives were pursued and a further three concept boards were developed. The island was positioned as a place that intrinsically provides high-quality products, a place that provides an ideal environment for growing high-quality products, and finally as a place where you could count on the people to provide high-quality products. The 'people' concept consistently outscored the other two in terms of credibility and the slogan: 'Growing well is a way of life' was developed to underpin the concept of high-quality foods from sustainable production systems.

This slogan works at many levels. Environmentally it embraces sound principles of growing and production practices. Socially it embraces a community that is healthy and vital. Intrinsically it embraces the optimization of good, safe, and healthy practices in production processes. And from a consumer perspective it embraces the desire to consume foods that are good for you. Above all, the slogan is seen as an inspirational one that must continually be improved upon. In all these vital areas, it represents a call to action for FoodTrust and its members. The name FoodTrust itself was a contraction of an earlier statement in research focus groups that initially read: 'Food you can trust from Prince Edward Island, where growing well is a way of life.'

Brand standards

When FoodTrust first began looking towards establishing brand standards, it quickly became evident that there were many protocols involved across different commodity groups in environmental and societal issues, and the organization quickly became bogged down in a multitude of standards ranging from soil, crop, and pesticide management to animal welfare issues. What was required was an interface that the consumer could understand and that would be easy to manage and control.

A number of qualitative research reports on concerns consumers have about food safety and production were reviewed. From these reports, issues were identified where FoodTrust could make a difference. Food safety, quality, and health were immediately selected as these are givens for any product. These minimum standards have to be met by any food product. Branding is about positioning and differentiation. In addition FoodTrust had to find credible levers that it could legitimately claim in its practices to give it a competitive edge. From the research, environmental and social standards were selected as areas in which FoodTrust could make a difference.

On the basis of these five issues, the FoodTrust Brand Standards Matrix was conceived. At the top of the pyramid, these five consumer concerns were listed. The expected FoodTrust standards that would deliver on these promises were elaborated next. Underpinning these were all the various agricultural and food safety protocols with which to measure compliance with the expected standards. The consumer issues in food supply are addressed and the producer understands the methods that ensure good farming practices. FoodTrust is the link that connects the consumer with the producer and monitors the supply chain to ensure compliance with the brand standards. Put simply, producers can concentrate on producing high-quality foods from sustainable agricultural standards, while consumers enjoy the peace of mind that their concerns about food quality, origin, and safety are being simultaneously addressed.

Going to market

The first challenge for any brand is to find a compelling reason for consumers to buy; this requires a careful study of the market and the competitive landscape. Differentiation has to be meaningful, relevant and of genuine value to the consumer. It is important also to position a brand within the consumer's perception of reality, whether that reality is flawed or not. Brands should not seek to exploit such perceptions as the truth will eventually come out. A belief that organically grown food is healthier or that locally grown produce is safer is an example of such perceptions. Furthermore, price competition should not erode the brand equity, as is starting to happen with the distribution of organic produce in North America. Growth is being fuelled by reductions in retail pricing as big box stores start to focus on this market segment, making it less attractive as an entry option for smaller producers who do not have the economies of scale to compete.

Values-based brand propositions must be sustainable in the long term. Ultimately a brand proposition should take the entire value chain into consideration, beginning always with a defined consumer need and proposition. Partnering throughout the supply chain ensures consistency in delivery of quality.

Case study: Potatoes

Prince Edward Island is renowned for its potato fields. Each summer, tourists encounter a patchwork of leafy potato canopies and multicolored blossoms. Over ninety varieties of potatoes are grown each season for various uses, from chipping and French-fry production to tablestock potatoes for the fresh produce market. Traditionally potatoes have been viewed as a commodity. With tablestock potatoes, some differentiation takes place through the forms of packing, either in a paper or poly bag or sold loose. Grading is progressively more stringent across the above formats, but the specifications are fairly broad.

Some differentiation in the market has occurred by focusing on varieties that display different properties, the yellow-fleshed Yukon Gold potato probably having achieved the most success with this approach to date. More exotic species like blue-fleshed, a traditional potato used with a salt cod supper or creamer and fingerling potatoes are also gaining favor.

Per capita consumption has been declining slightly but not significantly, apart from when the low carbohydrate diet fad went through the market in 2003. Between 1992 and 2002, potatoes fell from the number two revenue generator in the produce section of US supermarkets to the number six position. With sales volumes static or stagnating only slightly, much revenue has been ceded and the price per pound has dropped to maintain the status quo. This has led to a crisis at the farm gate. Producers are battling to recover their input costs in the marketplace. The glut in production in recent years has seen commodity prices below cost and the industry has its back to the wall. Should this trend continue, there will ultimately be only a few large players left in the market who can compete on the basis of size and least cost provider, further fueling the industrialization of agriculture.

FoodTrust met with several potato growers in a series of workshops to address these issues. Available research on the consumer and the market was reviewed and a marketing model based upon usage and cooking method was elaborated. Research on different varieties was conducted with the Culinary Institute of Canada and potatoes were grouped according to their suitability for baking, boiling, mashing, or roasting. Broadly, it was found that the solids and moisture content of the raw potato did much to determine their application. Further development took place in the design of a display bin to keep the potatoes fresh and to minimize glycoalkaloid production and the undesirable greening that occurs in potatoes. From a consumer perspective, the problems addressed were size and consistency in quality, variety selection, and freshness. This new approach to the marketing of potatoes was presented to a strong regional retailer in the market and a partnership was immediately formed to commercialize the system. In the three years since launch the category has performed well, with all stakeholders in the supply chain, from the consumer right back to the grower receiving an equitable return. The program has been rolled out and a second regional player has come on board. Over 45 potato growers are currently participating in the program. FoodTrust potatoes are now being sold in over 300 retail outlets in Canada.

Rewards

Rewards are being achieved across all three areas of the sustainability triangle. Environmentally, participating producers are committed to an environmental farm plan that is inclusive in the number of protocols embraced. Good science is finally being tempered with good sense in farming practices. Socially, as the program rolls out, there is an impact on the community as the economic benefits of the program trickle down. Economically, FoodTrust is starting to define a marketing system that can work within the vagaries of the commodity model and bring stability to the system. With this in place, longer-term programs that will improve marketable yield quality in a more environmentally friendly fashion can be addressed. Much effort is currently being directed toward growing, harvesting, handling, and storage systems to achieve this.

The Future

Big business today is also embracing the 'triple E' bottom line – economic viability, environmental friendliness, and social equity to its customers, its staff and the community. Partnerships that reconnect business with the community are actively being sought and in this respect FoodTrust can offer many unique opportunities. By applying classic consumer marketing practices to fresh produce, a winning formula has been developed. The programs elaborated by FoodTrust to date differ from others in that they do not rely on a product or packaging innovation, but go right back to the basics of cooking and culinary skills. Consumers are rediscovering the lost art of cooking in this age of microwavable convenience. This is as it should be from a bucolic province such as Prince Edward Island. The thought of massive capital investment and infrastructural transformation of the island is neither credible nor desirable. Prince Edward Island, with its small size and finite resources, has to find an economic model that preserves its character. For an agricultural community that is seeking to preserve a unique way of life in today's modern distribution systems, the successes achieved to date by FoodTrust show that there is a place in the market where producers can be rewarded for doing the right thing.

Chapter 9

Beyond Profit Making: Combining Economic and Social Goals in the German Organic Agriculture and Food Sector

Martina Schäfer

Based on the ideas of the founders of organic agriculture in the early twentieth century, the organic movement has grown by opposing the industrialisation of agriculture and similar trends in the modern food industry. Like enterprises in the solar, wind energy and ecological construction sectors, in the 1970s and 1980s many pioneering organic farming enterprises were involved in the environmental movement, which seeks to develop alternative forms of production and living (Ripsas 1997; Faltin 1998; Byzio et al. 2002). Combining economic with social and ecological goals – this being the cornerstone of efforts towards achieving sustainable development – has therefore been the starting point for producing, processing and trading organic food.

Current debates on sustainable enterprises and corporate social responsibility take up the idea that enterprises have a social responsibility that goes beyond merely making a profit. A recent research project, 'Regional Wealth Reconsidered'[1], aimed at analysing whether the German organic agriculture and food sector can truly be described as an exemplary economic sector that strives for forms of production that respect natural resources and take social constraints into consideration.

This chapter discusses the socially oriented activities engaged in by some members of the German organic sector, highlighting their motives as well as the difficulties they face in realising their ideals. Their objective conditions are portrayed and their own personal perspectives are given voice. The chapter closes with some recommendations concerning how such enterprises could be supported by government and wider society as they strive to develop and implement sustainable practices.

---

1 The research project was carried out from 2002 to 2007 in a cooperative effort between the Centre for Technology and Society at the Technical University of Berlin and the German Institute for Economic Research in Berlin. It was funded through the Social-Ecological Research Program by the German Ministry of Education and Research. For more information, see <www.regionalerwohlstand.de>.

Regional Wealth Reconsidered

The main hypothesis of the project Regional Wealth Reconsidered was that a combination of market and non-market motives and activities is necessary to be able to achieve sustainable economic forms. Key questions included the following: what indicators are capable of capturing the contribution of an economic sector towards 'sustainable regional wealth'? Which activities engaged in by members of the organic sector contribute to 'sustainable regional wealth' and what are the motives of the entrepreneurs in carrying them out? Are these activities market oriented or non-market oriented? Do the enterprises face difficulties in striving to achieve sustainable economics? How can those enterprises that are heading towards sustainability be supported by adequate policy measures?

The research project developed an analytical framework, 'sustainable wealth' (Schäfer et al. 2004), and an indicator set (Schäfer 2004; Schäfer and Illge 2006). Quantitative and qualitative analyses were carried out in 2004 and 2005. Questionnaires were sent to all 1000 organic farms, processors and retailers in the Berlin-Brandenburg region of Germany, enquiring about structural data (such as size, kinds of products, number of employees, trading channels) and the socially oriented activities engaged in by the enterprises.[2] Data was obtained from around one-third of the enterprises, thus achieving a representative sample of the regional organic sector. In a second step, the motivation of the entrepreneurs, the synergies between economic and social activities and the difficulties of combining them were studied in more detail through nine qualitative case studies. The case studies included interviews with manager-owners and employees of the enterprises as well as people from the local and institutional surroundings. The project did not aim to compare the organic and conventional sectors, but rather sought to identify commonalities and differences within the former.

The Organic Sector in the Berlin-Brandenburg Region

Berlin-Brandenburg in northeastern Germany has experienced rapid growth in organic agriculture since German reunification in 1990, resulting in almost 10 per cent of the agriculturally cultivated area being organic by 2005. However, the processing and consumption of organic food in East Germany has not kept pace with production. Raw organic products (mostly grains and meat) are to a large extent processed and consumed in other German regions, which means that the economic value generated through the processing of raw products is mostly created beyond Berlin-Brandenburg.

The rural areas of Berlin-Brandenburg are mired in a difficult economic situation and have a high rate of unemployment. This results in a high rate of emigration,

---

2 The sample contained processing enterprises that process 100 per cent organically and others which only process part of their products organically. Regarding the retailers, we included organic food stores and organic supermarkets that sell exclusively organic products as well as health food stores that sell a rather wide range of organic products. We did not include conventional supermarkets or discount stores in the sample.

especially among young people. As a result of these tendencies, the infrastructure for education, mobility, health, culture and social services is in a state of decay. The rural areas need to look for new development strategies.

Societal Contributions of the Berlin-Brandenburg Organic Sector

Based on the discussions of sustainable regional development and the constraints of the Berlin-Brandenburg region described above, the project's analysis focused on four key issues:

- whether the organic enterprises studied contribute to creating jobs, income and regional economic value
- whether the entrepreneurs act in a socially responsible manner with respect to their employees as well as the local and regional environment
- the efforts they make regarding conservation of nature and environmental protection
- the efforts they make towards spreading information and sharing experience about environmentally sound agriculture and healthy nutrition.

The main findings are outlined below.

Economic contributions of the organic sector

Unlike the conventional agriculture and food sector, which is stagnating or even shrinking, the organic sector in Berlin-Brandenburg has grown in the past two decades and is creating new jobs and income. In 2005, the organic sector in Berlin-Brandenburg employed approximately 6000 people (full time and part time), of which half were women. More than one-third of the enterprises are directed by women. Almost two-thirds of the enterprises have only five employees or less (Illge and Schäfer 2007). Since organic farming remains a niche sector it only makes a small contribution towards alleviating structural unemployment in the Berlin-Brandenburg region. Yet, for single villages an organic enterprise located nearby can have a significant impact on local employment opportunities.

With respect to economic outlook, more than two-thirds of the manager-owners estimate that their enterprises will continue to exist for at least the next five years. However, around one-third of the entrepreneurs are neither content with the economic situation of their farms nor with their incomes. The main reason for this is that they are not able to obtain satisfactory prices for their products on the market.

Concerning the economic value that is created in the region, more than one-third of the farms and the majority of the processors have regular trading partners in the Berlin-Brandenburg region. Almost half of the farmers sell more than 80 per cent of their products within the region, whereas a third estimate that they only sell one-fifth of their products regionally. Apart from producing food and selling to middlemen, a quarter of the farmers engage in direct marketing, a fifth in landscape conservation and, to a lesser extent, in tourism. These activities also contribute to the creation of regional economic value.

Organic processing enterprises market their products to a great extent within the region, with over two-thirds of them selling more than 80 per cent of their products there. One reason for this is the high percentage of bakeries in this group. Regional retailers state that, in the summer, they order up to 40 per cent of their fresh products from within the region; in winter this percentage is, however, much lower.

Socially oriented activities

The entrepreneurs contribute towards the stabilisation of social structures by becoming engaged in local or regional organisations or supporting them. More than half of the organic entrepreneurs (farmers, processors and retailers) support non-profit organisations through financial or material assistance. Over a third of the manager-owners are engaged in environmental organisations or village associations, grassroots movements or networks that are trying to stop, or at least strictly regulate, genetic engineering. In rural areas, some of the farmers and processors participate in regional initiatives such as LEADER, a European programme for the development of rural areas. Engagement in these networks sometimes leads to joint regional projects in the field of regional marketing, natural preservation or tourism – initiatives that cannot be realised by a single enterprise.

Solidarity between organic entrepreneurs is quite high, with over 40 per cent stating that they help other regional enterprises in difficult situations with advice, manpower, material or financial aid. Between the farms there is much reciprocal non-monetary exchange of fodder, dung, products or machines. Along the food production and distribution chain, the enterprises help each other by, for example, leaving payment terms flexible.

Although they are quite active on the regional scene, the firms are not outstanding in terms of offering social benefits for their own employees. Only a minority of enterprises offer special conditions for their employees, such as flexible working hours or additional retirement benefits, or give jobs to the long-term unemployed. Interestingly, the processing enterprises are more active in this regard than the farms and retailers (see Figure 9.1).

Protection of nature and the environment

There is already strong evidence that, by conforming to existing European Union (EU) regulations on organic agriculture or the more stringent regulations formulated by organic agriculture associations, organic agriculture contributes to maintaining high-quality groundwater and soil as well as biodiversity (Stolze et al. 2000; Köpke 2002; Stokstad 2002). Given this, the project was only concerned with learning about additional ecological measures undertaken by the region's enterprises that go beyond the EU regulations.

The three types of enterprises – farms, processors and retailers – have very different kinds of opportunities to contribute towards the preservation of nature and environmental protection. Many farms focus on maintaining habitat and species diversity by planting hedges and trees, cultivating biotopes or installing 'buffer zones' beside watercourses. In harvesting their crops, many farms take extra precautions to

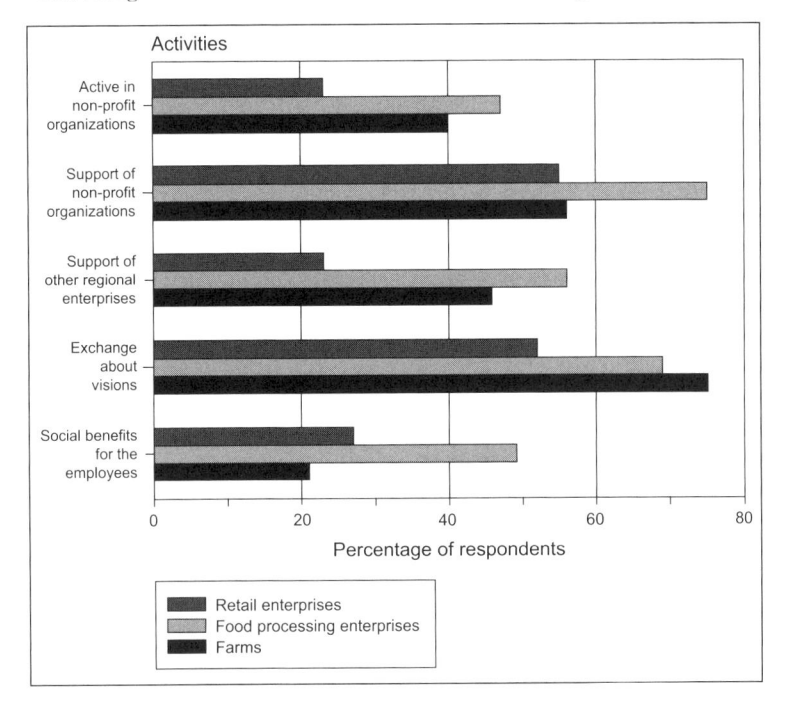

Figure 9.1 Social activities of organic enterprises in Berlin-Brandenburg

ensure the protection of wild animal and plant species. Some of these measures are financially supported by EU agri-environmental programmes. Furthermore, nearly a third of the farms cultivate heirloom plant varieties or breed rare animal species, which are then used by one-third of the processing enterprises. By taking these measures, enterprises contribute towards maintaining the genetic diversity of cultivated species.

Organic processing enterprises concentrate mainly on ensuring the ecological optimisation of the production process. Almost half of them make efforts to save water, and almost two-thirds employ energy-saving measures. One-quarter of the processors participate in an independent environmental auditing process. Retailers have fewer opportunities to apply additional environmental measures: 40 per cent use energy-efficient machines, while the majority uses environmentally friendly cleaning agents.

Disseminating information and sharing experience

Disseminating information and sharing experience regarding environmentally sound agriculture and healthy nutrition is an important way in which organic enterprises contribute towards the diffusion of sustainable lifestyles. They do so via formal educational measures as well as through more informal means.

While only a minority of the enterprises are active in the educational development of young people (through apprenticeships), half of them offer external formal training opportunities for their employees. The project case studies made clear that there is also much additional informal knowledge transfer from the manager-owners of the enterprises to their employees.

Most of the informal measures for passing on information are marketing oriented, directed at consumers and the local community, who are addressed through open days, guided tours, local or regional events or informational flyers and websites. Around one-fifth of the enterprises also offer seminars or participate in public discussions. Considerable information is disseminated through informal conversaton while selling products in their own stores or at open-air markets. A key element of these communication efforts is that they are not only verbal or written, but also rely on the other physical senses to create 'hands-on' experiences for (potential) customers, through product tasting or bringing customers into contact with animals and plants on the farms, for example.[3] With these practices, the enterprises aim to 'build bridges' between city and countryside and to strengthen regional identity. Figure 9.2 presents some typical activities.

To sum up: the organic sector in the Berlin-Brandenburg region contributes, albeit modestly, towards creating new jobs and prospects, especially for rural areas. There remains great potential for increasing the economic value created in the region by establishing more regional organic processing operations and expanding the multifunctionality of the farms. Except for some of the few existing processing enterprises, the regional organic sector is not outstanding with regard to social benefits for its employees. However, there is a high level of engagement in regional non-profit organisations and networks, which can be supportive in creating strategies for rural development. Moreover, the efforts already being made towards spreading information and sharing experience could be used more strategically not only to confront the contemporary lack of knowledge concerning sustainable agriculture and healthy nutritional practices, but also to strengthen regional identity.

Motivation of Organic Entrepreneurs

Many entrepreneurs have individual or social goals related to leading an organic enterprise that go beyond ensuring a livelihood or making profits. Some stress their motivation regarding the type of work they are doing and their sense of achievement; for others it is important to contribute towards environmentally friendly agriculture or healthy nutrition. For many of them, working in the organic sector is a means of realising their personal visions or goals. While motives concerning health are especially widespread amongst the processors and the retailers, environmental motives for working in the organic sector are mentioned by all actors: farmers, processors and retailers.

---

3 More detailed information about the learning processes that may arise in organic farms is available in Boeckmann 2007.

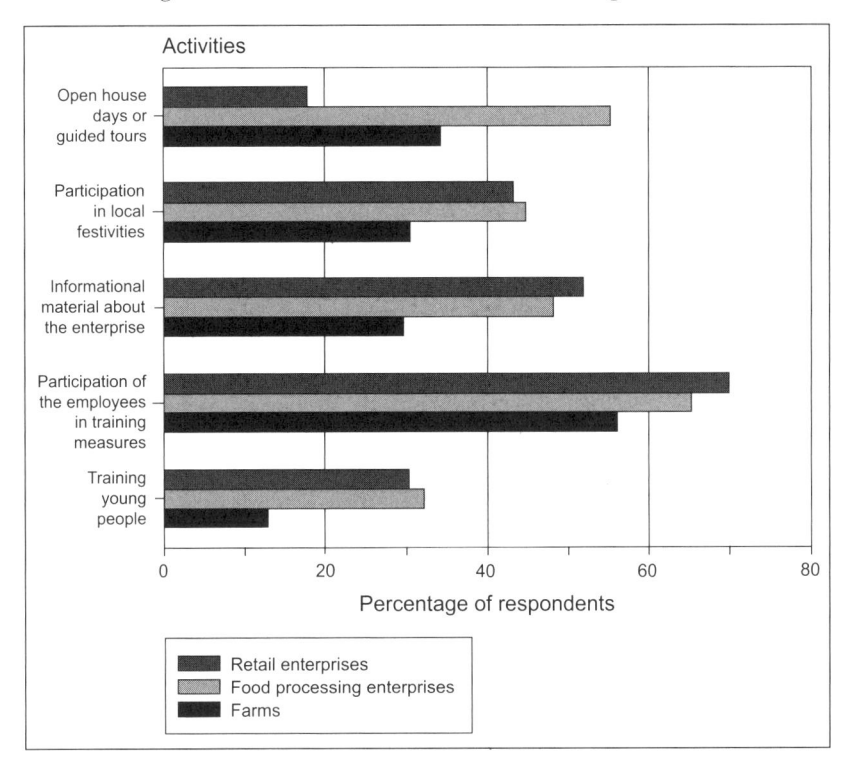

Combining Economic and Social Goals in the German Organic Food Sector   115

Figure 9.2   Activities related to passing on knowledge and experience by organic enterprises in Berlin-Brandenburg

Regarding the quality of their work, one of the bakers described his motivation as follows: 'The main goal is not to make a profit. The main thing is to focus on what kind of work we have. That was our motivation for starting this business in the first place'. Asked about the vision that keeps her enterprise together, the owner of a natural food store responded, 'to offer a group of people [employees] meaningful jobs and a pleasant working atmosphere'. Several entrepreneurs stress a strong identification with their work, as the following statement of an organic baker makes clear: 'I am fully convinced that this is the right kind of work for me – just making money is not my thing. Working with organically produced grains is my heart's desire'.

Making a contribution to healthy nutrition and sustainable consumption is important for a substantial sector of respondents. A retailer commented, 'I originally wanted to promote healthy nutrition in the [former] German Democratic Republic'. For some entrepreneurs, organic agriculture is part of a sustainable vision for society: 'I do it out of conviction, because I think it is the only way for children to learn how to live sustainably and to pass on other values to them. They should learn about more than just making money, and they can learn this best on an organic farm'.

Complementarity of Market-oriented and Non-market-oriented Activities

As a result of the special orientation of organic enterprises and the types of products they handle, different motives for combining market activities with non-market activities can be identified. This section illustrates the variety of motives these entrepreneurs have, discussing the ecological, social and communication activities that are part of their business practices.

For example, their additional ecological engagement – beyond existing regulations for organic agriculture – results, in part, from their ideological backgrounds. On the other hand, it can also be used to develop a positive image of the enterprise. Customers who buy products from an organic producer or processor expect the enterprise to be up-to-date as far as environmental management and eco-efficiency are concerned. For example, one of the bigger organic bakeries in Berlin, Märkisches Landbrot (<www.landbrot.de>), has established an image of itself as an ecological pioneer through installing solar power systems, operating with alternative fuel, being the first European bakery to submit to independent environmental auditing, and also by sponsoring reforestation of the rainforest in Madagascar as compensation for the enterprise's carbon dioxide emissions. There are also some farms that are regionally well known for their ecological commitment. The motivation for being active in this field can be linked to the desire to experiment with alternatives and to minimise the dependency on unsustainable resources such as fossil fuels. Furthermore, producing or processing rare animal species or heirloom plant varieties can be motivated by a wish to preserve heritage species as well as by a desire to create new, innovative products and improve the firm's image.

Aspirations to have good and fair relations with customers and employees are often based on ideas about what it means to be a responsible entrepreneur. 'I want to have a decent relationship with the people I purchase products from. I expect mutual understanding and reciprocal give and take', said one retailer. Creating a special atmosphere in natural food stores can, on the other hand, be used as a means of differentiating them from conventional retailers. Some of the entrepreneurs surmise that their social engagement has indirect, positive effects for their enterprises. For example, one retailer seeks out and trains young people who have alcohol- or discipline-related problems. She commented that, 'All of these things that don't bring in money – promoting tolerance, supporting women, or helping young people to obtain qualifications – nevertheless provide a sense of satisfaction for me as well as for my employees and customers. ... And, in the end, they all have some impact'.

Engagement in regional networks can be prompted by both economic motives and other aspirations (Schäfer 2006). Regional networking can be a starting point for joint projects, for example in the field of regional marketing – including establishing farmers' markets, organising events for regional restaurants and hotels, publishing regional shopping guides, and so on, which in the long term may lead to economic success. However, since the establishment of regional markets has been a slow process in northeastern Germany, it is necessary to uncover additional motives in order to explain entrepreneurial engagement there. One possible reason, which seems to be especially important for those entrepreneurs who have moved into the region recently, is to gain greater local acceptance and support. Particularly in rural areas, organic enterprises are still confronted by prejudice, as one mayor reveals: 'Originating from West Germany and doing organic farming – that was something very new for the people here. I think that, for them, it was at first unimaginable. But then the locals sensed the willingness [of the farmer] to make contact with the village and, slowly, the relationship has grown'. In towns, engagement in local initiatives or associations can help to gain acceptance, as a natural food store owner describes: 'Engagement with the association for retailers has had the consequence that we are no longer treated as eco-weirdos. Now some local retailers even come and buy in our store. That's a big form of success in the business world – they are multipliers I want to make contact with'. Another motive for engaging in regional networks or grassroots movements is that it provides a means to lobby collectively for their own interests (environmentally friendly agriculture, healthy nutrition, regulation of genetic engineering, and so on) with people who are not necessarily from the organic sector.

Finally, many of the practices related to spreading information that the enterprises are engaged in – holding open days or guided tours, participating in regional events or offering product tasting – originate in the necessity of explaining to (potential) customers the special qualities and the higher prices associated with organic products. Since the social and personal advantages of organic products cannot easily be recognised by customers, establishing the credibility of an entrepreneur's products is essential for success on the market (Clausen 2004, 151). Many farmers therefore provide opportunities for customers to have first-hand experience of their products through tasting, touching and smelling them. The motivation for engaging in these types of customer-oriented marketing activities is often mentioned by entrepreneurs, like this health food store owner: 'I am present at regional festivities. This is not an occasion to earn money, but rather to attract new clients to the store. I bring a lot of products to taste with me'.

However, beyond economic motives, some of the entrepreneurs want to combat what they perceive to be a historical loss of knowledge in the field of nutrition and agriculture. 'Twice a year I offer baking courses. By doing so I don't want to earn money, but I like it when people know how to bake their own bread', explains a baker. When engaged in direct marketing, farmers find themselves confronted by a surprising lack of knowledge about agriculture among city-dwellers. 'I offer guided tours on the farm', said one farmer, 'At the beginning I was rather shocked; I thought it couldn't be possible that the average person can be so far removed from agriculture'.

In sum, the study shows that the boundaries between economic and non-economic activities in the organic sector are fluid. Although economic development of the enterprise – marketing products and reaching new clients – is always an essential aspect of their entrepreneurial thinking and acting, social and environmental motives often play a supporting role in the overall plans of the organic entrepreneurs.

In many cases, it is difficult for the entrepreneurs to estimate the possible economic benefits of their socially oriented activities. But it is clear that they are fundamentally grounded in a desire to produce in a sustainable manner and contribute towards improved quality of life and healthy nutrition in the region. The economic benefits resulting from this attitude are twofold: the enterprise itself benefits by gaining better acceptance or improving its image, as well as by reaching new customers or establishing new economic branches; and the local or regional context benefits from actors who are able to initiate new projects in the fields of regional marketing, tourism or natural preservation. Further regional benefits are derived from measures that maintain the attractiveness of the local landscape, and activities that seek to strengthen regional identity and build bridges between city and countryside.

Challenges to the Holistic Economy

As has been shown, organic entrepreneurs in Berlin-Brandenburg often pursue ambitious entrepreneurial and social goals. This section explores the difficulties of combining market and non-market activities, while bearing in mind that this combination might result in middle- or long-term synergies for the enterprises and the region.

Limitations on available time coupled with economic pressures are endangering this more holistic type of economy. Although the European organic sector is experiencing a boom, the individual farmer or processor is confronted with severe economic pressure due to recent structural changes. Conventional supermarkets and processors have entered the market that not only are very efficient logistically, but also import cheaper products from other countries. More diversified, small-scale enterprises are tending to come under great economic stress as a result of these changes. Furthermore, the prices of organic products are dependent on the world market prices of conventional products and, therefore, sometimes suffer from great fluctuations, adversely affecting small producers the most (Thomas and Groß 2005, 63).

Economic pressure can result in the enterprises drawing back and concentrating on their 'core business', with the willingness to engage in some additional activities being put at risk. On one hand, activities like landscape preservation or habitat conservation, which are financially supported by the agri-environmental programmes of the EU, can still be carried out in a difficult economic situation. Meanwhile, other activities that are not financially acknowledged tend to decline or are eliminated altogether, as this farmer explains: 'In the beginning I carried out experimental cultivation of heirloom grain varieties. But then I gave up everything that didn't bring in money, because when the business is in the red it doesn't make much sense'. Also, activities such as giving lectures or participating in public discussions or offering guided tours tend to be reduced or modified in response to financial pressure.

While it may be economically rational for farmers to reduce their range of activities and to set priorities, some entrepreneurs are uneasy about trends towards increasing specialisation. They have expressed concern that the rationalisation of the organic sector is resulting in a continuous undermining and abandonment of the original ideals upon which the organic movement has always been based. Since the concept of sustainable development aims at an expansion of the number of enterprises that combine economic with social goals, policies are required to support those enterprises that are already attempting to achieve sustainability.

Developing and Supporting Sustainable Economies: Ways Forward

Sustainable development requires a blend of economic and altruistic entrepreneurial behaviour and, thus, incentives for a combination of economic and non-economic activities. Measures that support 'altruistic entrepreneurship' need to be established at several policy levels.

An important condition for achieving changes in this direction is a greater acknowledgement of the social benefits that result from mixture of economic and non-economic activities on the part of a range of actors: government, local and regional administrations, individual retailers and customers. Until now, neither the number of people employed nor the effects on natural resources and regional quality of life have been used as critical indicators in discussions concerning political measures for supporting the economic activities. Particularly with regard to agricultural policy, a clear signal needs to be sent that only those enterprises contributing to sustainable regional development, in a broad sense of the term, should be supported by subsidies.

Promoting a more holistic type of economics also means questioning the hard differentiation between market and non-market activities and recognising that entrepreneurs are acting not only as 'homo oeconomicus', but also as citizens with individual social goals that go beyond making profits (Biesecker 2000; Biesecker and Kesting 2003). This acknowledgement of the organic sector's societal value needs to be accompanied by efforts towards communicating the vision of an economic model that can succeed in being symbiotically embedded in both society and the natural environment. The efforts of pioneering sectors should be supported, being strategically used as 'good examples' for other economic sectors.

Greater acknowledgement of the contributions of the organic sector should, however, also result in 'prices which tell the ecological truth' (von Weizsäcker 1994). Sustainable consumption cannot be properly facilitated when conventional products that are responsible for water and soil pollution, as well as the loss of biodiversity, cost much less than organic products. At present, through their taxes, all consumers are paying for the social costs generated by conventional agriculture, regardless of whether they consume organic or conventional food. The internalisation of external costs that are due to conventional agriculture, and their reflection in product prices, has long been a demand directed at the political realm.

At the regional and local level, it is possible to support the social activities of enterprises by strengthening cooperative structures. From the survey, it became clear that the enterprises of the organic sector could play an important role in spreading knowledge and sharing experiences regarding agriculture and healthy nutrition. Organic enterprises could therefore be better integrated into strategies concerning health and environmental education: facilitating cooperation with schools, children's day care facilities, health insurance organisations or providers of adult education. Integrative networks comprised of enterprises, the public sector and NGOs – all acting towards improving rural or regional development – could also be strengthened through political or administrative measures.

At the level of the individual enterprise, consultants could advise farmers and other actors in the food chain on how to combine types of social engagement, bearing in mind the structure of each enterprise and its individual goals. This has good chances of resulting in synergies not only for the enterprise itself, but also for the local or regional context.

Finally, advertising the socially oriented activities undertaken by organic firms via suitable labels could facilitate consumer choice at the point of sale. In several European countries, efforts are being made to indicate additional social aspects of organic products that go beyond existing EU regulations. One example is labels that are given to enterprises that are involved in 'fair' trading relations with their suppliers in a region, including, for example, fair prices, long-term contracts, preferences for raw products from that region as well as additional social or ecological commitments. Labelling products in this way allows consumers consciously to choose organic products that may result in manifold benefits for the region concerned.

If combining economic with social goals is supported on all of these different levels – by politicians and administrators, by public discourses and adequate communication measures, through regional networks and individual consulting – the chances are good that a wealth of ways to achieve a sustainable economy can become more widespread.

References

Biesecker, A. (2000), Arbeitsteilung und das Ganze des Wirtschaftens—die Produktivität sozio-ökonomischer Vielfalt. In: Nutzinger, H. and Held, G. (eds), 204–33.

Biesecker, A. and Kesting, S. (2003), *Mikroökonomik. Eine Einführung aus sozial-ökologischer Perspektive* (Munich: Oldenbourg).

Biesecker, A. and Elsner, W. (eds) (2004), *Erhalten durch Gestalten – Nachdenken über eine (re)produktive Ökonomie*. Institutionelle und Sozial-Ökonomie 15 (Frankfurt am Main: Peter Lang).

Boeckmann, T. (2007), Bio-Betriebe—Vielseitige Lernorte im ländlichen Raum. In: Schäfer, M. (ed.), 113–35.

Byzio, A., Heine, H. and Mautz, R.2002), *Zwischen Solidarhandeln und Marktorientierung* (Soziologisches Forschungsinstitut an der Georg-August-Universität Göttingen (SOFI)).

Clausen, J. (2004), *Umsteuern oder Neugründen? Die Realisierung ökologischer Produktpolitik in Unternehmen* (Norderstedt: Books on Demand).

Eberle, U., Hayn, D., Rehaag, R. and Simshäuser, U (eds) (2006), *Ernährungswende. Eine Herausforderung für Politik, Unternehmen und Gesellschaft* (Munich: Ökom Verlag).

Estes, R. (ed.) (2006), *Advancing Quality of Life in a Turbulent World* (Dordrecht: Springer).

Faltin, G. (1998), Das Netz weiter werfen—Für eine neue Kultur unternehmerischen Handelns. In: Faltin, G., Ripsas, S. and Zimmer, J. (eds), 3–20.

Faltin, G., Ripsas, S. and Zimmer, J. (eds) (1998), *Entrepreneurship. Wie aus Ideen Unternehmer werden* (Munich: Beck).

Glatzer, W., von Below, S. and Stoffregen, M. (eds) (2004), *Challenges for Quality of Life in the Contemporary World*. Social Indicators Research Series, 24. (Dordrecht, Boston and London: Kluwer).

Grunwald, A., Coenen, R., Nisch, J., Sydow, A. and Wiedemann, P. (eds) (2001), *Forschungswerkstatt Nachhaltigkeit. Global zukunftsfähige Entwicklung—Perspektiven für Deutschland, 2* (Berlin: Edition Sigma).

Illge, L. and Schäfer, M. (2007), Beitrag der Bio-Betriebe zu „Zukunftsfähigem Wohlstand'—Ergebnisse einer Unternehmensbefragung in Berlin-Brandenburg. In: Schäfer, M. (ed.), 81–112.

Köpke, U. (2002), Umweltleistungen des Ökologischen Landbaus. In: *Ökologie & Landbau* 122: 2, 6–18.

Nölting, B. and Schäfer, M. (eds) (2007), *Vom Acker auf den Teller. Impulse der Agrar- und Ernährungsforschung für eine nachhaltige Entwicklung* (Munich: Oekom).

Nutzinger H. and Held, G. (eds) (2000), *Geteilte Arbeit und ganzer Mensch. Perspektiven der Arbeitsgesellschaft*. (Frankfurt am Main: Campus).

Ripsas, S. (1997), *Entrepreneurship als ökonomischer Prozess. Perspektiven zur Förderung unternehmerischen Handelns* (Wiesbaden: Gabler).

Rösch, C. and Heincke, M. (2001), Ernährung und Landwirtschaft. In: Grunwald, A., Coenen, R., Nisch, J., Sydow, A. and Wiedemann, P. (eds), 241–63.

Schäfer, M. (2004), 'Das Ganze' der Reproduktion im Blick behalten – was bedeutet das für die Entwicklung regionaler Nachhaltigkeitsindikatoren? In: Biesecker, A. and Elsner, W. (eds), 113–49.

Schäfer, M. (2006), The Role of Organic Agriculture in Networks for Rural Development, paper for the Joint Organic Congress in Odense, Denmark, 30–31 May 2006, <http://orgprints.org/7233/>.

Schäfer, M. (ed.) (2007), *Zukunftsfähiger Wohlstand—Der Beitrag der ökologischen Land- und Ernährungswirtschaft zu Lebensqualität und nachhaltiger Entwicklung* (Marburg: Metropolis).

Schäfer, M. and Illge, L: (2006), Analyzing Sustainable Wealth – The Social Contributions of a Regional Industrial Sector. In: Estes, R. (ed.), 85–103.

Schäfer, M., Nölting, B. and Illge, L. (2004), Bringing Together the Concepts of Quality of Life and Sustainability. In: Glatzer, W., von Below, S. and Stoffregen, M. (eds), 33–43.

Stokstad, E. (2002), Organic Farms Reap Many Benefits. In: *Science* 296, 1589.

Stolze, M., Piorr, A., Häring, A. and Dabbert, S. (2000), *The Environmental Impacts of Organic Farming in Europe*, Organic Farming in Europe: Economics and Policy, 6 (Stuttgart: University of Hohenheim Press).

Thomas, F. and Groß, D. (2005), Von der Bewegung zur Branche. In: *Kritischer Agrarbericht 2005* (Rheda-Wiesenbrück), 61–70.

von Weizsäcker, E.U. (1994), *Erdpolitik*. (Darmstadt: Wissenschaftliche Buchgesellschaft).

Chapter 10

The Cornwall Food Programme

Roy Heath and Mike Pearson

For many years hospitals in the National Health Service (NHS) have utilised the vast purchasing power of the collective hospitals to realise economies of scale; this meant that in many cases prices could be driven down to a level that was most advantageous to hospital caterers working to very tight budgets. This practice, however, led to problems. Sometimes quality was sacrificed in the interests of achieving a low price. The 'national contracting' ethos prevalent in the 1990s meant that the small local food suppliers were disadvantaged in other ways. They had to compete at a national level even if they were only interested in supplying their local hospital, which was possibly just down the road. The principles of sustainable purchasing that have been embraced by the Cornwall Food Programme (CFP) have meant that this way of purchasing food has changed.

The Cornwall Food Programme was developed to address the food supply needs of the NHS in the county of Cornwall. It was set up in 2000 and is run by Cornwall Healthcare Estates and Support Services (CHESS), a shared service across all three Cornish NHS Trusts. One of the CFP's core objectives is to incorporate local and organic food sourcing initiatives. It is funded by the UK's Department for Environment, Food and Rural Affairs (Defra); Organic South West, the local branch of the Soil Association; and Objective One, a programme set up to reduce differences in social and economic conditions within the European Union. The EU funding could be secured because Cornwall is the poorest region in the United Kingdom. In 2003, its GDP was only 62 per cent of the national average. Within the county, the NHS is a significant employer and procurer of food and thus its purchasing decisions have a major impact on the local population and economy.

The CFP has two broad aims. First, it aims to work in partnership with local producers, suppliers and distributors to purchase and process a significant percentage of Cornish produce for use in patient, visitor and staff meals. Secondly, it aims to recognise the pivotal role of the NHS Trusts within their local communities. The Cornish NHS Trusts, through the CFP, work to promote health and tackle obesity, as well as assisting in the education of the community with regard to the necessity for good food and nutrition.

The CFP seeks to deliver these significant benefits to the community in the following ways. First, economically, by increasing the percentage of its food budget spent with local producers and suppliers. Secondly, by having a positive environmental impact through reducing the distance that food supplies have to travel in order to reach hospitals, and through forging a closer working partnership throughout the supply chain in order to minimise packaging. Thirdly, through having a positive social impact. The CFP is already helping to secure current employment levels and is also generating additional job opportunities both in the NHS and with local producers. Job security contributes to both the wealth and the social health of the community. Fourthly, the CFP promotes sustainable methods of farming and food processing by working on collaborative projects with local colleges, farmers and producers. Finally, by providing better quality food to patients, the NHS Trusts have a direct impact on the social and physical well being of the clients they serve, aiding their recovery and lessening their dependence on NHS services in future years. Health services are therefore coming to be seen within the county of Cornwall as an integral part of the community. They have an important part to play in supporting and benefiting the local population.

Origins of the Cornwall Food Programme

The Cornwall Food Programme was conceived in 1999 when Mike Pearson, then the catering services manager, began to think about making greater use of local food suppliers and producers rather than using companies from 'up-country'. The high quality of Cornish food was obvious and work was started to make greater use of food produced within Cornwall. This was given a boost when, in 2001, the Royal Cornwall Hospitals Trust (RCHT) took over St Michael's Hospital in the small town of Hayle. The RCHT was required to provide food to its patients without the benefit of a kitchen; the concept of producing 'cook-freeze' meals in-house at the main acute site was formulated. The success of the in-house cook-freeze meals was such that it became obvious that the community hospitals in Cornwall (controlled by four separate Trusts at that time), which were at the time sourcing their cook-freeze meals from a company in Wales, could, if they so chose, purchase their cook-freeze meals according to sustainable purchasing principles. The idea of setting up a food programme supported by all five Trusts within Cornwall to increase the purchase of local ingredients was born.

It is interesting to note that the humble sandwich also helped to bring the CFP into being. A hospital patient read all the data on his sandwich label and upon being discharged wrote a letter to the then chief executive asking why his sandwich had travelled so far – approximately 200 miles, querying whether 'we had lost the recipe for sandwiches in Cornwall!' A discussion ensued over the absurdity of transporting sandwiches over 200 miles, six days a week, every week of the year.

A feasibility study was commissioned using grant funding from Objective One in order to examine whether food could indeed be sourced from local suppliers to provide food for patients. The main conclusion of the study was that the best option over the long term would be the construction of a central food production unit sited within the county. The Cornwall Food Production Unit (CFPU) is now being built and its likely effect upon food sustainability in Cornwall is discussed below; first, though, we discuss what has happened so far to help underpin the whole programme.

As well as identifying a local sandwich producer, the CFP began to source local ice cream and cheese. Callestick Farm ice-cream producers, based near the seaside town of Newquay, were able to take advantage of an Objective One grant to purchase a new ice-cream maker. They worked with the local NHS Trust to provide ice cream in a tub size that the tight budgets operated by the RCHT could afford. An 85ml pot of excellent high-energy ice cream can now be chosen from the menu by the patients twice a day.

In order to develop these and other initiatives, a new CFP post – that of sustainable food development manager – was created in 2004. This procurement post has been crucial in enabling the CFP to meet its aims. Over time it had become clear that many of local suppliers would need additional support to help them develop their businesses if they were to supply foodstuffs successfully to the NHS. The appointment of the sustainable food development manager, Roy Heath, has also enabled the CFP to become more proactive in identifying additional sourcing opportunities such as local yoghurt, more cheese products, milk and locally caught sustainable fresh fish and fish products. This has resulted in a significant increase of the proportion of the food budget spent locally and the added environmental bonus of a reduction in food miles being achieved.

The Impact of Local Sourcing Upon Local Businesses

Sustainability criteria have been introduced at every level of the procurement process. One of the driving factors behind this decision was the foot-and-mouth outbreak in 2001, which resulted in heightened concern over the source and transportation of food.

Tenders now include the phrase, 'offers showing benefit to the economy of Cornwall will be viewed favourably'. How can criteria like these be realised in practice, given that under UK and EU procurement laws, procurers cannot specify that food is local? It is possible because procurers are permitted to apply 'outcome-based specifications' to different parts of the food chain in order to increase local supply. A good example of this is the procurement of fresh fish. Although the procurement team cannot specify that it needs local fish, it can write criteria into the tender specifications that increase the likelihood of the tender being won by a local supplier. For example, criteria might require that the fish must be fresh and delivered within a certain timescale from the time at which the fish was caught. Not all work to increase local supply is done through direct contracts; procurers may work with current contractors who can provide the transport and distribution services to new local suppliers who do not have the infrastructure to deliver the product.

As a consequence of utilising outcome-based specifications in tenders, there has been a steady increase in the proportion of the food purchased locally. Although it is difficult to assess the full impact on the Cornish economy, current figures suggest that in excess of £400 000 is currently spent with local producers. Another £400 000 is spent with Cornish companies. These figures mean that approximately 80 per cent of the £1 million spent annually on food and catering by RCHT in Cornwall remains within Cornwall.

One fish supplier has commented that the CFP has significantly raised his company's profile. Before the setting-up of the CFP, the supplier had no contracts with the NHS in Cornwall since frozen fish was supplied under a nationally agreed contract. However, even though the fish supplier is now supplying fish to just one hospital – the Royal Cornwall Hospital – he anticipates that the upcoming introduction of the CFPU 'county-wide' delivery service will enable his company to increase significantly the size of its fish deliveries to the NHS units within Cornwall.

It is by working with local suppliers like these that close business relationships develop and flourish, resulting in a better product. For example, when the CFP was working with a local fishmonger on a recipe for fishcakes, several key factors had to be addressed. These included the requirement that only sustainably sourced fish be used, that a practical recipe in line with the facilities and ingredients available be developed, that an appropriate nutritional content be maintained, and that it would be possible to control the amount of ingredients such as salt in the recipe. Despite the positive work on the fishcake recipe, it soon became apparent that the white breadcrumbs used to finish the product were inappropriate since the CFP does not deep fry fishcakes. As a consequence they looked insipid and unappetising to patients. The fishmonger's solution was to source a fresh wholemeal breadcrumb, making the product much more visually appealing as well as tasting good. As a consequence of the strong working relationship between the supplier and the CFP, the problem was solved within days – rather than the weeks it would have taken to convince a national supplier to change their production techniques.

Another example of the positive impact on local businesses is that of Trewithen Dairy. The NHS contract with Trewithen Dairy required that milk be delivered in trolleys rather than in the crates previously used, requiring the supplier to modify the delivery vehicles. This adjustment, however, enabled the supplier to meet the contract requirements of a second customer, making the dairy more flexible. The NHS contract represents around 4 per cent of the dairy's output and has resulted in a need for an additional delivery vehicle and driver. Bill Clark, owner of Trewithen Dairy, won the contract against stiff opposition and supplies a quality product range that is produced just 20 miles from the Royal Cornwall Hospital from herds adjacent to the processing unit: truly a Cornish product.

Finally, working with the CFP has encouraged a local frozen food supplier to the NHS in Cornwall to source more local ingredients over the last seven years. The supplier had initially produced a separate Cornish product range to enable smaller caterers to purchase products containing local ingredients. However, it has now incorporated the Cornish list into the main company product portfolio. The supplier highlighted how this work had been helped by good communication with the CFP, with added support from external agencies such as Taste of the West and the NHS Supply Chain.

The Wider Impacts of the Cornwall Food Programme

The purchasing of an increasing volume of local produce has resulted in a decrease in food miles. It has been calculated from an analysis of previous national contracts and supply chain routes that by working with local suppliers, who provide the bulk of RCHT's commodities, approximately 100 000 food miles have been saved.

At the same time, budgets for the new food contracts have remained constant. Indeed, in some cases savings have been made through buying local produce. For example, a local cheese maker supplying multiple retailers found that he could not sell his cheese if it was under or over the specified weight required for the cheese;[1] the CFP now purchases these 'under/over' weights of high-quality award-winning goats' milk cheese from the cheese maker at a similar price to that previously paid for an inferior processed product from a national contractor. This is an example of the CFP making use of a product that prior to the contract was being thrown away as the producer could not sell it in the commercial retail sector. Moreover, patients particularly enjoy the taste and quality of the local cheese.

In 2007 suppliers and other local partners were given the opportunity to advertise in the hospital bedside menu books. This was important as it enabled the menu books to become self-funding. Local producers have experienced increased sales due to the advertising and patients can relate better to the produce being used in their meals. Indeed, the local yoghurt producer has experienced an influx of enquiries from patients enjoying it in hospital and wishing to purchase it for home consumption. In addition, all suppliers continue to receive positive publicity from the project as a result of local press coverage of contract awards and increasing national press awareness of what is being achieved with regards to hospital food in Cornwall.

How can the NHS contribute to creating food awareness regionally? In partnership with the Soil Association and directed by its 'Food for Life' targets, one of the objectives identified is to promote and set up green organic box schemes. For smaller hospitals this is not difficult. They can simply contact the nearest green box supplier and promote their produce in the hospital to both patients and visitors. However, for larger hospitals such as the Royal Cornwall Hospital, a totally different approach is required. The Royal Cornwall Hospital has over 4000 employees at the site, and given these numbers the solution to promoting the benefits of locally sourced produce was to open a local and organic produce shop on-site. In May 2006 the hospital saw the opening of Roots and Shoots, a local and organic produce shop funded through the NHS 'Improving Working Lives' scheme and staffed by volunteers from Cornwall Partnership Trust's Social Inclusion scheme.

Future Developments

As mentioned above, work on a unique £3.6 million central food production unit, the CFPU started up in early 2007, following the approval of Objective One and NHS investment. This unit will be the first of its kind in the southwest to be run by the NHS. It will transform the way meals are provided in hospitals across Cornwall. At the same time it will further contribute to regeneration and economic sustainability within the region by sourcing local produce and this in turn will help the environment by cutting food miles. It is hoped that in the future the unit will also be able to expand commercially by supplying food to other organisations in the region. The facilities

---

1   Certain products for retail contracts such as cheese have to be weight specific. When the cheeses are made there are weight variances and once the product has been wrapped and labelled and then weighed any that fall outside the degree of tolerance become unacceptable.

will be completed in 2008 and will utilise state-of-the-art catering equipment to produce quality meals for patients in Cornish hospitals.

At the CFPU, everything will be prepared and cooked using locally grown and sourced ingredients wherever possible. Meals will be prepared and cooked by existing teams of chefs to an extremely high standard, then transported from the food production unit to hospitals in the county. These meals will be designed to provide a healthy balanced diet, catering for a wide range of special needs, and will be prepared so their nutritional value is maintained right to the point of serving.

As soon as the CFPU is up and running, other environmentally useful savings will be made. The CFPU will be able to utilise food, for example vegetables, that are visually unsuited for the commercial market. Such vegetables, referred to as class two products, do not lack taste or quality. More often than not, they are deemed 'unsuitable' as they do not fit the packaging. Through purchasing the vegetables, the producer will still benefit from the agreed contract price – without the added expense of wasted packaging and excessive grading. There may also be opportunities for the CFPU to produce quality frozen and chilled products based on local produce for distribution by Cornish businesses as part of its aim to provide 'food that makes you better' throughout the community.

The CFPU will also house a product development kitchen that will allow all recipes to be checked not only for their nutritional value, but also to test their suitability for the food service systems, ensuring that the meal will be perfect when the patient receives it. In addition to this, the unit will have some of the most up-to-date large-scale catering equipment in Cornwall, creating the opportunity to form partnerships with local colleges, allowing catering students to gather experience there and gain a greater understanding of large-scale commercial catering.

One of the main aims of the unit will be to ensure that the high standards of RCHT's catering are maintained. Regularly receiving 90 per cent 'good to excellent' scores in monthly patient questionnaires, the chefs and catering team are proud of their achievements, and will maintain their high standards.

Conclusion

The objectives of the CFP are being met. They are:

- To provide guidance and support to local suppliers/producers so that they can participate in the public sector tendering process.
- To continue to produce quality freshly cooked meals for patients, and to increase the volume of local produce used in producing these meals.
- To have a positive impact on the health of the local community by influencing what people eat through education and health promotion campaigns, using the CFP as the vehicle for this information. It is envisaged that the CFPU will play a large role in the local community; it will not only produce good food, but will become a focal point for training and education.
- To have a positive effect on food miles by significantly reducing the number travelled by food products and by maintaining this as a key requirement of the CFPU's purchasing programme.

- To recognise the concept of 'good corporate citizenship' by demonstrating that large public sector bodies such as the NHS can make a difference to the whole community in which they provide their service.
- To secure local jobs, both through the development of the CFPU, thus providing skilled jobs within the county, and also by providing local businesses with markets for their products
- To provide an example of 'best practice' to encourage other NHS Trusts to play a similarly active role within the community.

A critical factor in the success of the sustainability agenda of the CFP has been the commitment at the board level of RCHT to invest in sustainable food procurement. Without this belief in the CFP, and without the foresight of the Trust executive team, the idea would not have got off the ground. This is a key element that is essential to the success of any similar scheme within the NHS. The support of the chief executive is always required. The CFP hopes that its success will influence chief executives throughout the NHS to take on board sustainability issues.

The CFP team has already started working with other departments, both nationally and locally, including NHS Estates, NHS Supply Chain and the local supplies manager and team (CHESS) in order to help change the way NHS food purchasing is carried out.

Chapter 11

Ethics in French Wine Cooperatives: Part of a Social Movement?

Yuna Chiffoleau, Fabrice Dreyfus and Jean-Marc Touzard

Challenged by the development of Fair Trade and ethical sourcing and confronted with an ongoing crisis in the regional wine industry, wine cooperatives in Languedoc in the south of France are addressing their corporate identity: should an ethical approach to corporate responsibility be part of a marketing strategy or should it form the basis of a larger, renewed collective project?

Fair Trade and ethical sourcing are concerned with equity, solidarity and empowerment and so preference is given to democratic groups of producers. In the case of agrifood supply chains, Southern producer groups involved in these new trade relations are cooperatives, and their promotion of solidarity and small-scale producers' empowerment is not questioned. Since they share the same principles and values, some Northern wine cooperatives are interested in taking part in the overall Fair Trade and ethical sourcing movement, but find they need to 'earn' recognition. Puzzled by the numerous issues that participation in the Fair Trade and ethical movements raises, some French wine cooperative directors have asked social scientists to assess their capacity to respond to these new challenges.

The first part of this chapter sets out an analytical framework designed to assess the different aspects of ethics that may be at work in organisations such as cooperatives. In the second part, the analysis is illustrated through a study of the history of wine cooperatives in Languedoc from their inception up to the 1980s. The study highlights their relation to the major social movements at the beginning of their existence, and demonstrates how the principles that were prevalent in the early years are similar to those that form the basis of the current Fair Trade movement. This historical study also shows how the second segment of history examined here, which lies between the early and current periods, displayed a cooperative movement tightly framed by the productivist paradigm prevailing at the societal level after the 1960s. Cooperative ethics have thus altered from one period to another in response to wider economic and social change. The third part of the chapter presents the current situation and analyses how the nature and realisation of cooperative ethics are changing once again. Finally, the nature of an ethical project and the current conditions for its development in French wine cooperatives is discussed and operational proposals are suggested.

An Analytical Framework of Ethics: Combining Scales and Points of View

Ethical principles may be construed as the extension of group or individual solidarity towards others (Ricoeur 1994). Their application is determined by a set of values specific to this group or individual, which enable the selection of who is in need of solidarity and how the particular set of values should be implemented. Fair Trade is a contemporary way of applying ethical principles, whereby consumers and distribution agents include in their solidarity a wide range of stakeholders in distant territories all over the world. Ethical behaviour and discourse thus appear to be embedded in social action aiming at social change as well as control over the course of history (Touraine 1984). In this sense, the values that feed an ethical approach raise the question of the building of a collective identity through participation in a social movement (Castells 2000). Triggered by these social movements or prompted by inner needs, firms and corporations may fulfil their sense of responsibility to society through the design and implementation of ethical codes and standards. These codes and standards can be introduced in the rules and procedures as defined in the statutes and contracts of the firm. Their introduction may challenge the former balance of the firms, seen as 'organised action systems' (Friedberg 1993) in which participants coordinate with each other. Members of a wine cooperative may perceive these changes as constraints or opportunities, depending on their own individual strategy and view of cooperative identity.

Ethical codes also display a convention, that is to say a social agreement, about what is good or bad for the firm, allowing 'a satisfying level of co-ordination, inside the relevant collective identity' (Favereau and Lazega 2003). Throughout their trajectory, firms may follow different conventions that have evolved from different principles relating to the domestic, industrial, merchant or civic world and that have shaped judgements concerning corporate behaviour (Boltanski and Thévenot 1991). From this viewpoint, analysing the possible involvement of wine cooperatives in ethical projects may be performed through considering the organisation's founding conventions and its relationship with the current economic environment.

However, stake- or shareholders prompt firms to develop a consequentialist approach to ethics as well, by assessing the results of the implementation of these ethical principles. Since these principles are fundamentally concerned with the building of solidarity, economic sociology (White 1992; 2002) provides resources to assess the way corporate projects presented as ethical may be acknowledged as such. By understanding markets and organisations to be social networks shaped by values, economic sociology assesses previously disadvantaged people, marginalised members or stakeholders not only by their poor level of economic resources, but also by their social capital – their degree of inclusion in power, information and trade relations. Hence it is necessary to assess the ways in which ethical initiatives actually improve the position of these groups in relevant networks through the mobilisation of their resources. Noticeably, chief amongst individual resources, economic sociologists emphasise the mobilisation of skills (Favereau and Lazega 2003) and stress the cognitive dimension of organised action systems, through human capital and the conventions associated with them.

One way of approaching the ethical commitment of a firm therefore combines an analysis of the social context in which it is embedded, with an analysis at the micro-level of the coordination convention that frames the evolution of firm behaviour. Our work suggests that the tacit or overt selection, design and implementation of rules and procedures are closely linked to their historical context. In order to grasp cooperative ethics through different periods, we have analysed the different actions that they have implemented to promote solidarity and equity. We have sought to identify interior social practices among members and in relation to the product itself, and exterior practices, along the value chain in downstream economic relations, or through actions of solidarity towards external individuals or groups. Since ethics can be illustrated by objects or practices, we grounded our research in the analysis of speeches, mottos and songs, construed as reminders of the basic principles for the members. These, with other signals such as labels, awards and packaging, are useful indicators of what has been considered good or fair and what has been valued by the collective identity. Codes and regulations enable the delineation of spaces of responsibility and of common humanity where solidarity is at work.

Ethics in the Cooperative Project: An Historical Perspective on the Languedoc Wine Sector

The first wine cooperatives (1900–30): economic projects, social assertion, local and class solidarity

The first Languedoc wine cooperatives were created in 1901 by small winegrowers in the context of a very serious wine market crisis. The case of the Vignerons Libres de Maraussan (Free Winegrowers of Maraussan) illustrates how ethical perspectives have been strongly linked to the economic and social issues of these organisational innovations. Documents and information concerning collective decisions gathered during this period (Tarbouriech et al. 1996) show how the founding members presented and built their project. First, they stated that wine regrouping would improve their incomes, citing two reasons:

- It would bring about better and more regular prices through more negotiating power with traders and by progressively cutting out parasitic retailers and selling directly to consumers.
- It would introduce better control over the wine quality and reduced technical risks and costs, first by storing and transporting wine by their own means and then by processing grapes in a common cellar.

These economic arguments clearly rely on both market and technological scale economies (Temple et al. 1996). The records of discussions among founding members suggest that these economies were far from certain. Nevertheless, the first investment decisions were associated with an increasing turnover and showed that the project could be economically viable for the following reasons:

- The cooperative bought horses, rail tankers and wine warehouses near Paris.
- A new collective cellar was built in 1905 in front of Maraussan rail station.
- Wine prices awarded to members remained attractive and marketed wine volume increased until 1914.

These economic targets and activities were completed by a more implicit, but perhaps more powerful objective. The small growers wanted to assert themselves against the largest employing landowners and the traders who allegedly cheated them. Examples of this social assertion objective are numerous: the name Vignerons Libres de Maraussan given to the cooperative, leaflets reproducing traders' advertising, and the desire to build the highest wine cellar in the village. This collective assertion is based on imitative mechanisms, in which the landowner or the trader became simultaneously the rival and the model (Girard 1983). It can also be interpreted as a means of building a new social status within local networks as well as within wine market networks. Indeed, early cooperative texts identified the collective project more generally with the 'emancipation of small growers within the wine industry'.[1]

Grouping wine for marketing and processing grapes in a common cellar proved to be a successful innovation, aiming at economic and social assertion objectives. But formal rules, conventions and routines that allowed and stabilised the system were also linked to ethics, extending their concerns at both local and class levels. Solidarity, democracy and educational support were explicitly promoted and implemented within the organisation. The ethical identity of the Maraussan cooperative was affirmed by the motto written over the cellar door: '*Un pour Tous, Tous pour Un*' (One for All and All for One). In this case, the term 'all' can be interpreted as restricted to the selective circle of the co-op members. Formal internal rules also expressed the democratic and non-capitalist options of the organisation:

- Decisions had to be taken following the principle '*un homme, une voix*' (one man, one vote).
- Cooperative benefits were distributed according to the wine volume delivered by each member.
- The amount of grapes that could be processed per member was fixed in order to support the small growers.

Moreover, ethical principles were discernable in many other rules or actions and extended into the local community. Pragmatic decision making led to the introduction of more equity in internal rules, through overt recognition of members' specific contributions to the collective project:

- A commission was given to members who found new markets.
- Four wine qualities were identified by a tasting committee and paid at different rates.

1　The Maraussan cooperative earned the status of French political movement when Jean Jaurès, leader of the Socialist Party, visited the village in 1905 and subsequently published his well-known article, 'The Wine of the Social Revolution'.

Some cooperative rules or decisions were specifically issued to promote mutual assistance between members:

- Thirty-five percent of the benefits were dedicated to a local development fund.
- Mutual help for sick or absent members was organised, especially during the First World War.

Finally, explicit involvement in local solidarity and development activities were implemented through other organised action systems, presented as auxiliary organisations of the wine cooperative:

- The farmers' union delivered agricultural supplies to growers.
- The Maraussan Union was a very active consumer cooperative.
- The local branch of the Crédit Agricole provided credit, insured by the regional cooperative bank.
- The Proletarian Beehive invested in small but clean houses rented to winegrowers' families.

Thus, ethical concerns were core to the Maraussan cooperative project and were integrated in a political perspective. Responsibility seems to have been extended to the whole local community, perhaps in order to involve more members[2] in the cooperative networks or to become collectively and individually 'great', according to prevalent local civic and domestic conventions.

The Maraussan cooperative project was relevant to a more extensive area of solidarity: the lower social classes, which included French workers and small farmers. This category was defined and celebrated in socialist ideology and fitted the general perception of identity in many working-class movements. Indeed, the cooperative produced basic wine, drunk by low social classes. Thus, new markets were developing along with the development of ethical behaviour. Indeed, this solidarity extended to all low social classes:

- The cooperative aimed to provide consumers with natural wines and to connect small winegrowers and workers through the cooperative movement. Maraussan succeeded in selling a significant proportion of its wine to consumers' cooperatives. This involvement led to the inclusion of internal rules that stated that 25 per cent of the cooperative's profits must be given back to consumers, whose delegates were also invited every year in order to learn about the real conditions of production.
- Maraussan directors decided to support the development of the socialist cooperative movement, and some members actively participated in regional meetings, promoting the creation of wine cooperatives in other villages. Solidarity with low social classes was extended to national solidarity during the First World War, when the cooperative made a donation of 200 000 hectolitres

---

2 In 1905 the cooperative numbered 230 members among 280 winegrowers in Maraussan.

to the French army, who mainly came from the lower social classes. This action has also been interpreted as a clever marketing strategy (Tarbouriech et al. 1996).

In the case of the Maraussan cooperative, the ethical principles of solidarity, democracy and social progress were integrated into rules, conventions and routines through a pragmatic compromise between local conventions inherited from local networks such as worker groups, previous associations, mutual help relationships between neighbours or within families, and the socialist ideology brought by leaders such as Elie Cathala (Gavignaud-Fontaine 2001).[3] With the emergence of the first wine cooperatives, ethical principles could be considered as a source of coordination and networking within the economic organisation and along its marketing chain. They reduced uncertainty and promoted this social experience at the national level. The nature, the role and the extension of these principles were clearly determined by the historical context: a wine market crisis, the legal recognition of associations and the evolution of political ideas in a powerful social movement.

Thus the cooperative ethics of this period show many similarities to presentday Fair Trade ethics. They share the same principles: local solidarity and democracy, direct relations and solidarity between producers and consumers, transparency and fair pricing within the commodity chain. They are both part of a wider social movement, socialism in one case, alter-globalisation (Jordan 2005) in the other.

The development of table-wine cooperatives (1930–80): mass production and regional corporate solidarity

The expansion of cooperative cellars in Languedoc started after the First World War. Their number increased dramatically in the 1930s, reaching 550 in the 1970s. The number of members per organisation also grew in such a way that cooperatives took a dominant position in the Languedoc wine industry, producing at least 75 per cent of its wine. What conditions can explain this development and how could ethical principles have influenced it?

A favourable environment The cooperative's expansion was influenced by a more favourable environment. Facing a possible repeat of the 1900–7 national market crisis, the French government and regional wine leaders gradually negotiated the construction of a specific wine policy, aiming at the control of the wine supply by establishing a planting quota and rules that could frame the sales. From this new perspective, cooperatives were considered to be possible tools for implementing this economic policy, rather than as rebel organisations, as Vignerons Libres de Maraussan were considered to be before 1920. Subsidies and fiscal advantages were accorded for cooperatives' development and were increased in 1936 by the Front Populaire government, which was politically aligned with regional voters.

---

3 In other regions, religious morality played the same role in the emergence of agricultural cooperatives (Desroche 1976).

A new model of management In this context, the economic utility of joining a cooperative was greater and economic projects converged towards the same organisational model: the village table-wine cooperative. Directors and workers were appointed to manage the wine processing. Wine production was delegated to them by the members of the cooperative who then specialised in grape production. This resulted in a progressive separation between growers and the cooperative's staff within this mass production organisation. Technological and commercial scale economies were established and reinforced. After the Second World War changes in farming systems resulted in new investment, both in the vineyard and in wine processes undertaken in the cooperatives. As a result of the opportunity this presented, medium-sized winegrowers became members of these organisations.

Cooperatives as local institutions As noted in the Maraussan cooperative, economic objectives were also related to social assertion issues. The competitiveness between small growers and the biggest wine producers also existed between neighbouring villages (Bort 2003). Indeed, at this level, it often produced a rivalry that seems to have been more powerful than the need for inter-cooperative strategies. Each village wanted to get the biggest and highest wine cooperative cellar. The cooperative became an institution, a symbol of local identity for each village of the Languedoc vine-growing region.

Important changes in the implementation of ethical principles With regard to ethical concerns, the same formal cooperative rules were followed in accordance with the evolution of the national legal status of these organisations (Fontaine 2003). The basic principles of democracy, responsibility, territory linkage and solidarity between members, for example in terms of capital, formally shaped social interaction within wine cooperatives. In many cases, specific actions revealing solidarity between members and extended further into the local community are noticeable.

Table wine production changed the nature of cooperative conventions and ethical values. It strengthened egalitarian principles: wine was bought at a fixed price according to the one very basic criterion of alcohol content. Indeed, in the world of mass production, industrial conventions fit with egalitarian principles (Salais and Storper 1993). As a consequence, the specific skills or assets of members were not acknowledged, giving rise to debates about equity and, eventually, efficiency issues. Finally, grapes and vinegrowers tended to be valued as interchangeable production tools, which presented an important weakening of the ethical principle of valuing the individual for him or herself.

The boundaries of the ethical space also changed: solidarity towards lower social classes and consumers became relevant to fewer cooperatives. Through the specialisation of tasks, consumers had relationships with the retailers and traders who mixed Languedoc and Algerian wines. Temporary crises in the market could also be alleviated by corporate negotiations and lobbying rather than by investigating new market niches. Consequently, direct selling, connection and solidarity with consumers seemed to be less necessary. Moreover, the dynamics of socialist ideology itself were changing in society. The social representations of low social classes were not as widespread as they had been previously. In fact, they could appear more repellent than attractive to potential members. Thus the weakening of these ideological conditions allowed the integration of more vinegrowers.

Another reduction in ethical practice occurred within the wine cooperatives. In many cases, especially during the 1970s and 1980s, an increasing gap between members and staff, between vinegrowers' groups inside the cooperative and, more generally, between the founding ethical principles of the organisation and the social practices of its members became apparent. The management of wine cooperatives became nepotistic in many cases (Chiffoleau 2001), deferring more to domestic and industrial conventions than to the former civic conventions of the cooperative movement.

In sum, during the 1970s, the cooperative projects became institutionalised through a mass production model. They were linked to local space and were initially oriented by the cooperatives' founding values. Their apparent success hid important constraints such as dependency on mass technology, restriction of varieties in the production system, specialised routines and references to industrial and domestic conventions fitting with egalitarian principles.

Cooperative Cellars at a Turning Point

Before analysing the building of ethical projects in wine cooperatives today, it is necessary to understand better the consumers' behaviour in contemporary society and their awareness of different aspects of quality as well as ethics.

Hyper-modernity and ethical movements

In Northern countries, where sustainable development is seen as increasingly important, demands for quality are symptomatic of a crisis of trust between consumers, producers and science (Joly and Paradeise 2003). The consequences of overproduction, the recurrence of health scares such as BSE in the last ten years and the development of biotechnology have led to the emergence of a new type of customer: the citizen-consumer, concerned, even anxious, about the environmental and social friendliness of the products he or she purchases.

More fundamentally, it is necessary to refer to a broader analysis of social evolution to assess such new habits of behaviour. The modern society that followed the Industrial Revolution in the nineteenth century (Weber 1922) was built on a fundamental class divide. After the 1950s this evolved into a postmodern society. By providing, at least in Western societies, a temporary solution to the core contradiction between capital and labour, it stole the thunder from the major social movement of its time. The 1970s have been assessed as the era of individualism, consumption and fashion, where people's sense of the distinctions between classes declined and institutions were called into question (Dubet 2002). Consequently, some philosophers and sociologists interpret the current wave of ethical consumerism as a reaction against the loneliness, anxiety, loss of faith and loss of meaning that are the negative consequences of postmodernity. According to these scholars, since the 1990s we have been in the period of hyper-modernity. In order to find a sense of meaning in these circumstances individualism includes a humanist dimension (Lipovetsky and Charles 2004). Given that personal social responsibility now substitutes for traditional social institutions, responsible behaviour focuses around altruism and a belief in fundamental human rights. Beliefs and traditional values are reappearing, such as sociability, voluntary work, moral condemnation of violence, glorification of love and a sense of solidarity. Such values are materialising through the exponential increase of local associations and through public demonstrations on social and political issues, such as anti-war marches. This trend arises with the emergence of new kinds of institutions, more fluid and circumscribed, purportedly aiding cohesion and guaranteeing justice (Forsé and Parodi 2004). It is embodied in the numerous new social movements (Touraine 2005) that contribute to the overall alter-globalisation movement.

This period is thus grounded in the concept of ethics as developed by Ricoeur (1994).[4] It fosters the emergence of new figures concerned with responsible and ethical consumption. In this sense, it may not only be a fashion but may reflect a deep change in societies (Bajoît 2003). Further, it questions the strategy of the cooperative, confronting the ongoing changes in economic relations along the value chain, and it casts a new light on the cooperative identity as ingrained in its democratic principles that echo the hyper-modern ethics illustrated in Fair Trade.

Wine cooperatives facing globalisation and quality requirements

These tremendous transformations in the economic and political context have skewed table-wine cooperatives' trajectories and destabilised their regional corporate governance. Changes simultaneously affecting different dimensions of the context of wine cooperatives have followed. Social changes in ways of life in France such as driving habits and other health concerns are associated with economic and demographic change – including the decrease in the number of manual workers and rising incomes. These changes have led to a great overall reduction in wine consumption, of table wine in particular.[5] At the same time there has been a consumption shift to quality wines, aromatic varieties and wines with a well-defined origin, in particular *Appelation d'Origine Contrôlée* (AOC) wines such as Bordeaux. Moreover, the definition of wine quality has been progressively integrating new attributes such as environmentally friendly concerns, landscape management, health issues, traceability, packaging innovations and cultural image, as well as ethical concerns.

France's integration into European agricultural policy, the enlargement of the European Community and the internationalisation of the wine market have changed the conditions of competition and political negotiation for Languedoc wine cooperatives. The development of regional economies, which are increasingly based on new activities, have put vineyards under pressure. By 1995 the economic and

---

4   Ethics consist of 'individual behaviours aiming at a good life, with others, and in fair institutions'.

5   From 120 litres per adult per year in the 1960s, to less than 60 litres in 2000 (Laporte 2001).

regional political weight of the wine industry was reduced to less than 5 per cent of regional GDP. As a consequence, the retail price for table wine, and vinegrowers' income, have decreased. New economic policies, including subsidies for the permanent uprooting of vines, obligatory distillations and incentives for replanting with aromatic vine varieties and for technological investment in cooperatives have been promoted. At the same time, the evolution of the cooperative legal framework has offered new opportunities, for instance for creating subsidiaries.

In this more open and changing context, Languedoc wine cooperatives have chosen diverging paths. Some have continued table wine production without changing their inherited organisational model. This has generally resulted in cost cutting and a reduction in investment. In many cases defensive practice has led to exit trajectories at the cooperative level by implicit bankruptcy and absorption by a neighbouring cooperative, and at an individual level, with members leaving the cooperative in order to develop their own estates. However, the majority of table-wine cooperatives have progressively engaged in trajectories of innovation, including a large range of new activities along the processing and marketing chain wine chain, and also in tourism and local development. Innovative activities include the development of new wines, either AOC or variety wines, new internal rules, for example for payment for grapes, and new economic or marketing alliances (Touzard 2002). An analysis of these innovation strategies shows that economic objectives and arguments have radically changed (Chiffoleau et al. 2002):

- The economic project deals with many fields of innovation that must be combined and tested in the new context. Thus it stresses the fundamental role of new factors of production such as knowledge in each field of innovation, but also in project management, social capital, information, culture and values (Cohendet and Llerena 1990). These factors are the new strategic resources of post-industrial firms.
- Former references to scale economies have changed for cooperative cellars: the critical size of the cooperative has clearly become relative to the kind of wine, the activity or the choices of the alliance.
- The efficiency of a project combining complementary fields of innovation is also determined by actions and networks to announce the firm's specialisation.

Among such a diversity of economic strategies and objectives, social assertion objectives seem to take ambivalent forms. The positive identity of table wine production has disappeared both for growers' groups in each cooperative and for the regional corporate movement. This can be seen as an internalisation of consumers' repeated negative assessments of table wine, as well as those from the media and public figures. In many cases this has meant that the wine cooperative no longer fits the criteria for a social assertion project. Members have become ashamed of their cooperative and thus their involvement has diminished or is limited to economic opportunities. But in a minority of cases, a new identity has been created through new collective projects aiming for quality wine production. In these cases, relationships with wine writers and famous buyers have developed, as a result of the implementation of new technical practices and personal involvement in networking.

Over and beyond these developments, some cooperatives, already committed to quality wine production and aware of their ethical tradition, consider the current ethical trend in economics and society to be an opportunity to renew and strengthen their social assertion agenda.

Building an ethical project

For those cooperatives that were established in an attempt to impose socialist principles and ethics on the everyday life of their members (Jordan 2005), the question 'what does an ethical project mean today?' must be understood as 'are our basic principles still alive in the everyday behaviour of members?' Thus a diagnosis encompassing two dimensions is called for; one relating to the distribution of income and the other linked to the practice of democracy in the cellar.

Distribution of income Faced with the new requirements of the markets, and the new attributes of quality – which increasingly include social and environmental sustainability, the cooperative must undertake a growing number of new tasks well beyond mere grape production, such as the cleaning of dykes, the organisation of cooperative events or the short-circuited marketing of products. Equity between members within this new economic context requires an adapted remuneration system that must acknowledge the different contributions of their members. Indeed, distribution of satisfactory incomes to the members is another important part of cooperative ethics.

The practice of democracy in the cellar Beyond the issue of income distribution, an ethical diagnosis requires the acknowledgement of unfair and exclusive behaviour inside the formal organisation. In fact, cooperative cellars are not havens of peace, and power battles often bias their democratic functioning. For instance, part-time farmers or those who bring in small quantities of grapes are not always considered to be real producers. The younger generation who are unable to take over the farm from their elders, unemployed residents without economic means or social relations who are often moonlighters in the vineyards and older people whose table wine knowledge is usually discarded may prove useful and could complement the input of others. In many cases, these people have no input in the collective decision-making process although they could contribute to effective outcomes.

Furthermore, the question of the external relations of the cellar and its members needs to be addressed. An ethical project is aimed at the extension of group solidarity towards other social groups. The identification of these positions is the touchstone of such a project. There are a number of options that are consistent with the history of cooperatives:

- *A territorial rooting* Cooperative cellars, because of their history, their agricultural activities and their status, have always been deeply and durably embedded in their local, physical and social environment. Hence, cooperative ethics are relevant to the territory in which they operate, where various stakeholders are concerned in the different activities of the cellar.

- *A social thrust*   Nowadays in France, unemployment is perceived as the most worrying problem.[6] Following a consequentialist approach, cooperatives would have to take on board those trends and extend their solidarity beyond their members and employees to focus on job creation and the integration of new skills such as those concerning the environment.
- *A global turn*   Ethics in cooperatives that aim to take part in the wider social movement may target other cooperatives in the South involved in Fair Trade exchanges as potential partners in a renewed ethical project. Common communication, cross-training and the sharing of downstream networks are key domains in which Northern cooperatives may join the Fair Trade movement directly (Pollet and Develtere 2004).

Finally, there is the overarching question of the actual need for an ethical project in the cooperative. The choice between the niche option versus the social movement option is not clear cut, nor has it ever been. The major issue is the means employed, rather than the end itself. Since the cooperative *modus operandi* is based on equality in participative decision making, the cooperative institution itself should provide an ethical procedure to answer these questions. Nevertheless, members and other stakeholders are entangled in a set of strategic interdependencies that may impede the decision-making process. Moreover, the cooperative cannot commit itself to such an endeavour without building alliances with other agencies. This may be at the territorial level if such is the cooperative project, or with municipalities, other cooperative organisations, solidarity associations or any kind of local group dedicated to the reduction of poverty and exclusion. It must be downstream in the value chain, whatever the project. Relevant stakeholders and consumer organisations need to connect in order to highlight their different expectations, values and knowledge of ethical production and consumption and to identify dedicated venues, fairs and other commercial events in which alliances can be formed.

As with non cooperative firms, cooperative cellars may import and adapt standards and codes that they judge relevant, or they may develop this set of rules through different procedures. However, the touchstone of an ethical project must be the progressive identification of relevant internal and external others and the progressive understanding of their expectations. Such a process, enlisting new positions at each step and adapting its design to include newcomers, makes any precise prediction of the stabilised form of the project difficult. Thus, one must accept that the final outcome is unknown and that the movement is more important than the goal. Ultimately, developing an ethical project provides an opportunity to shape new social capital and, consequently, human capital.

---

6   BVA poll for IRSN 2006.

Conclusion

Throughout the different phases of their history, Languedoc wine cooperatives have developed their activities within an overt or tacit ethical framework, which above all has been consistent with a specific context. Their example thus shows how the practice of ethical principles is not a universal given, but a contingent co-building product, anchored in a social context, in meso-structures such as firms and territories and in interpersonal relations. During a first phase of development, cooperatives enacted their ethical commitment by being part of the social movement of the early industrial society, which was oriented towards the central conflict of this era, capitalists versus workers. The creation of fair institutions was the aim, and cooperatives were themselves a fundamental component of this process and message. During the productivist era, cooperatives, which were recovering from the war, like all parts of society, were primarily concerned with material production and distribution. They operated at the strategic instrumental level of action, backed by a strong political lobby and under the shield of favourable economic regulations. Today, wine cooperatives are standing at a turning point in their history. On one hand, they may wish to unload the burden of the past and move toward more usual firm management practices. On the other hand, rooted in their rich experience as a significant actor in a once powerful social movement, they may wish to use their inheritance to contribute to the struggle for the control and definition of a new interpretation of history, practising their ethics in the framework of new social movements such as Fair Trade.

When located in the South, cooperative organisations are widely considered a priori as legitimate actors in North–South fair trade. However, when located in the North, cooperatives must prove that they do provide the fair institutions that ethics-oriented Northern consumers wish to support when buying goods. Languedoc wine cooperatives present some sound arguments, developed throughout their hundred-year history. However, this demands more than the practice of a set of inherited habits of protest and political opposition (Crossley 2002). Whatever the difficulty in acting ethically and fairly within the cellar, cooperative cellars that are committed to an ethical project must weave in interaction with different partners. They must build a set of signals, labels and indicators that give substance to an identity.

Both the economic and social international trends towards short food supply chains dealing with the local Fair Trade issue present a great opportunity for the still human-size Languedoc cooperatives to lead and implement a renewed territorial governance of ethics, built by – and no longer against – markets. In the final analysis, however, the conflict between different expectations calls for a permanent networking effort, internally as well as externally, enabling both 'reflexive politics of localism' (Dupuis and Goodman 2005) and the collective design of a proactive cooperative identity.

References

Bajoît, G. *Le changement social*. Paris, Armand Colin, 2003.

Boltanski, L. and Thévenot, L. *De la justification: les économies de la grandeur*. Paris, Gallimard, 1991.

Bort, F. Du rouge au terroir: de la tactique coopérative à la coopération tactique. In Draperi, J.F., Touzard, J.M. (eds), *Les coopératives entre territoires et mondialisation*, Paris, IES–L'Harmattan, 2003, pp. 93–104.

Castells, M. *The rise of the network society: the information age volume 1*. Oxford, Blackwell, 2000.

Chiffoleau, Y. Pratiques et réseaux d'innovation en milieu coopératif. Doctoral thesis, Université Paris V, 2001.

Chiffoleau, Y., Dreyfus, F., Ewert, J., Martin, C., Touzard, J.M. and Williams, G. Qualité et solidarité dans les coopératives viticoles : des enjeux communs en Afrique du Sud et en Languedoc. *Revue Internationale de l'Economie Sociale*, 285, 2002, pp. 63–74.

Cohendet, P. and Llerena, P. Nature de l'information, évaluation et organisation de l'entreprise. *Revue d'Economie Industrielle*, 51, 1990, pp. 141–65.

Crossley, N. *Making sense of social movements*. Buckingham, Open University Press, 2002.

Desroche H. *Le Projet coopératif. Son utopie et sa pratique, Ses appareils et ses réseaux. Ses espérances et ses déconvenues*. Paris, Éditions Ouvrières, 1976.

Dubet, F. *Le déclin de l'institution*. Paris, Seuil, 2002.

Dupuis, M. and Goodman, D. Should we go home to eat? Toward a reflexive politics of localism. *Journal of Rural Studies*, 21, 2005, pp. 359–71.

Favereau, O. and Lazega, E. (eds) *Conventions and structures in economic organization*. Cheltenham, Edward Elgar Publishing, 2003.

Fontaine, J. L'insertion des principes coopératifs dans le droit français. In Draperi, J.F. and Touzard, J.M. (eds), *Les coopératives entre territoires et mondialisation*. Paris, IES–L'Harmattan, 2003, pp. 33–50.

Forsé, M. and Parodi, M. *La priorité du juste: éléments pour une sociologie des choix moraux*. Paris, PUF, 2004.

Friedberg, E. *Le pouvoir et la règle: dynamique de l'action organisée*. Paris, Seuil, 1993.

Gavignaud-Fontaine, G. *Les caves coopératives dans le vignoble du Languedoc et du Roussillon*. Montpellier, Université Paul Valery, 2001.

Girard, R. *Des choses cachées depuis la fondation du monde*. Paris, Essais, Livre de Poche, 1983.

IRSN, 'La perception des situations à risques par les Français', Résultats d'ensemble Barometre IRSN, 2006. Joly, P.B. and Paradeise, C. Agriculture et alimentation: nouveaux problèmes, nouvelles questions. *Sociologie du travail*, 45, 2003, pp. 1–8.

Jordan, T. *Social movements and social change. CRESC Working Papers Series 7*. Manchester, CRESC, September 2005.

Laporte J.P., *Evolution de la consommation du vin en France, 1980–2000 et projection 2010*. Paris, Inra-onivins, 2001.

Lipovetsky, G. and Charles, S. *Les temps hypermodernes*. Paris, Grasset, 2004.

McDonald, K. From solidarity to fluidarity: social movements beyond collective identity. The case of globalization conflicts. *Social Movements Studies*, 2:1, 2002, pp. 109–28.

Pollet, I. and Develtere, P. *Development co-operation: how co-operatives cope. A survey of major co-operative agencies.* CERA Foundation, BRS, HIVA, Leuven, 2004.

Ricoeur, P. *Soi-même comme un autre*. Paris, Seuil, 1994.

Salais, R. and Storper, M. *Les mondes de production*. Paris, Editions EHESS, 1993.

Tarbouriech et al. *Les vignerons libres de Maraussan, 1901–1918*. Maraussan, Les Vignerons du pays d'Enserune (ed.), 1996.

Temple, L., Touzard, J.M. and Jarrige, F. La restructuration des coopératives vinicoles en Languedoc Roussillon: du modèle communal à la diversité des adaptations actuelles. *Revue de l'Economie Méridionale*, 44: 176, 1996, pp. 69–89.

Touraine, A. *Le retour de l'acteur*. Paris, Fayard, 1984.

Touraine, A. *Un nouveau paradigme: pour comprendre le monde d'ajourd'hui*. Paris, Fayard, 2005.

Touzard, J.M. Coordination locale, innovation et Régulation, l'exemple de la transition vin de masse – vin de qualité, *Revue d'Economie Régionale et Urbaine*, 3, 2000, pp. 589–605.

Touzard, J.M. Recensement des caves coopératives du Languedoc Roussillon, diversité des stratégies et des résultats, *Agreste*, Ministère de l'Agriculture, 2002.

Weber, M. *Economie et sociétés*. Paris, Plon, (first published 1922) 1971.

White, H.C. *Identity and control; a structural theory of action*. Princeton, NJ, Princeton University Press, 1992.

White, H.C. *Markets from networks*. Princeton, NJ, Princeton University Press, 2002.

PART III
Changing the Rules of the Game

Chapter 12

Impacts of the Supermarket Revolution and the Policy and Strategic Responses

Julio A. Berdegué and Thomas Reardon

The impacts of the supermarket revolution are profound and worldwide. This chapter begins by analysing in particular the consequences for small farmers and agrifood entrepreneurs. The weight of evidence shows that asset-poor farmers are unlikely to supply supermarkets, and small entrepreneurs are largely excluded from the procurement system. Policy makers, civil society and the private sector have responded to the evidence of adverse impacts by identifying policies and programmes that address the challenges and maximise the opportunities. Our assessment of their potential to mitigate the impacts is somewhat pessimistic; however, decisive and early action can bring worthwhile gains and these are explored in the second part of this chapter.

Impacts of the Rise of Supermarkets on the other Actors in the Agrifood System

Competition with traditional retailers

The mirror image of the spread of supermarkets is the decline of the traditional retail sector in substantial part because of competition with modern retailers. The fastest decline in the traditional sector is of small general stores selling broad lines and processed foods and dairy products; fresh produce shops and wet markets have held out longer. In Indonesia, supermarkets sales are rising by 15 per cent a year while those of traditional retail decline by 2 per cent a year. Nearly all Indonesians, apart from a tiny pocket of rich consumers, shopped only in small shops and wet markets in 1990; by 2005, 30 per cent of food overall was bought in supermarkets and 15 per cent of produce (Natawidjaja et al. 2007). In urban Chile between 1991 and 1995 some 15 777 small shops disappeared, mainly in Santiago, a city of 4 million, representing a decline of 21 per cent in small shops selling fresh food, meat and fish, 25 per cent in delicatessen, meat and dairy product shops but only a 17 per cent decline in fruit and vegetable shops (Faiguenbaum et al. 2002).

Tensions and conflicts with suppliers

We suggest that the emergence of tensions and conflicts between supermarkets and suppliers are correlated with the modernisation of retail procurement systems (Reardon and Hopkins 2006). First, there is what can be called structural tensions. The modernisation of procurement systems by supermarkets, combined with the demands of the formal sector such as formal registration of and invoicing by suppliers, translates into increasingly demanding requirements with respect to volumes, consistency, quality, costs and commercial practices. These represent for supermarket suppliers substantial threshold investments and costs in maintaining relations. As the supermarket sector consolidates, only a small number of buyers remain for an growing range of products; the resultant bargaining power of the retailers confers the power to impose requirements on suppliers.

Recent studies show that as a consequence of these demanding requirements distinctive patterns of participation by suppliers are emerging. Supermarket chains source from medium and large suppliers where they are available. Supermarket chains also tend to source fresh products from medium to large farmers; however, this is rarely possible in most developing countries except for a few products like bananas and other export sectors where large and medium farms have developed strong supply positions. Most of the time supermarket chains thus source only indirectly from small farmers, through wholesalers and processors. These farmers tend to be the upper stratum of small farmers in terms of capital assets (organisation, equipment and training), infrastructure access and size (see Box 12.1). Where small farmers do not have the needed assets but the procurement system must still rely on them, it is common for the proximate intermediary to assist with training, credit and so on (Dries and Swinnen 2004; Berdegué et al. 2005).

Box 12.1   Family farmers as supermarket suppliers

Does the rise of supermarkets lead to the exclusion of small farmers as producers? Yes, it does. But small farmers who have access to the assets that are critical to meeting the conditions of the supermarkets can in fact be included in the procurement system. Do the included farmers increase their income compared to selling in traditional markets? Yes, they do: increasing their income by a tenth to double. Asset-poor rural households can indirectly gain by becoming hired labourers through the modernisation of procurement systems.

Recent studies based on household surveys of 150 to 600 farmers each have compared horticultural product producers participating in modern domestic market channels (in which supermarkets are key downstream actors) versus traditional market channels. These studies have looked at tomatoes in Guatemala (Hernández et al. 2007), Indonesia (Natawidjaja et al. 2006) and Nicaragua (Balsevich et al. 2006), kale in Kenya (Neven et al. 2006), lettuce in

Guatemala (Flores et al. 2006), guavas in Mexico (Berdegué et al. 2006) and produce in China (Wang et al. 2006).

Supermarket-chain buying agents prefer to source from large and medium farmers if they can, such as in the case of bananas in Central America (Berdegué et al. 2005), tomatoes in Mexico (Reardon et al. 2005) and potatoes in Indonesia (Natawidjaja et al. 2006). In all cases where medium and large farmers are available with sufficient quantity of product, small growers are simply not included in the supermarkets' procurement system.

When medium and large growers are not available or do not produce enough to meet the year-round needs of supermarkets, the domestic retail impact studies available so far – with the exception of the China study – tend to confirm that asset-poor small farmers are almost universally excluded from supplying supermarket chains. As a rule of thumb, it could be said that only the top third of asset-rich small farmers tend to participate.

Flores et al. (2006) describe Guatemalan lettuce farmers who are included in the supermarket channel, relative to the non-included, as follows: twice the farm size (2 rather than 1 ha); twice as specialised in lettuce (58 per cent compared to 23 per cent of cropping) and specialised in horticulture (91 per cent compared to 79 per cent in horticulture instead of basic grains); with 40 per cent more education; twice as close to paved roads; nearly twice as likely to have irrigation (51 compared to 37 per cent); four times as likely to have a truck; and twice as likely to be a member of a small-farmer organisation (focused on marketing and production) (79 per cent compared to 42 per cent). Because the included use more labour-intensive practices in response to the supermarkets' requirements (use of specific field practices, sorting, packing), and are four times more likely to double (rather than single) crop over the year, they hire 2.5 times more labour (typically from local asset-poor households) as the non-included. If for example 50 lettuce farmers shift from the traditional to the supermarket channel, the data show that they hire 20 additional full-time workers for the two seasons. There is thus a significant exclusion effect on the producer side and an inclusion effect on the farm hired-labourer side.

In Indonesia, Natawidjaja et al. (2006) show that the included tomato growers, relative to the non-included have 17 per cent more education; are 26 per cent more specialised in tomatoes; have small farms that are 38 per cent larger (but they are still below 1 ha per household of cultivated land); are 20 per cent more likely to crop thrice over the year by means of irrigation; have 10 per cent more irrigation compared to before entering the modern channel; have 58 per cent higher per hectare profit rates but hire 30 per cent less labour because of greater capital intensity (such as greater use of plastic covers for the fields, reducing weeding needs). In general, farmers in the supermarket procurement system tend to earn substantially more (from 10 per cent to double) in net terms, so the payoff to making the required threshold investments is substantial.Overall, in all regions, family farmers are not excluded on the basis of the size of their landholding or land tenure, except when these factors affect the farmers' capacity to implement certain technologies that in turn have an impact on quality, productivity, costs, or the ability to plant and/or harvest at the needed times during the year. Other assets appear to play a much bigger role than does land. In particular, the included have more education, more access to transport and roads, have greater prior holdings of irrigation (for consistency of supply) and other physical assets, depending on the product, such as wells, cold stores, greenhouses, good-quality irrigation water (because of more careful use of contaminants), vehicles and packing sheds. In the rare instances where family farmers sell direct to the supermarket they typically are members of an effective rural producers organisation (RPO). The mass of the excluded, such as most of the traditional tomato farmers in West Java (Natawidjaja et al. 2006), lack these assets.

We find only two exceptions in the domestic retail impact studies in the horticulture sector to the 'exclusion of the asset-poor' rule. The first is where procurement modernisation is as yet insignificant and there is a cap on farm size and a relative evenness of asset distribution. In our set of seven studies only the China case (Wang et al. 2006) fits these conditions. The second is where non-government organisations have assisted (by means of implicit or explicit subsidies) the participation of the asset-poor small farmers. This had happened only in the instance of tomato supply to the lead supermarket chain in Nicaragua (Balsevich et al. 2006), at a cost of US$ 800 a year of assistance per farm, about ten times the public budget for farm extension and assistance.

There also are what can be called behavioural tensions between supermarkets and their suppliers. We say behavioural because they are widespread but discretionary practices of individual chains that affect their suppliers. For instance, supermarkets often pay their suppliers after a substantial lag compared to traditional wholesalers who pay on the spot. Gutman (2002) and Brom (2007) note for Argentina that in the late 1990s the greatly delayed payments by retailers to suppliers were the means by which retailers financed their expansion with negative working capital, using the suppliers in practice as lenders. By 1999/2000, supermarkets were paying suppliers in 60 to 120 days (compared to no delays in consumers' cash payments to supermarkets or up to 25 days for credit card payments). This compares with the 30-day limit imposed by a law enacted in 2001. Supermarkets also impose a series of regular fees on suppliers, such as slotting allowances and promotion fees as well as fees and discounts imposed for special events such as store openings (Dries and Reardon 2005). Supermarkets further require a range of post-harvest services from suppliers (special packaging, product delivery and so on) and give little advanced warning about the need for these facilities. In addition supermarkets require that suppliers meet stringent quality and sometimes safety standards that can require a high degree of asset specificity; they often change the level of enforcement of the standards when it suits them commercially (Berdegué et al. 2005). Because supermarkets in developing countries usually use only implicit contracts in most of the produce categories, established by the practice of listing suppliers (Hueth et al. 1999), there is scope for ambiguity and discretion that transfers risk to the supplier.

Suppliers sometimes need to pay bribes to procurement officers to be included in the supermarket lists.

The above tensions, charges and counter-charges have costs for the system. As competition among chains heats up it is common for a contradiction to occur. Supermarket chains, trying to cut costs in their supply chains in order to lower consumer prices and to create a fund for financing competition with other retailers, lengthen the delay in payments to suppliers and increase fees, but at the same time expect more in terms of quality, packaging and services from suppliers. The suppliers begin to see a drop in profitability in selling to the supermarket procurement system and they are expected to make more investments at the very time that the set of buyers is shrinking (because of retail consolidation). The fact that supermarkets in general and the share of foreign hypermarkets in particular have grown extremely fast in developing countries over the past decade indicates that the net effect of policy and regulation has been to promote or at least facilitate rather than restrain their spread. An upshot of the intense investment competition is that the supermarket sector is increasingly and in most cases overwhelmingly foreign owned and consolidated.

Policy Contexts

At the early stage of supermarket take-off, modern retail poses an immediate and major challenge to traditional retailers serving the larger cities and the middle class as well as to processed food firms. Wholesalers, most small and medium-sized agrifood enterprises and most farmers scarcely notice the effects of supermarkets at this stage. A few farmers engaged in the production of higher value foods that the supermarkets need in order to start differentiating themselves from traditional retailers will spot increasing opportunities for themselves. It is at this stage that the foundations need to be established of a public policy to deal with the emerging supermarket sector. The key public policy issues and decisions relate to the regulation of the growth of the supermarket sector vis-à-vis any perceived public interest in preserving and modernising traditional retail, the institutional framework governing relations between supermarkets and suppliers and the development of capacities among small and medium entrepreneurs and family farmers who are likely to be threatened in later stages of the supermarket diffusion process. The key private policy issues concern the type of relationship that supermarket chains intend to build with those suppliers who are not yet readily capable of meeting their needs, that is, if there is going to be any proactive effort to build a broad supplier base.

At the intermediate stage of supermarket penetration, modern retail begins posing major challenges in many more cities, towns and consumer markets to traditional retailers, suppliers of processed and semi-processed foods, wholesaler and family farmers engaged in fresh produce that the supermarkets have chosen to include in the early stages of their new procurement systems. At the same time, the opportunities increase for producers of higher value produce. As the dominance of supermarkets in urban retail reaches the 30 to 50 per cent range, major tensions emerge between supermarkets and suppliers. Traditional retailers begin to modernise their procurement systems to compete better with supermarkets, which means that for processed and semi-processed products the challenge to suppliers begins to spread over entire market segments. The policy issues and challenges remain the same as in the first stage of take-off except that some policy options have been foreclosed. The political pressure under which policy needs to be designed is greater, not only from those affected by supermarkets but also from the chains themselves who have greater capacity to resist unfavourable policies as a result of the preference they enjoy from a very large consumer base. At this stage, it is also likely that some of the leading chains belong to large multinationals who have ample resources to engage in the policy process, resources that dwarf the capacities of most developing nations.

At the advanced stage of supermarket penetration that one finds in Brazil, Argentina, Taiwan, Hong Kong or South Korea today there is little that can be done to change the fundamentals of the social and distributional outcomes of the diffusion of supermarkets. Not only have supermarkets become the dominant actor in food retail, they are also well on their way to reshaping the whole domestic food system throughout the country. Policies may aim at only marginal improvements; the economic and political costs of challenging supermarkets' dominance are simply too large to be contemplated by most governments.

Programmes such as that of the Regoverning Markets consortium (<www.regoverningmarkets.org>) thus are advocating the adoption of 'pro-active, anticipatory strategies and policies' that require a global outlook in order to deal with what indeed is a global phenomenon. It is essential to understand that the window of opportunity represented by the first and second stages of the supermarket revolution in most circumstances are unlikely to last more than ten years or so. A major challenge is to convince donors, firms, farmers' associations and governments to act early.

Differentiated policy instruments

Policy instruments that address the social and distributional impacts (rather than the growth side) can be classified as those that aim at regulating the diffusion, dominance and behaviour of supermarket firms, those whose objective is to support the development and competitiveness of traditional retail, and those designed to develop the capacities of upstream actors (in particular, family farmers) to participate in the new food system that is created by the diffusion of supermarkets. Most donors interested in development and poverty issues prefer to focus on the latter; we propose that without a substantial investment in market regulation and reform, a capacity-development strategy is akin to rearranging the chairs in the sinking *Titanic*.

Regoverning markets Competition policy, regulation of the diffusion of modern retail and regulation of retail procurement practices are three important policy instruments that can serve the purpose of introducing public good objectives into what otherwise is exclusively a market-driven process. We consider each in turn.

Government can limit the growth of the supermarkets' power through competition policy that limits concentration and collusion (such as through the Competition Commissions that one finds in most large developing countries, including Brazil, Indonesia and Mexico). For example, in 2004 Chile's National Economic Attorney fined a leading supermarket chain (Santa Isabel) after it was found that it had abused its dominant market position.

Governments can use regulatory instruments to limit supermarkets' diffusion and market penetration as well as their convenience (for instance through legislation on zoning and hours). Various developing countries have introduced such regulations, similar to those common in the US and in Europe. Often these regulations arise from political pressures by traditional retailer associations and are designed to impede supermarket diffusion, often in particular that of the hypermarkets typically associated with foreign chains, low prices and targeted competition with small stores.

Both Thailand and Malaysia have introduced strong regulation of hypermarket diffusion. The intensity of regulation none the less has varied considerably over the past five years. In Thailand such regulation first were intensified (in 2003) then relaxed (in 2004–5) and in 2006 were intensified again. Malaysia similarly witnessed first a rise and then a relaxation (CIES 2006a, 2006b and 2006c). However, it is also common for governments to promote the spread of modern retail and to regulate strictly the location and marketing practices of traditional retailers such as wet markets in an effort to modernise the commercial services sector. It is common also for governments through foreign direct investment policy to facilitate foreign supermarkets' entry and expansion.

Regarding the third policy option, regulation of procurement, it would be fair to say that most developing countries undergoing rapid transformation of their food retail sectors do not have strong regulations and implementation systems in place for governing buyer–seller relations (such as the PACA regulation in the US). The relatively sudden and extremely rapid rise of supermarkets has tested the commercial law system and shown it wanting.

There are a few examples of innovative action in this field, particularly in Latin America, where a combination of legal and self-regulatory approaches is emerging, sparked by the successful experience of Argentina. Around 2001 a crisis emerged in Argentina in terms of relations between supermarkets and their suppliers. The Competition Commission (founding its judgment on three existing laws: Truth in Trading, 1983; Consumer Protection, 1993; and Competition Law, 1999) said that it would promulgate a national law to regulate supermarkets and their relations with suppliers closely if the retail, wholesale, processor and farming sectors did not formulate and implement a private code of commercial conduct. The Argentine private sector (and foreign firms such as Carrefour) responded in July 2001, with retailers and suppliers signing a Code of Good Commercial Practices, the first of its kind in Latin America and probably the first in developing countries (Brom 2007). It was complemented by public regulation to strengthen the code with the promulgation of a new decree in March 2002 to limit the payment period to suppliers of perishable goods.

The terms of the private code were in essence four: compliance with contracts by both retailers and suppliers; equal treatment among suppliers; prompt payment and cooperation in logistics development. There is evidence that the conflict resolution mechanism accompanying the code has been effective (Brom 2007). Brom (2007) argues that in many developing countries a private code may well be the most practical and useful approach in the short to medium run in that it harnesses private sector interest, will and resources and can be implemented in situations where commercial laws and institutions are still evolving. Variants of the Argentine code have spread to Colombia (signed in 2005) and to Costa Rica (where it is under discussion) and Mexico (signed in June 2006).

Developing traditional retail   It has been said that traditional retail is the sector that perhaps faces the most immediate and the most difficult challenges as supermarkets move in and grow. In addition to other important considerations, the erosion of the traditional retail sector narrows the options left for the small and medium-sized businesses and family farmers who cannot gain access to supermarkets. One line of work in this area are policies supporting improvements in wholesale markets as well as other commercial infrastructure in order to increase the range of market alternatives for small farmers, to aid traditional wholesale markets compete with emerging specialised wholesalers and to help the wholesale markets remain a viable and competitive sourcing base for supermarkets for as long as possible (Reardon 2005).

Goldman et al. (1999) provide an illustration of improvements in wet market and other traditional retailer operations in Hong Kong. In the 1990s the government of Hong Kong instituted an aggressive modernisation programme that included wide-ranging improvements in infrastructure and hygiene of wet markets, privatisation, centralisation of procurement and advertising. This programme, combined with the advantages of traditional retailers in fresh vegetables and fish, allowed wet markets to protect their high share in these categories despite the ubiquity of supermarkets and hypermarkets and despite the latter's gains in other fresh categories such as fruit, pork and chicken, where they could gain advantages of scale through relations with large processors and packers.

Chile has instituted a programme for the modernisation of '*Ferias Libres*' (mobile street markets, of which there are 700 in Chile, involving about 60 000 family-based micro-enterprises). It includes access to special credit lines for these retailers, investments in basic infrastructure and services by municipal governments, training in good business practices by specialised government agencies and greater cooperation from the police force to keep away the thieves and pickpockets that are a main reason why customers otherwise may prefer supermarkets.

Developing the capacities of supplies   Many donors and governments are now experimenting or mainstreaming strategies and programmes to improve the capacity of participating small and medium-sized enterprises and family farmers to gain access to dynamic markets such as that represented by supermarkets. The effectiveness of these programmes varies considerably. As a cautious generalisation it may be said that the effectiveness and sustainability of these market-access programmes is hampered by the low quality or even the inexistence of certain basic services for the mass of small and medium-sized businesses or family farms. Good-quality technical and business advisory services, financial services and support to rural producer organisations have in a sense become niche services that are provided only to tiny fractions of firms or households. They must bear the full cost of developing the capacity of a farmer or a business from a very low baseline (no services or services of low quality), all the way to the high standards required by a demanding market. The cost often cannot be sustained beyond the life of the project or programme. In Nicaragua, for example, Balsevich et al. (2006) estimated the direct costs of one quite successful niche service project to be of approximately US$850 per farmer per year, an amount between eight and 12 times higher than that typically spent by the Nicaraguan government on the provision of more broad-based technical assistance services.

In addition to generic technical and financial services there is a need for more customised services under most circumstances. There are four main policy options. One is to create business development services that provide market intelligence at the same time as they facilitate business linkages between suppliers and supermarkets. This includes at a minimum provision of detailed, customised market information as well as facilitation of face-to-face meetings and follow-up, usually in the form of subsidised investments to help suppliers meet the requirements of supermarket chains. An example is that of ASERCA (the Mexican market promotion service of the Secretariat of Agriculture) that offers a direct marketing programme that facilitates links between local suppliers of fresh produce and supermarket chains in Mexico and in other countries. ASERCA also stages trade shows where supermarket-chain buying agents and suppliers meet, and sponsors producer groups from the various states of Mexico to attend Mexico's supermarket association's yearly convention. In parallel, the state governments' secretariats of agriculture are developing programmes to link suppliers with supermarkets. For example, the market promotion programme of the government of Michoacan's Secretariat of Agriculture has facilitated the link of several organisations of small fruit growers with leading chains such as Wal-Mart, Marx Aguirre and SEDAGRO Michoacan (personal communication, May 2006).

Secondly, governments have the option of facilitating the development of rural producer organisations. Supermarket chains usually do not work with individual small farmers. Traditional cooperatives are usually not viable for these relationships because of free-rider problems. Governments thus need to think hard about the role of a new generation of cooperatives and other farmers' associations and how to design new programmes to assist them in new markets. This is easier said than done (see Box 12.2).

Thirdly, in order to match public standards with the private standards of processors and supermarkets and to induce a diffusion of practices that would meet those norms, some governments have begun adapting public standards to often more demanding private standards. The policy dilemma of course is that raising standards means exclusion of those without the means to invest.

Fourthly, governments have the option of supporting suppliers' access to financial services. The reduction of the market risk faced by retailers and increased access to financial capital are crucial elements for suppliers. Retailers and their specialised and dedicated wholesalers (such as Metro in Croatia and Gigante in Mexico) are themselves mediating between commercial banks and suppliers to solve problems of credit access by providing the equivalent of a collateral substitute for small and medium-sized farmers, by proffering the listing contract as evidence that suppliers will be able to repay the loans. Governments are moving to provide similar guarantees so that small and medium-sized farmers can gain access to commercial bank loans to upgrade their outfit to sell to supermarkets. The effort of the Mexican government to facilitate

Box 12.2   Cooperating to compete: Easier said than done

Since 1990 the government of Chile has made a sustained effort to support the participation of small-scale agriculture in one of the most liberalised and competitive economies in the developing world. Between 1990 and 2004 about US$2.3 billion were invested by the government for this purpose. A key element of the strategy has been the promotion of rural producer organisations (RPOs) and the development of their entrepreneurial capacities. Berdegué (2001) conducted an in-depth study of close to 500 RPOs whose main purpose was to improve the economic performance of their members.

The government's effort to promote the formation of these kinds of market-oriented RPOs was very successful. In less than a decade 780 were formed, involving about one-third of the market-oriented small farms in the country. Half of the RPOs had less than 30 small farmer members each, and annual sales of less than US$33 000. Over 70 per cent did not have paid staff. Close to half of the RPOs were successful in accessing national markets and 13 per cent exported their products. The RPOs provided a broad range of services to their members and to other small farmers, including technical assistance, financial, machinery, storage, processing, marketing, legal, market information and accounting services.

An econometric analysis of data from a 3000-household survey showed that membership in an RPO did not make any significant difference in terms of annual net household income. The effect of RPO membership on the profitability (net margin) of agricultural production, depended on the product: if the product was sold in spot markets, as in the case of wheat or beans, there was no positive effect, but if marketing the product required some level of processing and a degree of vertical coordination with the buyer, as in the case of milk, then a significant positive effect was observed.

The most important finding of the study was that after one decade of sustained effort by farmers, technical advisers and government agencies, only about one-fifth of all the RPOs could be considered to be viable organisations. In 1999 about 45 per cent of the RPOs had annual expenses that were higher than their revenues, one-third had extremely high debts (mainly with governmental credit programmes) relative to their assets, and one-third depended on subsidies for 60 per cent or more of their income. In short, it is easier to support the formation of RPOs than for them actually to make a difference to their members' economic performance or to become self-sustainable.

What explains the success of the 20 per cent of the Chilean RPOs that had managed to become strong, viable and autonomous organisations? According to Berdegué (2001, 253) three factors deserve special attention:

- RPOs as vehicles for change: RPOs can be effective vehicles for farmers willing to change their practices, but not for sustaining the status quo in a context of traditional commodity production.

> - Networking: effective RPOs are embedded in effective multi-agent networks that link the farmers to ideas, resources, incentives and opportunities that are located beyond the rural community.
> - Rules for allocation of costs and benefits: successful RPOs have over time developed a system of rules and incentives for an adequate allocation of costs and benefits among the members, and between them and the RPO as an entity. These systems of rules typically transmit undistorted market signals to each individual member and reduce the transaction costs of negotiating, monitoring and enforcing agreements between the collective and the individual.

direct commerce between suppliers and supermarkets is interesting. The government agency concerned, SAGARPA, is extending the existing factoring service (that is, the supplier gets immediate cash instead of having to wait for payment) in return for a share of the invoice paid to the factoring service. Also as part of the SAGARPA initiatives, the government is working to bring in the rural bank, Financiera Rural, to pay small farmers immediately and then invoice the local supermarket chains.

Final Reflections

The onset of the supermarket revolution has been abrupt; the rise of modern food retail extremely rapid and the scope for policy and strategic effort to pursue public good objectives in a market-driven process appears to be limited. Asset-poor small farmers are almost universally excluded from supplying supermarket chains. The top third of asset-rich small farmers might be included, with targeted and appropriate effort and policy support. The challenge of providing both generic and customised services that can be sustained beyond the life of special projects and programmes to the very large numbers involved has not yet been effectively met. Those who are included experience considerable advantages and benefits and their participation stimulates an increase in labour hiring. Decisive and early action by governments and donors in the early stages of supermarket take-off can increase the opportunities for small farmers and agrifood entrepreneurs by broadening the supplier base and conserving those elements of traditional retail favoured by customers.

References

Balsevich, F., Berdegué, J. and Reardon, T. (2006), 'Supermarkets, New Generation Wholesalers, Tomato Farmers, and NGOs in Nicaragua', Staff Paper 2006–03 (East Lansing: Department of Agricultural Economics, Michigan State University).

Berdegué, J.A. (2001), *Cooperating to Compete. Peasant Associative Business Firms in Chile*, published doctoral dissertation, Department of Social Sciences, Communication and Innovation Group (Wageningen, Netherlands: Wageningen University and Research Centre).

Berdegué, J.A., Balsevich, F., Flores, L. and Reardon, T. (2005), 'Central American Supermarkets' Private Standards of Quality and Safety in Procurement of Fresh Fruits and Vegetables', *Food Policy* 30:3, June, 254–69.

Berdegué, J.A., Reardon, T., Balsevich, F., Martínez, A., Medina, R., Aguirre, M. and Echánove, F. (2006), 'Supermarkets and Michoacán Guava Farmers in Mexico', Staff Paper 2006–16, April (East Lansing: Department of Agricultural Economics, Michigan State University).

Brom, J.F. (2007), 'Best Commercial Practices Code (Argentina 2000–06) as an Efficient Policy to Improve Relationship Between Suppliers/Manufacturers and Supermarkets. A Case Study', manuscript, Regoverning Markets Programme.

CIES Food Business Forum (2006a), 'Foreign Retailers Pursue Small–Format Investment in Thailand', *CIES Food Business News*, 4 June.

CIES Food Business Forum (2006b), 'Freeze on Hypermarket Licences in Malaysia may be Lifted', *CIES News of the Day*, 17 July, no paging.

CIES Food Business Forum (2006c), 'Retailers Faced with Prison/Fines in Thailand', *CIES News of the Day*, 4 October, no paging.

Dries, L. and Reardon, T. (2005), *Central and Eastern Europe: Impact of Food Retail Investments on the Food Chain*, EBRD Cooperation Program, Report Series no. 6, February (London: FAO Investment Center).

Dries, L. and Swinnen, J. (2004), 'Foreign Direct Investment, Vertical Integration and Local Suppliers: Evidence from the Polish Dairy Sector', *World Development* 32:9, 1525–44.

Dries, L., Reardon, T. and Swinnen, J. (2004), 'The Rapid Rise of Supermarkets in Central and Eastern Europe: Implications for the Agrifood Sector and Rural Development', *Development Policy Review* 22:5, 525–56.

Faiguenbaum, S., Berdegué, J.A. and Reardon, T. (2002), 'The Rapid Rise of Supermarkets in Chile: Effects on Dairy, Vegetable, and Beef Chains', *Development Policy Review* 20:4, 459–71.

Flores, L. and Reardon, T. (2006), 'Supermarkets, New-Generation Wholesalers, Farmers Organizations, Contract Farming, and Lettuce in Guatemala: Participation by and Effects on Small Farmers', Staff Paper 2006–07 (East Lansing: Department of Agricultural Economics, Michigan State University).

Goldman, A., Krider, R. and Ramaswami, S. (1999), 'The Persistent Competitive Advantage of Traditional Food Retailers in Asia: Wet markets' Continued Dominance in Hong Kong', *Journal of Macromarketing* 19:2, 126–39.

Gutman, G. (2002), 'Impact of the Rapid Rise of Supermarkets on Dairy Products Systems in Argentina', *Development Policy Review* 20:4, September, 409–27.

Hernández, R., Reardon, T. and Berdegué, J.A. (2007) 'Supermarkets, Wholesalers, and Tomato Growers in Guatemala', *Agricultural Economics*, 36:3, May, 281–90.

Hueth, B., Ligon, E., Wolf, S. and Wu, S. (1999), 'Incentive Instruments in Fruits and Vegetables Contracts: Input Control, Monitoring, Measurements, and Price Risk', *Review of Agricultural Economics* 21:2, 374–89.

Natawidjaja, R., Reardon, T. and Shetty, S., with Noor, T.I., Perdana, T. Rasmikayati, E. Bachri, S. and Hernandez, R. (2007), *Horticultural Producers and Supermarket Development in Indonesia*, UNPAD/MSU/World Bank, World Bank Report no. 38543, July (Indonesia: World Bank).

Neven, D., Reardon, T., Chege, J. and Wang, H. (2006), 'Supermarkets and Consumers in Africa: The Case of Nairobi, Kenya', *Journal of International Food & Agribusiness Marketing* 18:1/2, 103–23.

Reardon, T., Berdegué, J.A. and Timmer, C.P. (2005), 'Supermarketization of the Emerging Markets of the Pacific Rim: Development and Trade Implications', *Journal of Food Distribution Research* 36:1, 3–12.

Reardon, T. and Hopkins, R. (2006), 'The Supermarket Revolution in Developing Countries: Policies to Address Emerging Tensions among Supermarkets, Suppliers, and Traditional Retailers', *European Journal of Development Research* 18:4, 522–45.

Wang, H., Dong, X., Rozelle, S., Huang, J. and Reardon, T. (2006), 'Producing and Procuring Horticultural Crops with Chinese Characteristics: A Case Study in the Greater Beijing Area', Staff Paper 2006–05 (East Lansing: Department of Agricultural Economics Michigan State University).

Chapter 13

Supermarkets: A Force for the Good?

Robert Duxbury with Cathy Rozel Farnworth

Robert Duxbury worked at Sainsbury's for 24 years in their Technical Division, ultimately taking on the role of managing organic integrity. He helped to introduce the organic range to Sainsbury's and soon became known as 'Mr Organic'. In a discussion with Cathy Farnworth, conducted face-to-face and by email, Robert Duxbury discusses whether supermarkets have the potential to promote social and environmental sustainability. This chapter opens with a consideration of the relationship between supermarkets and their consumers and then examines the role of supermarkets in supply chains. The vexed question of the ability of supermarkets to instigate ethical practices in the face of market realities is then discussed. Of major concern to many citizen-consumers is the impact of supermarkets on local economies: what stands in the way of supermarkets engaging in local purchasing? Following a discussion of this point, the debate turns to a consideration of the role of supermarkets in promoting food cultures, as opposed to commoditising and cheapening food. Finally, in the face of potential ecological collapse worldwide, Robert considers how much of a role supermarkets can play in stemming that collapse.

The Supermarket–Consumer Relationship

Robert Duxbury: All along the supply chain there are agreements or contracts between trading partners. There is no contract, though, between supermarkets and their customers. In this respect the retailer–consumer relationship can be viewed as being quite tenuous. Despite their sophisticated data capture systems, eye-catching offers and innovative developments, it is not always easy for supermarkets to predict consumer loyalty and behaviour. Although they rely on mass marketing and huge numbers of sales, their success is based upon the reputation they maintain within the marketplace. Just one product recall or bad news story can significantly affect sales and ultimately reduce profits.

The UK food retail sector is one of the most competitive in Europe, with the six major supermarkets vying for the custom of a defined consumer base. Although each has its distinctive trading style, all the major multiple retailers have to compete on common key factors that attract and retain customers, the most compelling of these being price. Despite contentions that consumers' buying habits are related to a set of sophisticated criteria that take into account a range of ethical issues and responsibilities, most consumers still buy principally on price. It is the bargain, the special offer and the desire to save money or get a cheap deal that drives most consumers. Food shopping is considered by most people to be no different from the purchase of any other commodity. Indeed, in our modern society, the value that consumers attach to food is very different from that perceived by our forebears. Many of us treat food as a just another disposable commodity, to be used or discarded with no real appreciation as to its true worth. I suggest that it is just as important to regain our understanding of food as a means of maintaining or improving our health and well-being, as it is to know that food prevents us from starvation. We need to appreciate fully the true social and environmental costs that are expended in bringing food to our mouths.

There are many ways in which supermarkets seek to promote relationships with their customers. Some have customer loyalty schemes, such as the Nectar card, which accumulate redeemable points based on the amount of money spent at the tills. Others provide store credit cards, which may include discounts or exclusive offers. Supermarketing is geared to providing a one-stop shop and caters for a wide range of consumer needs. The largest hypermarkets offer almost everything and anything their customers should need so that they will not be seduced into going anywhere else for their shopping.

Cathy Farnworth: There is evidence to suggest that an important number of consumers distrust major multiple food retailers as vendors of ethical products, such as organic and Fair Trade. For example, a Swiss study (Tanner and Kast 2003) found that people who specifically seek out 'green' products have generally positive attitudes towards the environment, fair trade and local products. Tanner and Kast found that such 'green consumers' shopped in supermarkets if they needed to save time. Yet they rarely purchased green products in supermarkets, despite the great range of such products now on offer. The reluctance of these respondents to purchase green products in supermarkets could be related to the narrow focus by supermarkets on the conditions of production. Supermarkets, Tanner and Kast argue, have tended to neglect other factors affecting the 'green credentials' of products (origin, packaging and conservation), which are equally important to consumers. Grolleau and Caswell (2003) note that signals indicating that a product is eco-friendly can be damaged by a failure to provide other verifiable attributes. In this context it is interesting to note that Lockie (2002) and Lockie et al. (2002) report, in a wide-ranging focus group study, that though Australians frequently shop in supermarkets for convenience reasons, many are hostile to the values and practices supermarkets seem to embody, such as dominance of the retailer sector, a lack of seasonal products and a lack of 'thoughtfulness'. Blythman (2003) reports similar consumer views vis-à-vis supermarkets in the UK. Despite this ambivalence, supermarkets are responsible for the majority of organic sales in the UK (Allan 2004).

Robert Duxbury: Supermarkets respond to customer demand; if customers want to be ethical, supermarkets will be. Despite the fact that we might not like them, we are nearly all 'guilty' of perpetrating the practice of supermarket shopping – the only ultimate sanction is for consumers not to shop at those supermarkets that do not reflect the values they seek. At this point, I would like to point out that the term 'supermarket' is not particularly precise as it misleadingly lumps together a great diversity of policies, practices and approaches to mass retailing. In the UK, shoppers know that there are considerable differences between Waitrose, Tesco, ASDA, Sainsbury's, Morrisons and Marks and Spencer. Using the term 'supermarket', which is actually a catch-all description of physical structure and retail format, therefore fails to address the comparative values and competitiveness of the businesses involved. Consumer greed, convenience and lack of personal responsibility have made the worst supermarkets what they are, while in other cases ethical purchasing decisions by consumers and the conscience of citizenship have driven the best supermarkets forward. Consumers themselves make supermarkets what they are, either as shoppers or as investors in financial markets.

Let me shift the discussion. One of the most important and intriguing things about the power of the supermarkets is that they have the power to make changes for the good. This is often overlooked. In the absence of supermarkets the rapid development of organic farming and the organic market over the last ten years in Britain simply would not have happened. The supermarkets' love affair with organic produce started in 1980 when Safeway started selling the first organic fruit and vegetables. Consumers had begun to be aware that health food shops were finding their way into town centres and offering organic ranges. This prompted the supermarkets to consider how similar developments might add value to their range offers. Waitrose followed suit in 1984, with Sainsbury's ranging a selection of Welsh organic vegetables a year later. Sainsbury's response was initially focused on stores in the London and Bristol areas, where their customers had started asking for organic food to be stocked. Significant numbers of shoppers had expressed their disappointment that, in not offering organic foods, the supermarket was not keeping up with market developments. Sainsbury's discovered that its customer profile was closely matched with the type of consumers who sought organic and other ethically oriented products. It set about building a repertoire of organic foods and offered a number of UK supermarket firsts, including organic bananas and Green & Blacks chocolate.

In branding Sainsbury's own label organic produce, it enhanced its reputation for good quality and competitively priced food. In so doing it attracted customers who were not necessarily confident about the quality or integrity of some organic food found in independent stores. In other words, Sainsbury's applied the same rigorous quality assurance criteria to the organic foods it sold as it did to all its other own label products. Organic produce was attractively labelled, information was provided about where it came from, and was supported by customer leaflets and point-of-sale material. The current Sainsbury's '*SO*' organic own label range epitomises a well thought-through branding and marketing initiative with consequent advantages for the supply chain that supports it.

The support of supermarkets for organic foods has resulted in a greatly increased market opportunity for many organic producers in Britain and overseas. Although some producers have been critical of the way in which supermarkets do business, many have seen their products being sold to a customer base much wider than they had previously experienced.

Relationships in Supply Chains

Supermarket relationships to suppliers

Cathy Farnworth: There was an example of an apple grower recently whose entire apple crop was damaged by hail. The supermarket he was growing for would not take the crop and now the farmer faces bankruptcy. Surely the control of supermarkets over the destiny of farmers goes too far?

Robert Duxbury: You could argue that the apple grower was farming unsustainably by relying just on one apple crop. It would be better to develop a more diverse system, whereby farmers have a range of enterprises. They could cooperate with other farmers to offer a range of products and to spread their risk. Most supermarkets are public companies and are therefore owned by their shareholders. This means that they are, in a sense, owned by all of us. Our investments, pension schemes and the money market generally have shareholdings in supermarkets. It is not beyond imagination that a supermarket could be owned by an organisation that had novel ideas about developing new ways of retailing. Although probably not for the altruistic reasons that some may hope for.

However, it is probable that any organisation taking over a supermarket would be faced with the same challenges that the existing chief executives and their boards face. The more fundamental issue facing such ideas are to do with the way commerce is structured in modern society. No business exists in a vacuum and even the most laudable ideals have to face up to the rigours and realities of the market. An even greater challenge today is the reality of the world market. Most supermarkets now operate on an international level and are subject to the pressures of international currency exchange rates, bank rates and corporation taxes. The pressures of existing in the European market and being subject to EU legislation are enough to make any business think twice before embarking on an innovative new development.

Current ways of managing value chains are so engrained in how our modern society is structured that it is almost impossible to speculate how they might be changed to reflect social or ethical ideals better. The two most important questions that must be asked before any new retail business venture is embarked upon are 'will it sell?' and 'can we make a profit?'.

Supermarket relationships with their suppliers are fundamentally structured through market principles. A different relationship could only come into being through the force of the law, or as a result of some seismic shift in the way business operates in the free market. Therefore I do not believe that the current supermarket business model can fully embrace some of the more ambitious philanthropic ideals to support and energise local or regional economies. At best, we will see a gradual development of some of the existing initiatives whereby supermarkets feature regional products and work with particular supply chains to ensure their customers get the products they want.

At this point it is interesting to look back for inspiration at the earliest relationships between supermarkets and suppliers. For example, Sainsbury's and Lloyd Maunder celebrated 100 years of trading at the turn of this century. A century ago, animals were reared in the southwest specifically for sale in Sainsbury's stores to specifications agreed between the farmers and the retailer. Before the advent of the railways, stock was driven on the hoof to Smithfield in London to be slaughtered and butchered for the city's consumers. This kind of relationship has become much more tenuous over time. Today, the supermarkets are driven by their links with customers much more than with their suppliers. And indeed, it would be true to say that seller–buyer relationships have always been somewhat adversarial. The seller wants more money for his or her goods and the buyer seeks to pay as little as possible for them. Many deals are settled as a compromise with one party often feeling the worse off – usually the seller!

Other Relationships in Supply Chains

Cathy Farnworth: Even organic farms occasionally use cheap labour – immigrants with no rights living in appalling conditions and receiving low pay – supplied by gangmasters. Yet many people think that organic farms are about creating fulfilling jobs in the countryside and do not have a clear grasp of some of the realities of organic production. Of course, I acknowledge that most organic farms treat their workers well and that the organic movement as a whole is moving towards an embrace of social justice standards.

Robert Duxbury: Low standards of employment sometimes characterise packing stations. People work long hours for low pay. They are often sourced from immigrant communities as well. While we are talking about complicated relationships and lack of transparency, I would like to add that the organic movement itself is guilty of building complex, convoluted certification and inspection regimes. It was never meant to be like that. The whole system has ended up being inaccessible and difficult to understand. Perhaps it is human nature to make things as complicated a possible! Complex systems offer endless possibilities for people to make money as far as possible along a chain of events and this happens in organic certification too. Organic certification is a system that exists by voluntary subscription. No one forces farmers to go organic; they do so of their own free will. However, once farmers have made the decision to turn organic, they are faced with a bewildering array of rules, regulations and standards. Someone once said: organic farming is 95 per cent between the ears. No one pretends organic farming is easy – if it was, everyone would be doing it. However, we recognise that the premium is designed to reward the extra care taken over farming practice.

Cathy Farnworth: A Fair Trade Foundation-certified coffee grower in Costa Rica told me:

> We are just plain coffee growers. Do we need to provide all this information? People aren't trusting. Honesty is being lost. In my case I have been producing coffee for ten years. I have never applied fungicide or herbicide, but I can't prove this. I have to provide written registers. This is so much work. I feel they don't trust me. People take a decision that certification is needed, but they don't think about the farmer and all the work it means for them. Small coffee growers [here in Costa Rica] are leaving farming because they have to provide numbers all the time; they need to provide registers. It is too much for them. My grandfather used to tell me never to keep records of what I do. If you keep

records, he said, you will end up disappointed. He told me to work with optimism, with hope, to work with hope – but not with numbers. Farming is a feeling. You feel that you want to work on your farm.

This farmer continued by saying that since his children were under 15 years of age they could not work on his farm, since they would be classified as 'child labour'. He understood that Fair Trade and Sustainable Certification is trying to prevent exploitation, but he felt that the people who devise certification standards had an extreme view of child exploitation in poor countries. In rural parts of countries like Costa Rica, he argued, children generally have half-day schooling and then watch TV. 'What is more important, to watch TV and be lazy because you are not allowed to work, or to work on the farm? Anyway, you can't teach farming to someone when they are 15 years old. They won't want to learn at that age.'

Robert Duxbury: Let me make a small diversion into the world of international organic accreditation. The International Federation of Organic Agriculture Movements (IFOAM) is currently revising its organic standards – actually now called 'norms' – and is attempting to make them more accessible so that they can be used around the world. This will allow IFOAM to continue to maintain its organic standards rather than to see them disappear into irrelevancy, eclipsed by regulatory and private standards. IFOAM seeks to encourage farmers in developing countries to embrace its organic standards and to assist them in seeking out new markets to which their organic foods can be sent. However, IFOAM has very limited means to consult with the market about what it wants or what consumers want. Thus a potential disconnection in the supply chain emerges.

Fraud is another real difficulty. Once you have a regulatory standard it needs to be policed. But in fact very little work is being done on fraud prevention. As more conventional businesses have entered the organic sector the potential of fraud is becoming very serious. However, in the UK the Department for Environment, Food and Rural Affairs (Defra) has no direct powers to enforce the organic standard it is responsible for. This is because the enforcement of organic standards is conducted by an entirely different agency, the Local Authorities Coordinators of Regulatory Services (LACORS).

Cathy Farnworth: I know of a case in Cornwall of chicken eggs from intensive battery units being sold as organic when there are not enough organic eggs to meet demand. The people who know about this are the packers at the farm, who find it hard to blow the whistle because they could lose their job. Often those who know have the least resources to fall back upon and so they stay silent.

Robert Duxbury: It is interesting to consider the concept of due diligence. As a representative of Sainsbury's I had to follow working practices that would exonerate me, or Sainsbury's, should something go wrong. Supply chains are built to act in this way. To put it simply, everyone makes sure that they are covering their backs. Quality assurance often results in a lot of energy being devoted to creating a sham of accountability.

Cathy Farnworth: In Madagascar many organic farmers have not signed up to the understanding of 'organic' that the market they are supplying into has agreed. They are not part of the international discussion processes that define norms, standards and indicators. My research showed that producing for the export market poses significant challenges for Malagasy smallholders (Farnworth 2007a; 2007b), largely because they have to meet standards that other people have defined for them, and which appear, in their eyes, to be irrelevant to the social and agronomic conditions they face on a daily basis. The promotion of entrepreneurial, individualistic values by private players and NGOs, for example by seeking out and developing 'model farmers', appears to harm Malagasy norms that prize togetherness. For this reason farmers tend to decline the status of 'model farmer'. The promotion of certain types of agronomic practice, understood by the international organic agriculture movement to form the heart of good agricultural practice, is also considered by many Malagasy smallholders to undermine the basics of good farming. For example, slash and burn cultivation –'tavy' – is not permitted under organic certification, but has for centuries been employed as a weed and fertilisation management strategy by farmers because of the difficult but fertile terrain. Tavy is also an important method of removing cover for wild pigs that otherwise devastate the crops relied on by people who do not have the purchasing power to buy their food at market should their crops fail. Furthermore, manuring with animal dung is generally considered integral to organic farming, but handling dung can be 'taboo' in Madagascar. A final key issue is the fact that the farmers have to sign French-language documentation that they cannot read. The fear is very real for them that they might be signing away land. They are even supposed to maintain records and diaries about their farms in French under the regulations imposed by the certifying body – yet almost no farmer can read or write their own language, let alone French. Complying with the regulations of organic farming for export can therefore be stressful for smallholders, and change long-standing ways of relating to, and managing, land.

Robert Duxbury: These difficulties are compounded by the fact that many farmers have no understanding of the consumer, or of how much a particular product sells for in the marketplace. This is a key disconnect. We need to understand much more about how each of us lives, how precious all our lives are and to connect with each other.

Cathy Farnworth: A manager of a Fair Trade Cooperative in Costa Rica told me:

> Fair trade is not just about a fair price. It is about getting more money for people to work as a community. We are part of links and networks throughout Latin America. All that connection creates a chain of communication, knowledge and hope. There is energy. The flow of energy is important.

Ethics Versus Commercial Realities for Supermarkets

Robert Duxbury: There needs to be an appreciation that the real commercial world is a tough world; it is all about price and competitiveness. A supermarket cannot just have high-minded values and hope to survive on the basis of these; it has to be competitive. Supermarket margins are already pared down to a minimum. They are run very lean and they have high overheads. As far as buyers for supermarkets are concerned, basic formulas apply. Individual buyers may care a great deal about food and ethics, but they still have to make margins and meet their targets.

Raising the bar

Cathy Farnworth: How much should the state be involved in developing and enforcing ethical standards? In many countries there is a minimum wage, and organic produce from outside the EU has to meet EU organic standards etc. Some people welcome the idea of the state as an ethical arbitrator in the marketplace, but others resist this concept since they do not like the idea of the state being an ethical enforcer in the domain of consumption.

Robert Duxbury: Interestingly, there is currently some discussion about devising an EU regulation to define Fair Trade. With respect to how decisions, including decisions regarding ethical retailing, are made in supermarkets, there has always been a debate about which internal force drives the supermarkets. Is it their customers or their shareholders? Although supermarkets claim to put their customers first and eagerly respond to their demands, it is their investors who are the final determining factor in the commercial realities of multiple retailing. Supermarket boards suffer from continuous conflicts between company policies and business expediency.

The Contribution of Supermarkets to Local Economies

Local purchasing for local supermarkets

Cathy Farnworth: Could supermarkets find ways to strengthen local purchasing and in so doing energise local economies? Concern about the effect of supermarkets on local shops and local suppliers is very high in the UK. Purchasing from local suppliers would help to save food miles as well.

Robert Duxbury: Often small producers cannot meet supermarket demand for every day of the year; not least when seasonality is a limiting factor. Supermarkets have to source sufficient quantities at the right price so that their customers can find the same product on the shelves every week. However, there are some examples of successful local sourcing. Waitrose in Bristol is marketing local organic milk and West Country labelled fruit and vegetables. Sainsbury's has sold vegetables sourced from the Gower peninsula in its Welsh stores, with Welsh-language labelling.

To make local sourcing work there must be sufficient volume to meet demand and to cover the basic costs of marketing, including packaging, labelling and transport. A reasonable run of products is required, quality is critical and the price has to be right. It is simpler to source single-item products locally, such as potatoes and apples, rather than those with complex ingredients.

Supermarkets and place

Cathy Farnworth: Products sold at supermarkets seem disembodied from the value chains that produced them. My research with organic consumers in Germany showed that consumers who buy at supermarkets are more interested in the health benefits and rarely consider farmer well-being, whereas consumers who purchase from farmers' markets and at the farm gate express much greater interest in supporting farmers (Farnworth 2004). These findings are echoed by other researchers such as Tanner and Kast (2003) and Lockie (2002). Surely the very essence of organic product systems is about maintaining ecosystems and place-based livelihoods?

Robert Duxbury: For many consumers, organic principles are not generally understood and therefore their reasons for purchase may be rather narrow. There is nothing wrong with wanting good things for oneself and one's family. There may be a one-dimensionality about that, but there is no harm in starting somewhere. I would argue, though, that supermarkets are changing. They are now offering more than just disembodied products on the shelf. Sainsbury's, for example, are providing information that explains how organic milk and vegetables are sourced from the UK. Supermarkets have caught onto the idea that consumers are interested in local and British products and are responding to this interest. The Co-op now sells own-label Fair Trade chocolate and Marks and Spencer are selling own-label Fair Trade tea and coffee. They are setting markers in the sand. Also, supermarkets are considering novel ways to help consumers judge and select products, for example Tesco is working on a carbon footprint indicator for all its products. The traffic-light system for nutritional content has also been introduced. It is not hard to imagine an environmental traffic-light system being produced soon that will signpost the amount of energy that has been expended to produce each product.

Food is about connectivity with the wider world; we need to connect with other cultures to enrich our own. We would become the poorer without it. There is a challenge, certainly, around emotional connection with people internationally through food, and there is a need to engage on a very practical level with sustainability and sourcing locally, not least with the spectre of climate change and peak oil coming ever closer.

Supermarkets and Food Cultures

Cathy Farnworth: How far do supermarkets work towards actively creating food cultures? Do supermarkets really care about food, and have a passion for it, or would they be just as interested in selling table legs?

Robert Duxbury: The quality of the food has to be right. People do look for quality and pay accordingly. They soon complain if they feel they have not got value for money, or if a product fails to meet their expectations. Supermarket staff, and fundamentally supermarkets themselves, are people too. They are not faceless automatons without opinions. At the same time it can be argued that the culture of mass consumerism and its general detachment from the truths and realities of production brings about a lack of interest and, worse still, fails to instil a sense of responsibility that each of us should carry regarding our consumption choices. At its worst extremes, modern food culture eschews any respect for the food we buy and consume. In fact, it could be argued that great numbers of us are living in a non-food culture. For instance, the notion of food as body fuel is adopted more and more by people who have no interest in food cultures, or perhaps have no real interest in their own health and well-being. Evidence for this lies in the increasing amount of obesity and diet-related illnesses in our society.

If one thinks back to pre-industrial society, when most people's time was spent on activities associated with providing themselves with food in order to stay alive, society was based on a great respect for food. Food was highly valued and the idea of wasting it was completely foreign. People understood the true value of food because their lives were intimately bound up in ensuring they were adequately fed. This contrasts with our lives in modern Western societies where the money many of us earn in less than one day can provide all the food we can eat in a week – whether it is good for us or not! No wonder, then, that our sense of value and responsibility has diminished as food has become just another consumer commodity. This loss of values also manifests itself in other ways as well. Today in the UK up to one-third of all food bought is thrown away. If one considers how much food is wasted as it is grown, processed, packed and shipped, that overall figure rises to over 50 per cent.

In considering how food cultures are enhanced by supermarket activity, a good example would be the new product development activities of many of them. The most innovative, such as Marks and Spencer, Waitrose, Sainsbury's and Tesco, are constantly bringing new products to market, offering their customers new food experiences. While some of these foods may not be considered the best ethical or nutritional examples, it is this approach to food culture within supermarkets that provides opportunities to find new sources of supply and new ways to support producers. In taking on the risk of food innovation, supermarkets energise consumers to experiment with new products. This is reflected in the rising popularity of food in the media, with Sunday supplements dedicated to food, with celebrity chefs, and through the diversity of restaurants in our high streets. Another shift in food culture is shown in the increasing amount of nutritional information that supermarkets provide with their food products. A culture of watchfulness is being developed by initiatives such as the nutritional traffic-light labelling scheme. Consumers are being educated about which foods might be better for them and are being enabled to make positive choices for health through this understanding.

Yet in the end there will be a need to engage with consumerism per se. The planet is failing – witness the soaring prices of oil and failing money markets at the moment – and all these symptoms are related to the insatiable nature of consumption. Faced with this, we should not underestimate the intelligence and ability of supermarkets. They are already considering doomsday scenarios. The cleverest supermarkets have begun working on safeguarding their supply chains by developing local supply networks. They are considering a time without oil and how to survive in a time of collapse.

With the ability to muster vast resources if required, supermarkets are well placed to take a lead in carbon emission reduction. In fact, it could be argued that they provide a prime conduit for educating consumers about how to reduce their individual carbon footprint. With the UK government's world-leading ambition to reduce carbon emissions by 60 per cent by 2050, supermarkets will be under a lot of pressure to play a major role. Tesco has already announced its intention to energy-rate all its products and provide an appropriate label, thus giving their customers a more informed choice when it comes to comparing imported products with home-produced equivalents. Marks and Spencer have developed an environmentally orientated 'Plan A', which aspires to reduce carbon emissions throughout their business to zero within five years. Furthermore, although criticised for contributing to the mountains of packaging disposed of each year, supermarkets are beginning to make efforts to reduce this waste. Supermarkets already recycle a significant amount of materials, be they plastic bags, pallet wrapping or energy within their stores. They may also begin to sell more energy-efficient products with reduced environmental impact. One such example is the use of biodegradeable packaging by Sainsbury's, which has extended starch-based packaging materials to much of its organic produce range. However, there are problems with consumer resistance. People still are attracted to wasteful packaging – the Easter egg being a good example.

Often criticised for exerting undue pressure on their supply chains, supermarkets may end up having the largest positive effect upon the carbon emission changes that will be necessary to safeguard the future of our food and farming industries. Working with their suppliers, supermarkets can move ahead of legislation to safeguard their own businesses and remain competitive in anticipation of the dramatic effects of climate change and peak oil. The interest supermarkets are already taking in local food procurement and organic produce is not just a gesture towards green tokenism. It may signal the start of a very serious race to secure food supplies for the future. The supermarket that can continue to stock its shelves when food shortages begin to bite will claim a competitive advantage in a fast-changing marketplace.

References

Allan, B. (2004), *Social Enterprise Through the Eyes of the Consumer. A Think-Piece Prepared for the National Consumer Council* (London: National Consumer Council).

Blythman, J. (2003), 'Lords of the Aisles', *Guardian*, Saturday 17 May 2003.

Grolleau, G. and Caswell, J.A. (2003), 'Giving Credence to Environmental Labeling of Agro-Food Products: Using Search and Experience Attributes as an Imperfect Indicator of Credibility', in Lockeretz (ed.).

Farnworth, C.R. (2007a), *Well-Being is a Process of Becoming: Research with Organic Farmers in Madagascar*, Wellbeing in Developing Countries (WeD) ESRC Research Group, Working Paper 34 (Bath: University of Bath), published online 30 September 2007 <www.bath.ac.uk/econ-dev/wellbeing/research/workingpaperpdf/wed34.pdf>, accessed 30 September 2007.

Farnworth, C.R. (2007b), 'Achieving Respondent-led Research in Madagascar', *Gender and Development* 15:2, published online 30 July 2007 <www.oxfam.org.uk/resources/ issues/gender/gad_contents.html>, accessed 30 July 2007.

Farnworth, C.R. (2004), *Creating Quality Relationships in the Organic Producer to Consumer Chain: From Madagascar to Germany*, published doctoral dissertation, Agraria 483 (Uppsala: Swedish University of Agricultural Sciences).

Lockeretz, W. (ed.) (2003), *Ecolabels and the Greening of the Food Market*. Proceedings of a Conference at the G.J. & D.R. Friedman School of Nutrition Science and Policy, Tufts University, Boston, MA, 7–9 November 2002.

Lockie, S. (2002), 'The Invisible Mouth: Mobilizing the Consumer in Food Production-Consumption Networks', *Sociologia Ruralis* 42:4, 278–94.

Lockie, S., Lyons, K., Lawrence, G. and Mummery, K. (2002), 'Eating Green: Motivations Behind Organic Food Consumption in Australia', *Sociologia Ruralis* 42:4, 23–40.

Tanner, C. and Kast, S.W. (2003), 'Promoting Sustainable Consumption: Determinants of Green Purchases by Swiss Consumers', *Psychology and Marketing* 20:10, 883–902.

Chapter 14

Mixing is the Way of the World: A New Social Label

Cathy Rozel Farnworth

The Challenge

'Mixing is the way of the world. The world passes through us – food, books, pictures, other people' (Hustved 2003, 89). And yet, despite the rainbow blend of our lives with those of other people, current consumption patterns in the North frequently cause real harm to people, their livelihoods, and their environment in the South. The humanity of producer–consumer relationships in many international value chains is distorted and disfigured by power relationships that restrict the ability of many small producers in the South to live rich, fulfilling lives. The terms of trade are in the North's favour. At the same time, the harm caused by current levels and types of consumption is already rebounding on Northern consumers in the form of climate change, increased prices and the permanent loss of biodiversity. Nevertheless, trade between North and South is certain to increase, thus escalating a spiral of social injustice and ecosystem collapse. Engaging in ethical (as well as less) consumption is perhaps the simplest and most realistic form of action open to ordinary people who want to counter global trends of harm.

However, real world complexity muffles attempts by consumers to consume ethically. Consumers are engaged in functional relationships over which they have little control. They can rarely trace the 'real world' effects of their consumption choices, and are thus not rewarded through direct, tangible feedback on the impact of these choices upon the intended beneficiaries. Although it can be argued that Northern consumers are rewarded through a sense that they have 'done good', this is of course not the same thing. The feedback loop engendered by the hope that one has done good is very fragile.

The 'real world', as it is expressed in political and market mechanisms, frequently frustrates the desire of consumers to follow through on their synergistic, complex thought processes. For example, many retailers lack ethical consistency in their product range and in their relationship to producers, even though 'ethical concerns' increasingly thread through their bottom lines. Multiple retailers in particular often fail to exploit the potential of their role as heads of supply chains to influence ethical practice between stakeholders down the chain. Furthermore, there seems to be a kind of moral discrepancy in encoding 'things that really matter' – such as a living wage, the right to collective bargaining and other issues with a material bearing on quality of life – into codes of conduct, and labels, that can then be marketed as ethical propositions, rather than as a regulatory requirement, to consumers. It is plausible to argue that the resistance of a good many consumers to retailers as 'ethical arbitrators' in the marketplace may arise from unease at the idea that ethical behaviour can provide retailers with a selling point.

Indeed, the evidence suggests that consumers are driven to make trade-offs due to the frequent failure of food chain arbitrators such as multiple retailers to act successfully as intermediaries between what consumers want to achieve, and what they think they are actually able to achieve through their consumption choices. Consumers generally understand that the trade-offs they make corrode the ethical consistency of their personal value systems.

Although 'marketing ethics' is clearly problematic, credence (social) labels are able to actually change the way the function functions. Examples of social labels are Fair Trade and Organic Marks. They denote that an ethical practice is occurring at some point in the value chain. If they are accepted by consumers, they help to strengthen and entrench that practice. This chapter argues, though, that the current brief of social labels is often disappointingly limited. It is not clear whether the community projects that premiums support are always those that the producers – women as well as men – really want, or whether the projects are in fact selected with an eye to the preferences of the Northern consumer. Research carried out in Madagascar and Germany showed that Malagasy farmers would like to have funding for facilities such as dance halls and video salons to lighten an often-arduous life. Almost no German consumers agreed that they would support such aspirations through selective Fair Trade purchases; rather, they would only support educational interventions (Farnworth 2004; see also Clark 2002 for similar findings resulting from research in South Africa).

This chapter proposes that a new kind of social label that occupies quite different ground to labels dealing with the conditions of production or trading relationships is needed if understanding between producers and consumers is to be increased. To create such a label, profound attention would be paid to the values and aspirations that producers hold, the aim being to ensure that these are supported, rather than eroded, through production for the Northern market. An important feature of the label would be its ability to acknowledge and build upon the ethical values held by the consumer. Indeed, a central selling point of such a label would be its dynamic character. It should evolve as quality of life aspirations among organic producers and consumers change. An iterative learning process would need to be set up between producers and consumers to achieve the goal of a true social label.

Following a discussion of social labels, the chapter outlines how a new social label, capable of allowing the producer to arise as a 'legitimate other' in the eyes of the consumer, could be created. A prototype label is then put forward.

What Social Labels Do

Ethical values, in relation to foodstuffs, are deliberately created by particular production processes; they are not intrinsic to the product itself. A Fair Trade orange may be just the same as a non-Fair Trade orange in terms of colour, size and nutritional value. The 'added value' of the Fair Trade or Organic orange rests upon a production process that has been developed specifically to ensure desirable social or environmental outcomes. These ethical values are 'marketed' to the consumer in the form of social labels. Social labels are also termed credence labels, since the factor of belief in the claims of the label is vital.

Social labelling programmes operate as 'ethical verification' systems for enterprises. They use a highly visible means of communication – a physical label – to describe the efforts they are making to ensure that good social or environmental conditions are maintained, or even enhanced, during the production of a product or the rendering of a service. Labelling initiatives are often independently managed standards that use certifying bodies, such as the Soil Association Certification Ltd, as neutral intermediaries. If companies are able to comply with these independent standards they earn the right to use the label, or mark, as a proof of compliance (Blowfield 1999). However, self-declared claims by companies function as social labels too (Zadek et al. 1998). Labels are primarily targeted at export markets involving retail trade, 'niche' product markets and affluent consumers, and they are more readily developed for products associated with social identity, such as clothing and food, or for discrete production processes like tea (Diller 1999).

The aim of social labels is to influence the economic decisions of one set of stakeholders by describing the impact of a business process on another group of stakeholders. Generally, the term 'social' describes impacts on stakeholders who are not the audience of the labels. They tend to maintain a clear distinction between the producer (the beneficiary) in the South, and the consumer (the benefactor) in the North. Consumers are primarily viewed as a means of channelling benefits, via the mechanism of the social label, to a range of beneficiaries. Organic labels isolate ecosystems as prime beneficiaries – and via feedback loops, the consumers themselves. Fair Trade labels highlight quite specific and narrow aspects of the lives of beneficiaries.

A particular concern is that the typical social label works on the basis that consumers and producers occupy static categories. The agency, meaning the ability to act as one chooses, of both producers and consumers is confined by the intent and practice of current social labelling. The partners in the relationship do not engage with one another.

Nonetheless, social labelling arguably has the potential to act as a stepping-stone to a new consumer community (Allan 2004; Zadek et al. 1998). They could form part of a 'virtuous system' of consumers, producers and social labels developing new forms of cooperation and interaction. A powerful way of creating trust and understanding between producers and consumers would be through shortening chains by creating shared 'value spaces'.

A New Social Label

Through reimagining the producer–consumer relationship on the basis of creating mutual understanding of each other's shared, and divergent, values, each party could take on a new kind of reality. Given the imbalance in power relationships between wealthy consumers in the North and poor producers in the South, a key aim would be to enable producers to arise as 'legitimate others' in the eyes of the consumer.

How could such a label be created? To start with, practical logistical issues need to be addressed. Then, stakeholders in the process need to be identified. They should be 'representative'. Exploring 'what counts' in terms of values is the next step. It cannot be assumed that producers and consumers share the same values. This is important because, as mentioned above, an apparent lack of ethical consistency between stakeholders in the organic food chain often leads to disillusionment, not least among consumers. Given this, the final step is to promote conversations between stakeholders in order to develop mutual understandings and acknowledgement of difference. This chapter suggests sources for the rich information needed for this step, and outlines arenas in which conversations could be conducted. The discussion concludes by presenting a prototype label.

Logistics

Appropriate, diverse, and consistent information flows are critical to a well-functioning label. In order for communication systems to work, all parties must be able to interact effectively. They have to understand the information being transferred, have the ability to apply the knowledge gained, and be able to learn from experience. These provisos are not being properly met in the case of consumers. In contrast, there is usually plenty of informational activity, though of varying quantity and quality, in the producer domain – between producer organisations and their members, between producer organisations themselves, and between producer organisations and other stakeholders, such as extension services, certifying organisations and buyers. From there, a much-reduced flow of information takes place between processors, importers and retailers through to the consumers at the other end of the chain. Consumers themselves are mere recipients of information flows presented in summary form on labels and packaging. Their realm of action is limited to either purchasing the product, or not. For interested readers, Goodman (2002) elucidates in more detail the extent of consumer agency.

Despite the reduced information consumers receive, more cannot be argued to be better. Information overload is a real problem for consumers (Bougherara and Grolleau 2003). However, it is possible to negotiate one's way around the block posed by information overload by considering how to address information asymmetry. Research shows consumers want information that enables them to take proper ethical decisions, not more information per se (Lockie 2002). Redressing information asymmetry involves tackling not only what, but *how* information is mediated in the producer–consumer chain. Certifiers and buyers clearly occupy a top-heavy position here. The solution cannot be merely to expedite information flows between these stakeholders (and others) for two reasons: first, considerable vested power is bundled in the organisations occupying these nodes. Their power is derived from their role as creators and mediators of information to other organisations willing to pay for that information. Tackling their vested power is quite a task because information asymmetry is one basis of their existence. Secondly, 'Unsticking' the information that these organisations have by making it more accessible (in terms of content and flow) to consumers does not, in itself, resolve the problem.

Stakeholders

Developing a new social label would involve setting up multi-stakeholder negotiations. Multi-stakeholder negotiations are 'processes which aim to bring together all the major stakeholders in a new form of communication, decision-finding (and possibly decision-making) on a particular issue' (Hemmati 2002). The key stakeholders discussed here are the producers and consumers in the international organic chain. When considering which consumers to involve it is important to note that within the broad category of 'consumer', whole subcategories are easily ignored, for example poorer women, or Southern people in the North. The latter are often overlooked both as consumers, and as people with frequently profound expertise and insights into the South.

Two further potential candidates for stakeholder status – future people and 'the environment' – can be factored in to our preliminary categorisation of stakeholders. This is important because these two candidates can be argued to have a 'stake' in current consumption patterns. Although future people, and 'the environment' are voiceless in themselves, they can be construed to have a moral claim. On this basis, representatives may be appointed on their behalf (Goodpaster 1978; Stone 1974). Whilst the ethical debates on moral considerability and moral standing are complex, there is no doubt that, providing accessible terminology is used, consumers and producers can engage in sophisticated debate on these ideas. As one consumer said, 'For me, everything belongs together. The one cannot exist without the other – water, air, plants, animals, people. For me, that means that the whole belongs together, and no one thing is more important than another' (Farnworth 2004: 132). This person has already ascribed moral standing to features in the natural world.

Stakeholders have a 'stake' – a real, material interest, from their perspective – in the situation, activity or resource under discussion. 'Stakeholding' expresses the idea that individuals actively construct, promote and defend their stake. For our purposes, we can think of stakes in two ways. First, stakes can be identified by virtue of a person's (or group's) positionality with respect to the significant resource, activity or situation. For example, the positional stakes of consumers may revolve around food quality, taste and price, whereas the positional stakes of producers may centre on characteristics such as the disease resistance of particular varieties, and on the profitability of farming vis-à-vis other livelihood options. When thinking of how to develop a social label, it is important to consider the hindrances to action that 'positional stakes' may pose. Consumers and producers, on the basis of their position in the food chain, may not have sufficient stakes in common for 'positionality' to form the basis of multi-stakeholder negotiations.

Stakes can also come into existence through the flipping on of a kind of ethical light switch. That is, they are called into being by, and are highly dependent on, stakeholder interactions. For example, Northern consumers might come to consider that they have a stake in the biodiversity of the rainforest in Madagascar on the grounds that this biodiversity forms part of the global commons. It is quite hard to decipher what flips the ethical light switch to make people feel they have a stake in something, but certainly broad movements in civil society play a role. Changes across the human lifecycle, such as having children, or realising that one is getting older, may also help to flip an ethical light switch. Although value stakes are hard to capture and to understand, they are tremendously important to our work on social labels. They can enable people to override their positional stakes in the interests of creating a 'good' in which many stakeholders may feel they have a stake. This is important since clearly not all consumers, or producers, can be involved in the actual creation of a social label.

It would be quite wrong, incidentally, to consider that a 'value-free' social label can be produced. All labels reflect and transmit the values of their creators. In our work, the subjectivity of the new social label under discussion would be made explicit. The key to ensuring that it can somehow remain 'representative' for the time being is by involving a wide range of stakeholders. A further way of ensuring a moderately 'representative' label is by exploring, as part of the process, the value stakes that the label will embody.

Values

Federico Borromeo, Cardinal of Milan and patron of Jan Brueghel the Younger, spoke thus of the delight that the new Flemish style of painting brought him:

> I have decorated my room with paintings... And the pleasure that I feel looking at these painted views ... has seemed to me just as lovely as the open and wide views [of nature]... In their place, when they cannot be reached, pictures embrace in a small space earth and sky, and we go on long walks in spirit, standing still in our room. (Villa Huegel 2002)

Consumers need to take 'walks in spirit' in worlds and lives they will never personally know. Southern producers and Northern consumers, apart from a very few isolated instances, will never meet. Connections have to be made in the world of ideas to enable us to weave our worlds together. Labels help, for they tell stories and paint worlds on our inner eye. To do this they select items from the rich picture of real life and rework them into a 'social label narrative'.

A key question is whether this narrative should aim to be consistent in terms of the values it conveys. The author suggests that incommensurable values have to be recognised and built into social labelling initiatives if the ethical separateness of the stakeholders is to be acknowledged.

Is it possible to do this? In order to answer this question, this section examines the concept of values more closely. First, some general comments on values: 1) Values can 'hold true' in a variety of situations. They can override the specific nature of a particular situation without being shaped by it. 2) Nevertheless, values can be traded off against each other, and 3) Values provide individuals and organisations with a means of negotiating the real world. Conflict and misadventure is inherent in this endeavour since the real world is complex. At the same time, values are a means of dealing with unpredictability. They enable people both to cope with as yet unknown situations, and to try and configure situations before they actually happen. Values-in-action impose patterns and draw the world behind them, like a skein.

Social labels deal in value stories and seek to associate these with particular products. They try to achieve 'rich coherence' by knitting values into one story. The label for Gepa Fairena chocolate, for example, tells us that:

> ... today, chocolate is affordable for everyone and literally 'in every mouth'. For the producers of the most important raw materials, though, the sweet success story has a bitter aftertaste: speculation and worldwide overproduction of cocoa and sugar have caused world market prices to collapse. It's different with fair trade chocolate. Cocoa and sugar producers receive well over world market prices, premiums for ecological and social projects, long-term purchase contracts and partial advance payment before harvest. (Gepa Fairena Bio Praline product packaging, author's translation)

It is worth unpacking the idea of the coherent story a little. Social labels appear to act as go-betweens, bearing a story as a gift. In so doing, they act as 'vectors of value' between producers and consumers. If credence labels are successful go-betweens, the producer's value story weaves into the consumer's value story. That is to say, a 'fit' between the values that help guide a particular consumer's life and the values signified by the product is achieved. We can apply the vector of value metaphor more widely. Social labels are intended to be vectors of values such as transparency, credibility and accountability. Rather like a telescope, credence labels can foreshorten distance, giving the impression of nearness and of truthfulness.

Whilst these seem worthy goals for credence labels to follow, some issues arise. Above all, the story can be unravelled. Sutcliffe (2004) researched the product trail of Green and Black's Maya Gold fair trade chocolate and discovered that the actual growers had no understanding of Fair Trade – or 'unfair trade' – nor even of the difference that selling to Green and Black's actually made to their lives. As far as Sutcliffe could ascertain, though, Green and Black's made a great deal of positive difference to the producers' lives in terms of purchase guarantees and the price paid for the cocoa. Does it matter that the producers are not helping to weave the threads of the Fair Trade value story that is presented on labels? Surely it matters a great deal. If social labels ask consumers to support projects in producer communities selected because of their resonance with widely held values in the consumer's own society it is possible that the transmission of values across the food chain may have the real world effect of narrowing, as much as widening, the decision-making spaces of producers.

What is the way forward? An approach focused on capturing the quality of life needs and aspirations of farmers would enable certain values to be captured that may otherwise be eroded because discussion fora such as joint bodies often find it hard to capture such values. Research in Madagascar showed that an organic plantation owner instituted practices that unintentionally stifled locally important activities and the values associated with them. An example is the value that workers place on attending market days in order to meet and converse. These days represented the only real leisure opportunity for women, and were also a major shopping opportunity – important when time is at a premium. However, women and men had to work on market days if they wanted to achieve, or retain, permanent status on the plantation. Considerable benefits such as a higher wage, health care in times of need, and schooling for children were associated with permanent status. It was not possible for the plantation workers to resolve this dilemma adequately (Farnworth 2004).

Part of our task demands that we move beyond presenting the producers as beneficiaries of the consumers' good actions. It is necessary to dismantle the dichotomy that constructs consumers as 'doers' and the producers as 'being done to'. If consumers are going to take 'walks in spirit' with the producers then a means has to be found to enable the latter to arise as 'legitimate others' – as equal partners in the project – whether or not values are fully shared. It is helpful at this juncture to take a step back to consider again the importance of 'ethical consistency'. By ethical consistency the author means values that are recognisably shared by stakeholders across the chain. Is ethical consistency really a pre-requisite to building quality relationships between producer and consumer in the organic commodity chain?

A lack of resonance between stakeholders in terms of what values 'count' certainly seems to disturb. As mentioned earlier, evidence suggests that multiple retailers, in the eyes of some consumers, lack ethical consistency. As a consequence, these consumers distrust multiple retailers as mediators of ethical values (Farnworth 2004; Tanner and Kast 2003; Lockie 2002). A failure to achieve ethical consistency between consumers and producers therefore arguably places a considerable obstacle in the way of the discussion processes that are needed to construct a social label. Furthermore, the assumed universality of a particular stakeholder's value sets may confound understanding and, indeed, erode support by other stakeholders. Chrissiane, a Malagasy plantation worker said, 'Like everyone else, I want a cow' (Farnworth 2004). Northern consumers may, at least initially, refuse to support the realisation of a value that arguably harms the global commons, in this case through over-grazing and methane production.

Since achieving ethical consistency between stakeholders is neither tenable nor desirable in every case, one way forward is to consider how to 'extend the collective ethical boundary' in order to find ways of legitimising the value stakes of the 'other' in the value chain.

Promoting conversations

Extending ethical boundaries involves asking: who belongs to my circle of concern? Where am I drawing the boundary to show who is in, and who is out? Fair trade consumers may well be including different stakeholders in their circle of concern to organic consumers, for example. For the former, for example, the environment may not be included; for the latter, the producer may not be an active consideration. Midgley (2000) suggests that conflict can arise when different groups of people have different ethics relating to the same issue, resulting in different boundary judgements. Conflict situations tend 'to be stabilised by the imposition of either a sacred or a profane status on marginal elements. The words 'sacred' and 'profane' mean valued and devalued respectively' (Midgley 2000, 137). If we apply Midgley's approach to the development of a social label, the following practical objective can be developed: 'render profane values sacred'. This objective has as its aim the rise of the consumer, or the producer, as a 'legitimate other' who holds 'legitimate values'. Relabelling the values of other stakeholders as sacred does not imply that their values are absorbed or synthesised. Rather, the aim is to ensure that they come to be valued and legitimised by stakeholders who may not share those values.

The revised boundary judgements made in the process of creating a social label should not aim to be cohesive. Such a boundary would be highly permeable and subject to repeated challenge. This would enable new meanings to emerge, as a consequence of natural growth, change and learning. Profane ethics would constantly be produced around the edges, but, if managed well, could have an energising effect.

How might expanded circles of concern be realised? The task of the change agent is to find ways of altering boundary judgements to enable stakeholders to relabel the concerns of the 'other' as sacred. To do this, one should think of creating a variety of 'spaces' at varying scales of interaction, and offering varying degrees of intensity of interaction, and not only one grand space that is bound in some degree to favour one stakeholder interest over another. Examples, and the respective considerations of each, include:

- The space in which conversations are conducted can be associated with the ability of particular stakeholders to form agendas. In the UK, interviews that the author carried out with community groups demonstrated that ownership over agendas and places was vital: 'We don't want other people to run Saturday schools for us', says Williams, 'it is an African-Caribbean thing' (Farnworth 1996). In bringing together stakeholders for the purposes of creating a social label, it is important to consider the question of ownership over the physical space and agendas in which discussions are conducted, as ownership has a considerable bearing on outcomes. One way of resolving this issue is to employ 'virtual spaces'. The use of electronic communication in multi-stakeholder negotiations 'can provide a good basis for neutralising differences in status and personality, as related to gender, age and ethnicity ... representatives of groups with less status, such as women or members of ethnic minorities would benefit primarily from this filtering of personal characteristics' (Enayati 2002, 87). Against the empowering aspects of conversing in virtual spaces need to be weighed the objection that it is precisely these differences that should not be neutralised. Notwithstanding this, the potential of electronic communication to assist disempowered stakeholders to overcome their disempowered status in order to converse should be examined carefully.

- Individuals hold multiple identities. However, they are often placed in professional positions where they need to defend a particular identity, for example, that of farmer, or certifier. In these situations, it is possible that the ethics (values in purposeful action) held by other stakeholders cannot be taken on board. A way of resolving this impasse is to free up thinking by 1) drawing upon other identities that a stakeholder may have; 2) allowing the fluidity thus generated to enable the stakeholder to relabel the concerns of other stakeholders as 'sacred'; and 3) to capture and stabilise the learning that has occurred. When participants in stakeholder meetings have their 'official hats' on they cannot permit themselves to 'hear' the other side. However, when they conceptualise themselves as free-floating agents they are able to listen and to contemplate new ways of doing things without immediately ridiculing them. To allow this to happen, stakeholders need to be brought

together into discussion spaces that downplay the official nature of people's roles (Farnworth 2004, 346).
- It is possible to agree upon a value stake around which action to promote positional stakes can be coordinated. This is the converse of the examples above. Prince Charles in the UK has developed the concept of 'virtuous circles', by which he means the development of ethical trading partnerships between Northern businesses and small organic community projects in the South. His own brand, Duchy Originals, has established such a partnership with a cocoa producing cooperative in Guyana. The Prince asks governments, for their part, to be supportive of organic agriculture and also to support local marketing initiatives.

Rich information is required to ensure the multi-stakeholder discussions are effective and as representative as possible. One way of ensuring that the views of producers on the values they would like to see expressed and supported through a social label would be by designing a work package to capture their quality of life aspirations. The author piloted a quality of life toolkit to develop and capture criteria for well-being among organic smallholders and plantation with organic smallholders in Madagascar. One objective was to understand and measure producer well-being, thus providing a new method for social certification in organic agriculture. The toolkit aimed not only to record, but also to help bring into conscious awareness, local conceptions of well-being. At the same time, indicators derived from internationally agreed codes of conduct were considered. Discussing both ideas with producers can help ensure that they may be objectively agreed to have a life 'worthy of the dignity of a human being' (Nussbaum 1998). In this way, a powerful set of social standards – with corresponding indicators – in organic agriculture with meaning to stakeholders across the producer to consumer chain can be created and used for both the social label and for social certification. At all times the research would need to be gender-sensitive (Farnworth, 2007a; 2007b).

A new social label

The final form of a new social label would be the result of discussions between the stakeholders involved. Yet it is useful to conclude this discussion by putting forward a tentative vision: one can take up the image of spotlights converging upon a dancer on the stage. This signifies convergence between producers and consumers in terms of a quality relationship. A logo of overlapping circles, acting as spotlights could be developed. The overlapping areas would signify significant ethical consistency between stakeholders – on the importance of schools, perhaps. The non-overlapping areas would indicate significant discrepancies between stakeholders on values that they want to realise. A depiction of the label, for a particular product, on an internet site would enable people to click on to different parts of the logo. Through this they would discover what the circles might have in common with one another, and what is different in terms of their values-in-action. The indicative data upon which these claims rest would need to be backed up by data provided through the multi-stakeholder discussions. This proposal allows for dynamism since it would be possible to make the circles overlap in many different ways. A certifying body could provide a 'date stamp' that indicated the most recent review.

Conclusion

It would be necessary to observe carefully the multi-stakeholder discussion processes set up to create the social label in order to register, capture and fix some of its emergent properties. This would allow us to understand whether a quality relationship between producers and consumers was being achieved through the mechanism of the social label. What might these emergent properties be? One may hope that they could include love, care and respect for the 'other'. It would not, though, be possible for someone monitoring the process to get 'inside' the feeling that these words convey. They would have to content themselves with the limited advice given by Maturana: 'An observer says that there is love in a relation when he or she sees a behaviour through which another arises as a legitimate other in the living of that relation' (personal communication September 2004).

Zadek et al. (1998) outline seven criteria for effective labels. These are:

1. relevance
2. clarity
3. trust
4. accessibility
5. accuracy
6. financial viability
7. legal viability.

This is sensible advice; yet it seems necessary to move away from too much pragmatism. It is just as important to be brave and bold. It would be good to see a social label that brings the producer more fully into our world through allowing them to speak and shape what is important to them as well as to us. It is plausible to argue that the emergent properties of a social label – along the lines of the one presented here – like love, care, respect and knowledge are in themselves mechanisms capable of eroding real world structures of inequality. This is because, through the preferential purchasing inspired by the social label, they will start to create new weightings of relationships that actually pull and tug at what is wrong in order to make it right.

References

Allan, B. (2004), *Social Enterprise Through the Eyes of the Consumer. A Think-piece Prepared for the National Consumer Council* (London: National Consumer Council).
Blowfield, M. (1999), 'Ethical Trade: A Review of Developments and Issues, Natural Resources Institute, available at <www.nri.org>.
Bougherara, D. and Grolleau, G. (2003), 'Can Ecolabeling Mitigate Market Failures? An Analysis Applied to Agro-Food Products', in Lockeretz (ed.).

Clark, D. (2002), 'Development Ethics: A Research Agenda' *International Journal of Social Economics* 29:11, 830–48.

Crocker, D.A. and Linden, T. (eds) (1998), *Ethics of Consumption: The Good Life, Justice, and Global Stewardship* (Oxford: Rowman & Littlefield).

Diller, J. (1999), 'A Social Conscience in the Global Marketplace? Labour Dimensions of Codes of Conduct, Social Labelling and Investor Initiatives', *International Labour Review* 138:2, 99–129.

Enayati, J. (2002), 'The Research: Effective Communication and Decision-Making in Diverse Groups', in Hemmati (ed.).

Farnworth, C.R. (2007a), *Well-Being is a Process of Becoming: Research with Organic Farmers in Madagascar*. Wellbeing in Developing Countries (WeD) ESRC Research Group, Working Paper 34 (Bath: University of Bath) published online 30 September 2007, <www.bath.ac.uk/econ-dev/wellbeing/research/workingpaperpdf/wed34.pdf>, accessed 30 September 2007.

Farnworth, C.R. (2007b), 'Achieving Respondent-Led Research in Madagascar', *Gender & Development* 15:2, published online 30 July 2007 <www.oxfam.org.uk/resources/issues/gender/gad_contents.html>, accessed 30 July 2007.

Farnworth, C.R. (2004), *Creating Quality Relationships in the Organic Producer to Consumer Chain: From Madagascar to Germany*, published doctoral dissertation, Agraria 483. (Uppsala: Swedish University of Agricultural Sciences).

Farnworth, C.R. (1996), *Development Education in the Community* (London: Development Education Association).

Giraud, G. (2003), 'Organic and Origin-Labeled Food Products in Europe: Labels for Consumers or for Producers?', in Lockeretz (ed.).

Goodman, D. (2002), 'Re-Thinking Food Production-Consumption: Integrative Perspectives', *Sociologica Ruralis* 42:4, 271–7.

Goodpaster, K. (1978), 'On Being Morally Considerable', *Journal of Philosophy* 75:6, 308–25.

Hemmati, M. (ed.) (2002), *Multi-Stakeholder Processes for Governance and Sustainability: Beyond Deadlock and Conflict* (London: Earthscan).

Hustvedt, S. (2003), *What I Loved* (London: Hodder and Stoughton).

Lockeretz, W. (ed.) (2003), *Ecolabels and the Greening of the Food Market*, proceedings of a Conference at the G.J. & D.R. Friedman School of Nutrition Science and Policy, Tufts University, Boston, MA, 7–9 November 2002.

Lockie, S. (2002), 'The Invisible Mouth: Mobilizing the Consumer' in Food Production–Consumption Networks', *Sociologia Ruralis* 42:4, 278–94.

Lockie, S., Lyons, K., Lawrence, G. and Mummery, K. (2002), 'Eating "Green": Motivations Behind Organic Food Consumption in Australia', *Sociologia Ruralis* 42:4, 23–40.

Midgley, G. (2000), *Systemic Intervention: Philosophy, Methodology and Practice* (Netherlands: Kluwer Academic Publishers).

Nussbaum, M.C. (1998), The Good As Discipline, the Good As Freedom. In Crocker, D.A. & Linden, T (eds) *Ethics of Consumption: The Good Life, Justice, and Global Stewardship*: 312 – 341. Rowman & Littlefield Publishers, Inc., Oxford.

Stone, C.D. (1974), *Should Trees Have Standing: Towards Legal Rights for Natural Objects* (Los Altos, CA: William Kaufmann).

Sutcliffe, W. (2004), 'Counting Beans', *Guardian Weekly*, 20–6 August, 15–16.
Tanner, C. and Kast, S.W. (2003), 'Promoting Sustainable Consumption: Determinants of Green Purchases by Swiss Consumers', *Psychology and Marketing* 20:10, 883–902.
Villa Huegel (2002), 'Flamische Landschaften', exhibition board quoting Borromeo at Villa Huegel, Essen. Translated by the author.
Zadek, S., Lingayah, S. and Forstater, M. (1998), *Social Labels: Tools for Ethical Trade*, Final Report to the European Commission, Directorate-General for Employment, Industrial Relations and Social Affairs, Directorate –V/D.1.

Chapter 15

Responsibility in Value Chains and Capability Structures

Jérôme Ballet, Jean-Luc Dubois and François-Régis Mahieu

The construction of 'value chains' is part of the development process. Value chains can be beneficial for a great many people, whether considered as individuals or as social groups, but at the same time they may generate unexpected and adverse effects for some specific groups of people. We take the normative position that the risk of such negative effects should be taken into account in a preventive way. This position raises the general issue of responsibility for the harm that could be done in the future and, more precisely, the respective responsibilities of those who are involved at all steps in the design and the implementation of a value chain.

A socially sustainable development is, by definition, expected to 'guarantee an improvement in the capability of well-being, expressed in social, economic and ecological terms, for all people in the present and in future generations' (Ballet, Dubois and Mahieu 2005). To ensure such 'social sustainability', two pre-conditions are required: 'to ensure equity in the distribution of such capability within each generation'; and 'to ensure an equitable transfer of capability between the generations' (Ballet, Dubois and Mahieu 2005, 33). This definition is based on the concept of 'personal capability' as described by Sen:

> A person's capability refers to the alternative combinations of functionings that are feasible for her to achieve ... The concept of functionings, which has distinctly Aristotelian roots, reflects the various things a person may value doing or being ... Capability is thus a kind of freedom: the substantive freedom to achieve alternative functionings combinations or, less formally put, the freedom to achieve various lifestyles. (Sen 1999, 75)

Capability, according to Sen, relates an increase in freedom to the capacity and power of doing things and of being what is expected.

This chapter is organized in terms of three sections. In the first section, the general issue of responsibility is addressed and related to the analysis of value chains. In the second section, the notion of capability structure is used to measure the impact of value chain policies on the people concerned. The key question within this framework is: will the value chain contribute to the strengthening of individual and collective capabilities or could it jeopardize some of them?

In the third section a 'social precautionary' attitude is suggested, based on the elaboration of principles appropriate for encouraging all stakeholders to share responsibilities within the value chain. These three sections give rise to discussion of the way in which value chains might be designed or implemented, in order to ensure their social sustainability.

The Distribution of Responsibilities Within the Value Chain

Analyzing the distribution of responsibility within a value chain necessitates consideration of all agents acting in the chain and their corresponding roles. This is why, according to Wood (2001), the concept of value chain has to be limited to those directly involved in the coordination of the various activity levels in the chain, that is, to a relatively few forms of commercial governance, such as by a dominant firm or a coalition and network of firms that manages the chain. The case of an atomistic market has to be excluded.

Dealing with the issue of responsibility

Deardoff (1998) and Arndt and Kierzkowski (2001) point out that everywhere in the world, production is becoming fragmented, with increasing physical dispersal of the various steps in the production process, resulting in the scattering of the agents involved in any one production chain.

Hughes (2000), Henderson et al. (2002), and Dickens et al. (2001) emphasize the complexity of the relationships between firms in this context. They show how production coordination and control are established independently of any kind of direct ownership of the assets. This does not help to clarify the issue of who is responsible for what and thus this question remains largely unaddressed.

Gereffi, Humphrey and Sturgeon (2003) distinguish five types of governance for such value chains, each type influencing the form of stakeholder responsibility. The first type is related to the 'market'. In this case, the cost of changing partners is low for all stakeholders. The second type is a 'modular' value chain. The suppliers manufacture their products following more or less detailed specifications issued by their customers, and assume full responsibility for the manufacturing process because of their technological skills. The third type is associated with 'relational' value chains. It is characterized by complex interactions between suppliers and salesmen, who create a mutual dependence and a high level of shared assets. This type of governance is often built on reputation or family or ethnic bonds. In a number of such cases, proximity plays a key role in establishing these relationships. The fourth type of governance is the 'captive' value chain. Small suppliers are dependent on more powerful purchasers. Such suppliers are described as captive because it is they who bear the highest costs if there is a change in partners. This type of governance is characterized by a high degree of monitoring and control by the major firms. The fifth and last type of governance considered here follows the 'hierarchical' model. This corresponds to vertical integration and is characterized mainly by top-down managerial control.

These five types of governance, that is, market, modular, relational, captive, and hierarchical, can be characterized further by means of two criteria: the degree of coordination and the degree of asymmetry in power. Gereffi, Humphrey and Sturgeon (2003) summarize these results in Table 15.1.

Table 15.1 Determinants of global value chain governance

Type of governance	Complexity of the transaction	Ability to codify the transaction	Capabilities of the supply base	Degree of explicit coordination and power asymmetry
Market	Low	High	High	Increases from low to high
Modular	High	High	High	
Relational	High	Low	High	
Captive	High	High	Low	
Hierarchical	High	Low	Low	

Source: Gereffi, Humphrey and Sturgeon 2003

These five types of governance clearly involve differing degrees of power and consequently higher or lower levels of responsibility. The more power and control an agent has, the greater his share of the responsibility. Since the decision-making power is unequally distributed, the responsibility for the consequences of decisions cannot be shared equally either. In the market type of governance, responsibility is fairly equally shared among the stakeholders. At the other extreme, hierarchical governance implies that the decision makers in the driving seat have much more responsibility.

However, raising the level of responsibility of all stakeholders within the value chain is not the solution to the problem of power asymmetries. Responsibility implies a charge to somebody for something he did (or is expected to do) and whose consequences are estimated to be the results of his or her action. In other words, in addition to the question of the level of somebody's responsibility – the 'responsibility of *whom*?' – there is also the need to know for what action is the responsibility charged – the 'responsibility for *what*?' The case of the Nile perch production in Tanzania provides us with a good example for exploring this general issue further.

Sharing responsibility: Nile perch production in Tanzania

The case of the Nile perch production chain in Tanzania illustrates the social errors that can arise in value chains in the course of economic development. It is a perfect case of social unsustainability.

The Nile perch chain was booming in Tanzania in the early 1990s thanks to the fish farms set up in Lake Victoria. Traditional fishing had been carried out in Lake Victoria for many years prior to the development, assisted by international agencies, of the commercial perch fisheries. Garrod (1961) dates the first local unit producing nets for fishing to 1908 and provides evidence to show that traditional fishing began to expand after 1917. However, there were no Nile perch in the lake then. Nile perch began to appear only in the early 1960s following a fish replenishment program in the Ugandan part of the lake. Since then, the numbers have grown significantly.

During the 1980s the production of fresh and smoked Nile perch developed largely for two reasons: the increasing demand from local consumers and a supply-side effect – the nets were catching increasing numbers of perch. This species is carnivorous and so it proliferated to the detriment of others, which became progressively scarcer and more expensive. the first exports of frozen Nile perch took place in 1987, to Israel, by a Kenyan company. The main consumers were the Israeli armed forces.

The process of increasing fish numbers, increasing catches and increasing exports accelerated in the 1990s as a result of the conjunction of several factors. First, the Kenyan export companies increased their market share abroad and in so doing put pressure on domestic demand in Tanzania. Since the price paid by the exporting companies was higher than the local price, they exercised a stronger demand han the local market. The Nile perch became known as a fish destined mainly for export and difficult to find on the domestic market. Secondly, this process was reinforced by a number of economic policy decisions taken by the government of Tanzania. According to Gibbon (1997), the implementation of a structural adjustment program made a major contribution to the booming of the chain. The devaluation of the Tanzanian currency reduced production costs and facilitated the expansion of foreign companies. In 1996 the international financial institutions assessed the economic liberalization program and concluded that it had been a success in Tanzania. However, they did not attempt to assess the social consequences. Thirdly, a law promulgated in 1992–3 obliged foreign companies, including the Kenyan companies, to set up processing plants in order to reduce the exports of unprocessed perch.

The story so far shows how various players, with differing degrees of responsibility, interacted in the development of the Nile perch production chain. International institutions in particular, as a result of the policies they advised, produced a series of unexpected social consequences that resulted in exclusion and extreme inequality as the chain developed.

The corresponding responsibilities, distributed through the Nile perch chain, can be assessed through an analysis of the stakeholders' role within the chain. Gibbon (1997) distinguishes at the first level of analysis the fishermen whose camps on the islands in the lake were built with assistance from the export companies. They benefited from the presence of the processing and export firms who supplied them with fishing nets and boats although they do not sell directly to these companies. At the second level, there is the network of independent fish dealers who buy from the fishermen and who are used as intermediaries by the companies. At the third level are the processing and export firms who buy the fish from these independent dealers. At the fourth level, according to Gibbon, there exists a clique connected with Air Tanzania that monopolizes the air transport of the fish.

The multiplicity of social players indicates that the responsibilities cannot all be laid at the door of the processing firms, even though as the main decision makers they have real power and thus may be considered to have a larger share of the responsibility. The analysis rather indicates that each player in the structure of the chain shares some of the overall responsibility. Some may think that the fishermen are purely victims of the situation, suffering the high level of mortality in the camps, mostly related to HIV/AIDS. Yet, as Gibbon explains, the fishermen's camps are run according to strict rules about fighting, excess alcohol and sexual relationships. The processing firms introduced these rules in order to ensure an effective workforce, and procedures for sanctioning misbehaviour were put in place in all the camps. Compliance with the rules cannot be the sole responsibility of the firms; the fishermen have to be considered as primarily responsible for their own behaviour.

Naturally, if we want to assess the entire set of responsibilities, we also need to consider other stakeholders based in the countries of the North, such as the wholesale companies, the fish retailers and the consumers. The Nile perch is became familiar to consumers in the North because of the growing scarcity of local species as a result of intensive fishing and other practices that did not allow fish stocks to reproduce; the scarcity has increased the price of native species compared to that for the Nile perch. These causal linkages are systemic and imply that fishing policies and industries in the North also bear some indirect responsibility for the situation in and around Lake Victoria. However, it is also clear that the key players are relatively few and have a greater share of responsibility since they have more capacity to act and to control some parts of the chain. Any attempt to re-examine the production chain in terms of the social consequences that it may generate implies a clear identification of where the responsibilities lie. Allocation of responsibility in turn gives rise to questions of compensation, incentives and sanctions.

Capability Structures and the Analysis of Vulnerability and Fragility

The particular instance of the Nile perch underlines the social consequences that the implementation of value chains may produce. If we go back to the question of the 'responsibility of *whom*', it clearly appears that there are multiple responsibilities that are shared at various levels of decision making and at different points along the chain Therefore, the respective level of responsibility, and the commensurate charges that might be levied for social consequences, varies deeply from one stakeholder to another. In order to determine with equity the resulting degrees of responsibility, it is suggested that the notion of 'capability structure' (or 'structure of capabilities') may be helpful as providing an objective benchmark. Through the use of such a structure, a cross-analysis can be made of the linkages between 'responsibility of *whom*' and 'responsibility for *what*'.

Personal and collective capability structures

Our hypothesis is that organizations, like persons, have a set of capabilities (or capability set) at their disposal, which allow them to achieve various things that they value. The application of the capability concept to firms, and more generally to any organization, began with the work of Penrose (1959). However, its original meaning was more restrictive than that subsequently developed by Amartya Sen (1987, 1999) and Martha Nussbaum (2000; 2006) in the 'capability approach'. For Penrose, a firm uses specific skills to capture a share of the added value through its production process. These skills are developed through a learning, or learning-by-doing process in such a way that it cannot be replicated by easily competitors.

In considering the value chain, we can apply the concept of 'collective capability' to describe the interconnected links that exist between the various agents, that is, the productive organizations acting within the value chain. This makes it possible to distinguish between the set of capabilities that belongs to an agent – whether a person or an organization – and the set which belongs to the value chain.

In order to integrate the production and trade of some of their specific goods into the chain, the various firms that constitute the chain mobilize their respective assets and skills to function adequately, in the face of opportunities and constraints.

Value chain and collective capability

The concept of collective capability structure has been particularly highlighted by Boucher, Carimentrand and Requier-Desjardins (2003) in their analysis of the rural agro-industry development policies in Latin America.

The development of rural agro-industries often took the form of the geographical concentration of very small processing units of products such as sugar cane, cassava and other tubers, milk, cereals (Boucher and Requier-Desjardins 2002; Requier-Desjardins, Boucher and Cerdan 2003). Such concentrations within a specific territory facilitate the combination of internal and external resources, and catalyze the integration of individual capabilities in order to generate collective capabilities. These collective capabilities in turn produce collective skills, which are finally highlighted by appropriate certification and labels. This mechanism is particularly well illustrated by the case of the Cajamarca cheese production chain in Peru. It shows that the agents' localization, as well as their position within the chain, plays a key role in their capacity to contribute to the development of collective capabilities.

The production of Cajamarca cheese requires two major inputs. The first one is milk. It is produced in mountain areas where the quality of the pastures makes it possible to obtain it with a fat content higher than the one produced in valleys. This gives specificity to the cheese. The second input is the ancestral know-how of the cheese manufacturing, which originated more than two hundred years ago. Since then, a series of innovations in the overall processing, like the introduction of the mill, improved the quality.

To address the issue of differing quality standards, various processes of mediation were set up, but mechanisms of selection and exclusion appeared among the producers. In 1999, an association of producers was created to promote a common brand, but this excluded some stakeholders, like intermediary agents, informal cheese producers, street vendors, and so on. In 2002, the producers of milk byproducts decided to promote a coordination body in order to relate with NGOs and state institutions. It supported the debates on the quality of the products, therefore contributing to the reinforcement of the production chain and to the forging of a collective capability able to confront the competition of lower quality products. However, two negative consequences appeared. First, certain agents are de facto excluded from this process because of their extreme location or the difficulty they face in adjusting to new demands. Secondly, disparity increases in the distribution of the agents' capabilities, generating more heterogeneity among the chain stakeholders, as this happens usually during the growth process.

This analysis suggests that the changes that occur in the chain may affect various levels differently. Some changes, occurring at the level of the individual capability structure, may affect the structure of the whole chain. For instance, a crisis that may affect specifically the mountain producers at the level of milk production will affect, through the various levels of the value chain, the cheese producers. On the other hand, changes affecting the global structure may also have an impact on individual structures. For instance, the entry on the market of new competing products of good quality changes the production possibilities for all levels within the value chain. All this shows that it is necessary to question what the effects of any change may be, and to what extent these individual and collective structures would be able to absorb the corresponding consequences. This dual structure raises three types of questions.

First, can the chain be upgraded? According to Gibbon two types of upgrading process may occur:

> The first of these forms is the capture of higher margins in exports of existing forms of unprocessed raw material, by moving up the quality grade ladder, increasing volumes and reliability of supply, securing more remuneration contracts through forward sales and becoming active in hedging risk via utilising futures and option instruments. A second form of upgrading involves the production of new forms – as opposed to higher grades – of unprocessed raw materials. The most obvious example is gene-manipulated food crops, with their strongly positive implications for saving on inputs. (Gibbon 2000, 12)

Secondly, any change can be due either to an exogenous player or to a decision taken at one level of the chain. This raises the question of the agent's responsibility for structural changes, and for the consequences that may result. Thirdly, the changes and the capacity to absorb them will depend upon the fragility and vulnerability of both the individual and collective structures. We will now discuss this issue.

Vulnerability of the agents and fragility of capability structures

A clear distinction should be made between vulnerability and fragility. Vulnerability is related to the agent's set of capabilities (Dubois and Rousseau 2001; Dubois 2003). It is the way in which agents combine their capabilities, within their personal structures, in order to enable them to face any current risk and overcome the related consequences (Rousseau 2001). Poor people, for instance, focus more on capabilities such as work, education, and social bonds, since they lack other potentials such as financial assets, power relationships, and so on. Their capability structure is concentrated on certain assets, and this limits the possibility of substitution between their capabilities.

Vulnerability can be assessed at two levels of agency: the individual level of the player, and the global level of the chain. This means that the degree of vulnerability of a chain is determined by the relevant combination of the individual capability sets, in order to generate the capacity of resilience required to face potential risks. Fragility, on the other hand, is related to a specific capability. Some capabilities are more fragile in a given context, whereas others may seem to be more robust, and can be used on a permanent basis. A specialized technology that requires lengthy training is, for instance, more fragile when confronted by unexpected situations than a generic technology, which is quite easy to acquire, and remains usable in various circumstances.

Assessing the fragility of capabilities to some sort of disruption is as important as analyzing the vulnerability of an agent. There is a direct link between the two, since the destruction of a specific capability implies a readjustment within the structure of capabilities, which inevitably has an effect on the agent's degree of vulnerability.

Such an analysis shows that development strategies can lead to unsustainable situations by affecting the structure of capabilities through destroying some of them or changing the way they are combined. To absorb shocks, readjustments are required within the structure of capabilities by substituting some capabilities for others. But such substitutions are not systematic, because of threshold or ratchet effects. The capability structure may not be able to cope beyond a given level of destruction of capabilities. In this context, it may either become ineffective or actually have a negative impact. This means that it is important to assess the capabilities of the agents, to review the possibility of substitution between these capabilities, and to determine adjustment thresholds.

The destruction of capabilities is unavoidable and irreversible in a number of cases, especially when changes are occurring in the technology, knowledge, and legal spheres. However, in a majority of cases, such as those related to the organization of the production process, reversibility can often be achieved, by taking time to rebuild the capabilities in the long term.

Responsibility and Social Precautionary Attitude

The stability of the capability structure is an important issue that may be affected either by the decision of some agents belonging to the chain, or by external phenomena. The responsibility for the changes that may happen in the value chain is thus related to the way in which the chain is structured. Therefore, the key question that remains for such an approach is on the ways responsibility can be shared amongst the various players.

The importance and the role of capability structures

The interaction that exists between capabilities within the capability set, held by a firm or the value chain as a whole, defines a 'structure of capabilities'. At any given time, this structure displays a particular pattern that expresses the individual or collective ability of the agents to adjust to specific constraints and opportunities. If we consider that these structures are managed rationally, in the sense that their configuration is the result of optimization in response to constraints, then any change, no matter how small, will result in readjustment in the structure.

Any shock on the capability set may destroy some of the capabilities, and therefore impose an internal reorganization within the capability structure. Some impacts are negligible, and can easily be overcome without changing the current structure; in this case there will be no disturbance. But others may actually destroy one of the capabilities and therefore have consequences for the overall structure. This is why it is necessary to evaluate the degrees of fragility of the structure, and the players' vulnerability, in order to assess the resistance to external shocks and, more generally, the structure's resilience. The structure within which capabilities interact is the key to understanding how the various players react to external events and shocks. The ability to adjust their capability set, and to change the corresponding structure, is mainly what determines their vulnerability and their resilience when faced by economic and social changes.

To be socially sustainable, development must take into account the capability structure and its capacity to adjust, that is, its plasticity. This requires setting up principles of carefulness that define the norms and standards to respect, which includes 'precautionary principles', applied before undertaking an action, and 'prudential principles' derived afterwards.

Social precautionary principles and the sharing of responsibility

When confronted by situations of brittleness and vulnerability, with the serious consequences that may result, all agents are required to apply their own responsibility. However, to what extent would one agree to modify the capability structures in designing a development strategy in the light of the risks of exclusion or social uprising that are related to the brittleness of capability and the vulnerability of the players? Without knowing the exact thresholds of effects, would one be able to propose the appropriate set of principles that could provide useful guidance to ensure that the value chains do indeed result in sustainable development?

In this framework, it is clear that any kind of development strategy should start with a preventive assessment of the consequences of the scheduled policy measures, whether they are likely to be positive or negative. In this domain, where the level of uncertainty is high, harmful social consequences can result, such as an increase in poverty traps and exclusion, social conflicts and unrest, urban guerrilla warfare, gender inequalities, and so on. Given such risks, everyone would want appropriate social precautionary, or social prudential mechanisms, to be implemented.

There is, however, always uncertainty about such risks. This is why further research into risk is required, in order to assess the damage that could arise from various scenarios and solutions. It may be difficult to review and assess all possible alternatives properly. However, the worst scenario envisaged may provide enough information to set up a standard for the lowest acceptable threshold. In this case, the policy decision chosen would be the one that is expected to lead to the least bad outcome. Such a 'maximin' way of proceeding, that is, choosing the best of the worst alternatives, defines a social precautionary principle for decision. However, criteria other than the 'maximin criterion' could also be used.

All the possibilities, in the form of various scenarios that have differing levels of relative risk acceptance, will have to be discussed and assessed by all the stakeholders. This implies embacing an ethics of discussion between partners (Habermas 1991) in order to reach a satisfactory consensus.

Box 15.1 shows the various steps in the process leading to the implementation of the social precautionary principle. To begin with, a reference to the ethics of responsibility is required to take into account the respective roles of the various parties in the decision-making process. The next step is to assess what could be the probable consequences of decisions on the agents' capability structure, in a world of uncertainty. Several scenarios should be then envisaged by reviewing the probable consequences, and by considering alternative criteria for the social precautionary principle. On the basis of such scenarios, and with reference to the chosen principle, the level of responsibility for every agent involved in the development strategy of the value chain can then be established.

Because of the serious consequences of some decisions, the social precautionary principle has to be accepted by all the key decision makers involved in the development of the value chain. Respecting this principle engages the players' responsibility for their interventions that affect the overall structure of the production chain.

Rethinking the design of fair trade value chains

'Fair trade' is an interesting example of a value chain for the analysis of responsibility because it is, precisely, an attempt to modify the rules of the international trade game in favor of the most underprivileged producers of the developing countries. It raises

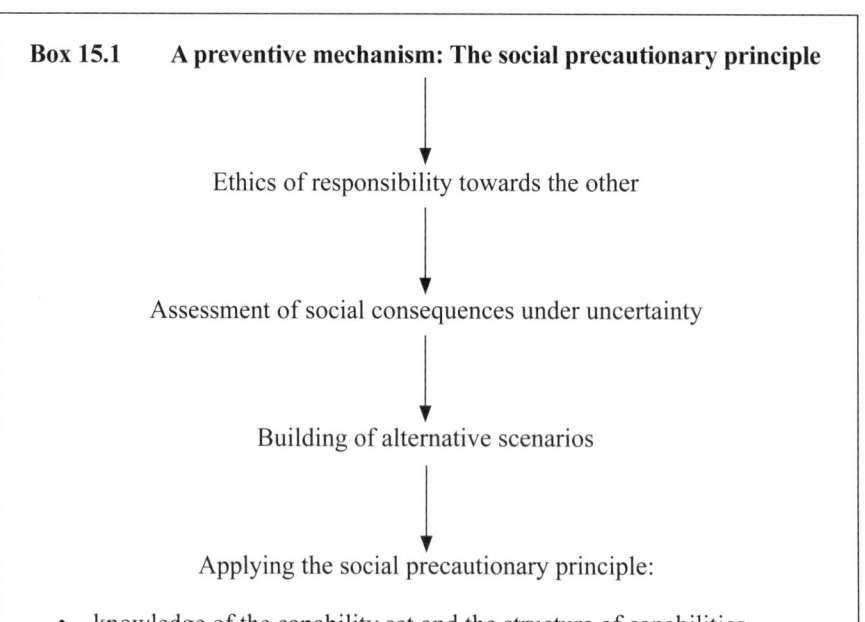

Box 15.1   A preventive mechanism: The social precautionary principle

↓

Ethics of responsibility towards the other

↓

Assessment of social consequences under uncertainty

↓

Building of alternative scenarios

↓

Applying the social precautionary principle:

- knowledge of the capability set and the structure of capabilities
- ethics of discussion and debate on the sharing of responsibilities
- implementing responsibility: incentives and sanctions

the questions of the structure of the value chain and its mode of governance. However, one should not consider fair trade in a naive way, fair as a homogeneous practice. In that field, Ballet and Carimentrand (2007) distinguish four categories of value chains: those specialized having specific networks: those labeled with certification, those specialized and distributed by the middle and large commercial stores, and those made by traditional firms. None of these categories have the same commitment toward the sharing of responsibility and the definition of common standards.

Only the specialized value chains can prevail in a discussion of the guarantees and rules of production. In the other cases, these rules are imposed onto the producers by the actors controlling the value chain, that is, in fact, the certifiers. In addition no responsibility with respect to the negative consequences is clearly defined and established, whatever the value chain that is considered. This attitude raises a serious problem about how the actors who control the value chain impose their rules, sometimes modifying deeply the organization of the production at local level. For instance, the value chains that are certified by the Fairtrade Labelling Organization (FLO) and benefit from the labels Max Havelaar or Transfair, have to be connected, at the producer level, to appropriate producers' organizations. Such a constraint is not neutral for the capability structure of the individuals, or for the value chain's structure of capabilities. On the one hand, the creation of such organizations of producers modifies the local social fabric. Sometimes the consequences are quite positive, but they may be also negative, depending on the sociocultural context. On the other hand, not all producers are members of these organizations and thus some cannot be connected to the value chain. Therefore, the risk of systematic exclusion as the the value chain develops is far from being negligible.

Moreover, the entry of new actors in the fair trade option, for instance the middle and large commercial stores, may significantly modify the building-up of a value chain. These actors often dominate the value chain without assuming any responsibility (Renard 2005). The harmful effects, which may result from shocks on the capability structures, are therefore totally ignored.

It appears clearly that fair trade is far from being equitable as regards responsibility. All responsibilities rest on the producers of the developing countries, at the end of the chain, and absolutely not on those actors who are at an upper level, yet dominating and controlling the whole chain.

Conclusion

In economic terms, production and value chains are extremely important in generating growth, employment, and added value that can be assigned to all the players involved in the chain. They are also a source of economies of scale, productivity, and innovation, and so can be expected to be of benefit to a country, and to its population. Unfortunately, there can also be some negative consequences on people, perverse effects, or unexpected social externalities, and this has happened in many development projects, programs and policies. We have cited the case of the Nile perch as one example of how development can have a negative impact on some stakeholders, such as the poor fishermen of Lake Victoria.

Designing a social precautionary principle from the outset may be a way of avoiding such social issues. This implies simulating the impact of development policies, assessing various scenarios, and alternative approaches, and discussing how responsibilities should be allocated. An ethics of open discussion between the various stakeholders will assess the level of freedom of all the players in order to appreciate the various responsibilities. This may also be a way of empowering the poor by improving their participation as stakeholders in assessing the respective responsibilities of the various players.

In this way, the poor will not be treated as though they have no responsibility for their plight, or as though they have no responsibility for what has happened to them and are not able to live their lives rationally. Other people involved in development, who are assumed to be better informed and sufficiently rational to make development decisions, may also share responsibility for the negative externalities generated by development projects in a vulnerable society.

Once the responsibilities have been assigned, the stakeholders might decide to prosecute the agents with the greatest responsibility within the chain. This would require the availability of appropriate lawyers and courts able to deal with the information available about capabilities, their limits and fragilities, the acceptance of social risks, the issue of shared responsibility, and, more generally, all the issues related to socially sustainable development.

Applied in this way, there is no risk that the social precautionary principle will become a conservative principle, but it will help to rehabilitate the ethics of responsibility in everyday life. It would be a useful tool for the design of development strategies that can be expected to be sustainable in social terms.

References

Arndt, S. and Kierzkowski, H. (2001), 'Introduction', in S. Arndt and H. Kierzkowski (eds), *Fragmentation: New Production Patterns in the World Economy* (Oxford: Oxford University Press), pp. 1–16.

Ballet, J. and Carimentrand, A. (2007), *Le Commerce Équitable* (Paris: Ellipses).

Ballet, J., Dubois, J.-L. and Mahieu, F.-R. (2005), *L'Autre Développement: Le Développement Socialement Soutenable* (Paris: L'Harmattan).

Boucher, F. and Requier-Desjardins, D. (2002), 'La Concentration des Fromageries Rurales de Cajamarca: Enjeux et Difficultés D'une Stratégie Collective D'activation Liée a la Qualité', proceedings of the SYAL Conference, 'Les Systèmes Agroalimentaires Localisés: Produits, Entreprises et Dynamiques Locales', Agropolis, Montpellier, France, 16–18 October.

Boucher, F., Carimentrand, A. and Requier-Desjardins, D. (2003), 'Agro-industrie Rurale et Lutte Contre la Pauvreté: Les Systèmes Agroalimentaires Localisés Contribuent-Ils au Renforcement des Capabilities?', Third International Conference on the Capability Approach, 'From Sustainable Development to Sustainable Freedom', University of Pavia, Italy, 7–9 September.

Deardoff, A. (1998), 'Fragmentation in Simple Trade Models', Discussion Paper 422, School of Public Policy, University of Michigan.

Dickens, P., Kelly, P., Olds, K., and Yeung H.W.C. (2001), 'Chains and Networks, Territories and Scales: Towards a Relational Framework for Analysing the Global Economy', *Global Networks* 1:2, 89–112.

Dubois, J.-L. (2003), 'Food Security, Vulnerability and Social Sustainability', *Cahiers de l'IFAS*, Institut Français D'Afrique du Sud, Johannesburg.

Dubois, J.-L., Lachaud, J.-P., Montaud, J.-M. and Pouille, A. (2001), *Pauvreté et Développement Socialement Durable* (Bordeaux: PUB).

Dubois, J.-L. and Mahieu, F.R. (2002), 'La Dimension Sociale du Développement Durable, Réduction de la Pauvreté ou Durabilité Sociale', in J.Y. Martin (ed.).

Dubois, J.-L. and Rousseau, S. (2001), 'Reinforcing Household's Capabilities as a Way to Reduce Vulnerability and Prevent Poverty in Equitable Terms', First International Conference on the Capability Approach, 'Justice and Poverty: Examining Sen's Capability Approach', St Edmund's College, Cambridge, 5–7 June.

Garrod, D. (1961), 'The History of the Fishing Industry of Lake Victoria in Relation to the Expansion of Marketing Facilities', *East African Agricultural and Forestry Journal* 27:2, 95–9.

Gereffi, G., Humphrey, J. and Sturgeon, T. (2003), 'The Governance of Global Value Chains', *Review of International Political Economy* 12:1, 78–104.

Gereffi, G. and Korzeniewicz, M. (1994), *Commodity Chains and Global Capitalism* (Westport: Praeger).

Gibbon, P. (1997), 'Of Saviours and Punks: The Political Economy of the Nile Perch Marketing Chain in Tanzania', Working Paper 97.3, Centre for the Development Research, Copenhagen.

Gibbon, P. (2000), 'Global Commodity Chains and Economic Upgrading in Less Developed Countries', Working Paper 00.2, Centre for the Development Research, Copenhagen.

Habermas, J. (1991), *De L'éthique de la Discussion*, French translation 1992 (Paris: Cerf).

Henderson, J., Dickens P., Hess M., Coe N. and Yeung H.W.C. (2002), 'Global Production Networks and the Analysis of Economic Development', *Review of International Political Economy* 9:3, 436–64.

Helleiner, G. (1992), *Trade Policy, Industrialisation and Development* (Oxford: Oxford University Press).

Hughes, A. (2000), 'Retailers, Knowledges and Changing Commodity Networks: The Case of the Cut Flower Trade', *Geoforum* 31, 175–90.

Martin, J.Y. (ed.) (2002), *Développement durable? Doctrines, Pratiques, Évaluations* (Paris: IRD Editions).

Nussbaum, M.C. (2000), *Women and Human Development: The Capabilities Approach* (Cambridge: Cambridge University Press).

Nussbaum, M.C. (2006), *Frontiers of Justice: Disability, Identity, Species Membership* (Cambridge, MA: Belknap Press).

Penrose, E. (1959), *The Theory of the Growth of the Firm* (Oxford: Basil Blackwell).

Renard, M.C. (2005), 'Quality Certification, Regulation and Power in Fair Trade', *Journal of Rural Studies* 21, 419–31.

Requier-Desjardins, D., Boucher, F. and Cerdan, C. (2003), 'Globalization and the Evolution of Production Systems: Rural Food-processing and Localised Agri-food Systems in Latin-American Countries', *Entrepreneurship and Regional Development* 15:1, 49–67.

Rousseau, S. (2001), 'Capabilités, Risques et Vulnérabilités', in J.-L. Dubois, J.-P. Lachaud, J.-M. Montaud and A. Pouille (eds).

Sen, A.K. (1987), *Commodities and Capabilities* (New Delhi: Oxford India Paperbacks).

Sen, A.K. (1999), *Development as Freedom* (New Delhi: Oxford India Paperbacks).

Wood, A. (2001), 'Value Chains: An Economist's Perspective', *IDS Bulletin* 32:3.

Chapter 16

Food, Environment, and the Good Life

David E. Cooper

There is now a massive literature on the relationship between food, environmental issues and the well-being of both humans and animals. Ecologists, for example, examine the effects of arable farming methods on sustainability and biodiversity; other scientists investigate the contribution to global warming of gas emissions from cattle, with its implications for flooding and desertification; economists study the long-term results of liberalised international trade in food for the traditional economies of developing countries. Research of these kinds clearly has an important bearing on matters of a broadly moral type, for processes such as those mentioned – loss of biodiversity, say, or desertification – do have an effect upon the well-being of creatures, upon their capacity to lead good lives.

At another level, however, the literature on food in relation to environment and well-being is relatively modest. In part, this is because the focus has been upon the production of food, on agriculture, to the relative exclusion of other practices involving food. As two writers observe, 'the geographies of food preparation, cooking, recipes, meals and diet have received scant attention from scholars' (Atkins and Bowler 2001, 274). And in part it is because the bulk of the research – ecological, scientific and economic – assumes a rather particular notion of environment. This notion is, in fact, derived from an older one that still informs everyday thought and talk about environment and is central to an important range of issues concerning well-being and the good life.

My topic in this chapter is the relationship between food practices at large (not just food production), environment (in a sense to be explained in the next section), and the good life (not in the sense of the fun-packed life, but in the sense of one that goes well for the creatures whose life it is). In more detail, I aim, in the four following sections of the chapter: first, to explain the relevant notion of environment and its relation to that of well-being or the good life. Secondly, I aim to show the historically important relationship of food practices to environment in the sense explained in the first section. Thirdly, the aim is to discuss some ways in which, in developed societies at least, this relationship has been perverted or degraded, ways in which, therefore, well-being is itself compromised, and fourthly, to discuss some proposals – especially the call for a 'reconnection' with local environments – for halting or reversing the processes discussed in the third section and make a proposal of my own.

Environments and the Environment

One may safely predict that ecologists, natural scientists, environmental ethicists and so on, when writing on environmental issues, will frequently refer to *the* environment. The dangers they discuss, typically, are ones to *the* environment; it is *the* environment that needs protecting. The definite article suggests that there is just one environment – something very large and encompassing that all of us, humans and animals alike, are located in. Quite what *the* environment is identified with is often left vague and varies among authors. Sometimes it is equated with nature, sometimes the biosphere, sometimes everything 'from the street corner to the stratosphere'. But whatever exactly it is identified with, *the* environment is something very different from what was once understood by 'environment', and from what clearly still is understood by it when, for example, people speak of a school or office environment and talk about the 'atmosphere' or 'ambience' of the place. In this latter sense of the term, there is no single environment, but countless ones – mine, yours, an African farmer's, a fox's, a cod's.

It is tempting to think that *an* environment – the fox's, say – is just a small portion of *the* environment, a physically bounded space within a gigantic one, *the* environment, which contains all such portions. But this would be wrong. Environments should not be understood in physical or spatial terms at all – as, for example, geographical areas of limited size that surround creatures. While a creature is 'in' an environment, this is not in the way a pea is in a pod or a tree is in a forest. The way is more akin to that in which a person is 'in' the world of fashion or even 'in the office'. (Contrast the way I am 'in the office' today, even if I've popped outside for a smoke, to the merely spatial sense that an intruding fly or wasp might be in it.)

It is not easy to spell out this older sense of 'environment', to specify what constitutes *an* environment for a person or animal. (For an attempt to spell it out, see Cooper 1992.) But the little word 'for' is indicative. An environment is an environment *for* a creature, something it is not simply in, but something it has understanding of. One's environment is what one knows one's way around – and in an unreflective, implicit manner. The geographer, with the help of maps, may know his way through the rainforest, but not in the manner of the woman who lives there, whose environment the forest is. An environment, however, is not simply something a creature knows and understands: it is what the creature engages with. Or better, the understanding of the environment that the creature has is implicit in and constituted by intelligent engagement with that environment. The things that belong in the environment are encountered and understood in relation to the creature's practices and purposes – as things to eat, to avoid and so on. One could put this another way by saying that the objects and places that belong in a creature's environment are meaningful for it: its relation to its environment is what phenomenologists call 'intentional', not simply spatial or causal. And one could then characterise an environment as a 'field of significance' for the creature whose environment it is.

This makes it clear why a creature's environment cannot be equated with what is more or less spatially close to it. Some barely accessible outcrop of rocks a few metres from the fox's den will not belong to its environment, whereas the rabbit-rich field several kilometres away will. My university belongs in my environment even though it is much further from my home than the housing estate I speed by on the train, which doesn't so belong. (I never go there and would be quite 'lost' if I did.) That said, there is indeed likely to be some correlation, other things being equal, between a creature's environment and what is geographically fairly close to it. For example, what impinges upon a creature's sense organs, with their limited range, is more likely to belong in the creature's environment than what does not: impingement on the senses is often crucial to engagement with things and the development of unreflective knowledge of them. But, especially in the case of human beings, other things are not always equal. The 'field of significance' that jet travel, television and other technological products open up for a person may be very large and scattered. 'Global cities', such as London and Tokyo, may belong in the environment of an executive in a way that the hills a mile away from his or her house do not.

The environment is not a place any creature can be outside of, for it must be somewhere, not nowhere. Environments, by contrast, can be lost by creatures, for they can be deprived of what they know their way about, engage with and encounter as significant. The captured fox placed inside a bare laboratory cell is deprived of its, or perhaps any, environment: for there is nothing it understands there, nothing with which it can be 'at home'. We naturally speak of an environment being lost to us when the changes inflicted on our surroundings – by new building, say – render those surroundings strange. What was meaningful has gone, replaced by things and places whose significance we have yet to make our own.

The vocabulary of 'loss' and 'deprivation' indicates that the notion of environment as a 'field of significance' is evaluatively charged. An environment, in this sense, is something a creature ought to have: for any creature, if it is to live well – indeed, if it is really to have a life – must have, or be 'in', somewhere it is 'at home', somewhere it understands, engages with, and is replete with significance for it. It is possible for a creature – a battery hen, perhaps, or a man whose work and family farm have suddenly been taken over by an agro-industrial complex – to be in a place, but hardly 'in' it. The animal or the man has been deprived, to a greater or lesser degree, of the conditions required for the pursuit of a life that embodies purpose, understanding and a sense of the meaning of what impinges on it. The life deprived of, or poor in, environment is not, at any rate, a good life.

Food Practices and Environment

The relationships between food practices, from growing turnips to dining at the Ritz, and environment, understood as a 'field of significance' – a theatre, as it were, for the enactment of a life – are bound to be many and diverse. Any food practice could contribute to, reflect, or otherwise relate to that meaningful milieu in which, with unreflective understanding, a creature engages, knows its way about and is 'at home'. So any general account of food practices in relation to environment would be impossibly encyclopedic. Still, it will be helpful to indicate some broad and important ways in which, historically, food practices have served to relate people and animals to their environments, to shape or even create the 'fields of significance' within which they move.

In the case of most wild animals, the connection between food practices, notably the obtaining of food, and environments is very tight. It would hardly be exaggerated to equate a wild animal's environment – the world it knows its way about – with its feeding habitat. Again, physical proximity is not the crucial consideration. Going back to the fox, the bare, hardly accessible outcrop of rock close to its den is not part of its environment in the way that the more distant rabbit-rich field is. That is because the latter, unlike the former, provides food for the fox. Even so voracious an animal as a fox cares, of course, about things other than eating: its young, for example. But no one would deny that the availability of food and the animal's manner of feeding are the main shapers of the animal's environment, of what it notices or ignores, is drawn to or avoids in its 'world'. Even the manner in which it cares for and interacts with its young is powerfully constrained by its food practices.

The relationships between human beings and their environments are, naturally, much more complex: factors other than food practices – work, for example – structure what matters to men and women. But it is worth recalling that there have been peoples, among whom 'work' is itself a food practice, whose environments are scarcely less identifiable with feeding habitats than in the case of wild animals. Hunter-gatherers, for example, were not rootless nomads: they occupied a place, a territory – however large and scattered – that was at once their provider and their environment, a place 'known in extreme detail' with which they were on 'intimate terms', and outside which 'their knowledge – of place, creature and spirits – [would] probably fail them' (Brody 1999, 11).

One constituent in almost every creature's environment is its home, a place to sleep, find protection and eat (or digest) food. Indeed, a home is an environment *par excellence*: a place 'where we know – and are known – through accumulated experience' (Tall, cited in Pretty 2002, 110), where, more than anywhere, we know our way about and understand the significance of things and actions. The human home is a richer, more versatile theatre than the animal's den or nest. Nevertheless, the traditional home environment, like those animal accommodations, was powerfully shaped by food practices. Not only the lay-out of the home (pantry, kitchen, dining-room) but the form of family life within it were structured by food practices. Mealtimes – 'ordinary' ones and 'special occasions' – structured the daily and longer-term life of the family, helping to cement or even define relationships within the family, relationships further confirmed by 'the division of labour' called for by food practices (bringing home the bacon, peeling vegetables, cooking, serving and carving). The contribution of food practices to the home and family environment was especially salient, of course, in the case of those homes that were also the sites of food production – the small 'family farms', for example, that are still the norm for rural households in some developing countries (see, for example, Norberg-Hodge 2005). For, here, as with the hunter-gatherers, factors that also serve to shape home environments – work, weather, dangers, hopes and ambitions – are inseparable from food practices.

The productive food practices of a family farm are paradigmatic of practices that involve engagement with nature, and thereby of ones that more broadly serve to make environments out of the areas by which people are physically surrounded. For family farmers, but also for farm labourers, hired gardeners, fishermen and gatherers of wild berries or honey, it is their practical, purposeful engagement with natural life that constructs environments from the spaces in which they move and work. The point is not only, or mainly, that what they do physically alters these spaces by, say, turning a area of jungle into a vegetable patch or a meadow into a lawn. More crucially, what they do, even when the physical impact is slight, 'humanizes landscapes' (Atkins and Bowler 2001, 323), turns them into 'fields of significance', theatres for meaningful activities. In one sense of that elastic expression, such activities promote 'oneness with nature'. For the person who gathers berries and honey there, the forest is not a place simply to stare at, or hurry through on the way to the next village. It is a place that enters into the person's life, a place one is 'at home' in, a 'book of signs', as it were, of sounds, smells and sights that are immediately and effortlessly understood.

Gathering honey, fishing, cooking and eating may be solitary activities, but often food practices are communal activities. I do not mean, simply, that they are conducted alongside others – people who may be casual day-labourers or passing tourists in one's local pub. Rice harvesting in an Indian village and a 'garden-day' lunch on an English village green are communal activities because they involve a community, people who know one another and enter significantly into one another's lives. The communities in which a person participates are an integral aspect of his or her environment, for it is not just things and places that belong to a 'field of significance', but other people and their ways. Indeed, one's understanding of just about everything in one's environment is 'public', since it is an understanding one shares with and inherits from others. As the German philosopher, Martin Heidegger, put it, each person's world is a 'They-world', one 'always already' interpreted by others (Heidegger 1980, 190).

One central way, therefore, in which food practices may shape environments is by fostering, reflecting or otherwise bearing upon communal relationships among people. And it is clear that, historically, food practices have emphatically done this. In *The Rituals of Dinner* (1991), Margaret Visser argues that castes, kinship groups and other communities may be partly defined in terms of food practices: a kinship group, for example, being one whose members share food without hesitation. On a smaller scale, one thinks of the roles played in structuring and lending character to communities of practices such as communal harvesting, drinking and eating in local pubs and exchanging seeds with neighbours or fellow horticultural enthusiasts. The communities, and therefore environments, that food practices help to define and shape need not be 'local', for there can be 'community without propinquity' (Bell and Valentine 1997, 94). The community of dahlia growers, the gardening milieu to which I belong, may be far flung. Indeed, a community of which one feels oneself to be a member, in part through sharing a diet, may be a diaspora – as with the Jewish community or perhaps the 'veggie' community.

Here, then, are some of the important ways in which, historically, food practices, from growing produce to eating meals, have served to shape and stamp those 'worlds', those 'fields of significance', of people and animals that I am calling 'environments'.

Food and Environmental Impoverishment

It is possible for a creature to be without an environment, to be in no 'field of significance' – to be alive, in effect, but without a life. Such was the condition, for example, of the monkeys placed by experimental psychologists at the bottom of long, featureless aluminium tubes ('wells of despair') in order to induce insane depression. Though less drastically deprived of environment, the condition of geese force-fed to fatten their livers and of battery broilers approximates to that of the monkeys. One reason for saying that these animals are (virtually) devoid of environment is that they have no scope for engaging in significant food practices, ones central to the existence of animals who are leading natural lives, for these serve to organise the animals' lives, to make an environment of their surroundings. (Ingesting pellets dropped down a metal tube, let alone having food funnelled down its throat, is not a way in which a creature engages with its world.)

Few human beings are so drastically deprived of an environment: but, in less dramatic ways, they too can experience environmental 'impoverishment'. Maybe there is no nowhere they fully know their way about with unreflective ease, nowhere rich and replete in significance for them, nowhere they are 'at home', nowhere they feel engaged. Those great themes of twentieth-century literature – anomy, alienation, disenchantment – are, as often as not, themes of environmental impoverishment. And familiar announcements of 'the breakdown of the family', of the atrophy of community life and 'spirit', of 'disconnection' from the land or nature are variations on those great themes. There is no need, here, to dwell on the usual suspects deemed responsible for the anomic, disenchanted character of modern life. But any shortlist is likely to include: rapid technological change; high mobility in jobs and housing; the 'compression of time and space' (through television, jet travel and the like) that makes 'global citizens' of people at the cost of rendering them citizens of nowhere in particular; a serendipitous 'neophilia', induced by advertising and the cult of 'difference' that drives people to try anything and anywhere without the time to identify with and understand something and somewhere in particular.

Food practices, we saw in the preceding section, can help to provide and shape environments. But they can fail to as well. They may, in the lives of many people, become irrelevant, so that, for them, 'food itself is considered less "significant", and carries less symbolic weight than in the past' (Gofton, quoted in Bell and Valentine 1997, 5) – no longer, for example, providing occasions for family gatherings. Or they may even militate against the having of an environment, thereby compounding environmental impoverishment – by, for instance, turning a once rich and varied landscape into featureless 'monoscape'. This failure of food practices to contribute positively, as historically they have done, to forging and structuring environments can occur in all the areas discussed in the previous section: those of home and family, of community and of engagement with nature.

It is, of course, the perception of many observers, including contributors to this book, that prevailing modern food practices – of producers, retailers and consumers alike – are guilty of this failure. These observers would endorse the environmentalist and organic farmer, Sir Julian Rose's, judgement that such practices have contributed to 'alienation' – not only that of people from their 'means of survival', but 'alienation from fellow workers and therefore from society' (Rose 1999, 132). If, as I assume, there is truth in this perception, then the modern food practices in question fail to contribute to the good life, for a condition of the good life is having and engaging with an environment; a condition that, according to the above perception, is degraded by practices that contribute, instead, to what has been called 'gastro-anomy'.

The many food-related processes accused of contributing to environmental impoverishment can, at a pinch, be subsumed under two umbrella labels – 'levelling' and 'abdication'. By 'levelling processes', I mean those that tend to homogenise food practices, to flatten out local and other differences among those practices. At the level of production, one thinks, for example, of the transformation of a diversified agriculture into a monoculture, with a corresponding transformation of a variegated landscape into a 'monoscape'. One thinks, too, of the increasing 'commoditisation' of agricultural produce, especially of what has been called 'appropriationism': 'the persistent transformation into industrial activities of certain farm-based labour processes, and their subsequent reintroduction ... in the form of ... processed food outputs' (Atkins and Bowler 2001, 60) – the turning of poultry, for example, into raw material for such 'outputs' as 'nuggets' and 'twists'. Levelling processes of production can impoverish environments, first, by accelerating the tendency to what Jules Pretty (2002, 110) calls 'place neutrality'. A patchwork of diverse farms, offering scope for a wide range of engaged activities, is replaced by a featureless landscape of cereal crops or gigantic poultry factories, indistinguishable from those to be found a hundred or a thousand kilometres away. Secondly, these processes can degrade the work environments of those who work in monocultural, industrialised enterprises. Philip McMichael, drawing on Deborah Barndt's research, gives the example of Mexican workers shunted around tomato-packing plants in a region entirely taken over by monocultural tomato growing. Denied any satisfying, meaningful participation in and control over agricultural production, the workers have suffered, as Barndt puts it, a 'spiritual loss ... a loss of knowledge of seeds ... of sustainable practices ... that had maintained the land for millennia' (McMichael 2000, 24).

Levelling processes are familiar, as well, at the level of consumption. In this connection, one inevitably thinks of 'McDonaldisation', the inexorable spread of chains of barely distinguishable outlets, serving the same food in the same surroundings. The contribution, here, to environmental impoverishment is once again through engendering 'place neutrality'. This may confer the 'ability to come and go as you please, without reference to ... ties of places and localities', but place neutrality 'implies all the facilities but none of the heart, none of the natural connections between people, and between people and the land' (Pretty 2002, 110).

By 'processes of abdication', I refer to those in which people hand over responsibility for food practices to faceless others – to biochemical experts, say, or the managers of the production lines that package the frozen dinners that people thaw out at home. Like levelling processes (with which they are often connected and sometimes coincide), these processes of abdication are visible at all levels of food practice. At the productive level, they are at work in the ever-increasing reliance of farmers on hi-tech machinery and chemical inputs, both of which substitute for traditional skills and 'know-how'. Writers from John Steinbeck to the present have recorded the poignant experience of farmers to whom the environments in which their forebears were integrated and 'at home' have become alien. One novelist, for example, describes a Polish farmer who, unlike his neighbours, still refuses to substitute a mechanical harvester for his scythe, whose use had been taught to him by his father and grandfather: for 'what mattered was belonging to a history that attached itself to a stretch of land' (Powers 1997, 100). These processes are at work, too, in the 'appropriation' of agricultural produce by industrial enterprises, for the farmer then abdicates responsibility for growing anything that resembles what actually gets eaten. The environment once shared by growers and consumers – a context of mutual understanding and reciprocal recognition of needs and benefits – will suffer further atrophy if, as some predict, 'agriculture ... [is] reduced in its function to little more than the provision of feedstocks to the bio–industrial complex' (Atkins and Bowler 2001, 233).

Abdication is evident, too, in food practices other than agriculture. As two authors note, 'functional specialisation', which implies handing over responsibilities to the specialists, has, in conjunction with 'globalisation', 'penetrated to the household level, where even farmers ... have become consumers of food ... with limited knowledge of how and where most of their food is being produced, transported, processed, and distributed' (Koc and Dahlberg 1999, 113). This is not the only way, of course, in which consumers' engagement with and understanding of food has been degraded. One reads, for example, that in the northeast of England 94 per cent of the meals eaten by the families studied took less than ten minutes of preparation (Atkins and Bowler 2001, 268) – just one indication of the manner in which responsibility for the preparation and cooking of food has been handed over to faceless others, such as the makers of instant, ready-made dinners. One can indeed appreciate how food becomes 'less significant', of 'less symbolic weight', for people whose dealings with it – and, one predicts, whose manner of actually eating it – are so quick and casual. The preparation and eating of food in the homes of such people are no longer ingredients in a 'field of significance': they have become incidental, a mere means, one imagines, to topping up energy levels.

Here, then, are some of the many processes, subsumable under the headings of 'levelling' and 'abdication', that mark the failure of modern food practices to perform their historic role of shaping environments – of enriching the 'fields of significance' in which people conduct their lives. Unless compensated for by practices of a different kind, the implication of this failure is that people's environments and so, to a greater or lesser degree, their lives have been impoverished.

'Reconnecting'

Responses vary among the many writers who have commented on the processes described in the previous section and appreciated their implications for what I called environmental impoverishment. For some – a minority – there is nothing to lament. This is partly because of new freedoms these processes enable; the freedom, to recall an earlier quotation, from 'ties of places and localities' and the freedom from work in the kitchen that women in particular may welcome. It is also partly, according to these authors, because the lost or impoverished environments have been replaced, and compensated for, by new ones. The global city, with its global diet, affords its own kind of know-how, intimacy and community: those of people who are adept (and recognise one another as adept) at eclectic shopping in all-night supermarkets, at choosing from menus in every sort of ethnic restaurant, at putting together ready-made ingredients for a 'creolised' dinner party, or at keeping up to date, whether out of conviction or out of political correctness, with the products it is morally permissible to buy (coffee 'direct' from peasants, nothing from Monsanto).

But for many other writers, expressions such as 'global citizen' and 'global diet' only put an optimistic spin on what might more reasonably be regarded as 'gastro-anomy'. For these writers, there is no sufficient compensation for the loss of older environments, for the atrophy of the role of food in shaping people's environments. What we hear from these writers is a call for reconnection. Jules Pretty's (2002, ch. 5) slogan 'Only reconnect!' can, of course, be variously taken – as, for instance, an exhortation to grow and eat organic, thereby promoting a less 'mediated', less 'abdicating', relationship to natural processes. But the call for reconnection has primarily been heard as one for connecting once again with the *local*. How better, the underlying thought goes, to resist the processes of levelling and abdication than to reconnect food practices with locality? Hence, one is told, people should heed a 'proximity principle', sometimes interpreted to mean that the food you eat as you travel across a country should enable you to tell where you are (see Raven 1999, 139ff). Examples offered (and praised) of 'the reinstatement of the local as resistance to the homogenising global' (Bell and Valentine 1997, 190) include vegetable 'box schemes', the eschewing of non-regional cheeses and of vegetables out of season in one's own country, and the Slow Food Movement's encouragement of 'local rootedness and decentralisation' in food practices.

It is certainly not my purpose to decry such locality-sensitive practices, but I wonder whether enthusiasm for local reconnection, when considered as an antidote to environmental impoverishment, is not guilty of the equation – challenged early on in this chapter – of a person's environment with a more or less circumscribed physical area. The 'field of significance' within which a person is at home may or may not coincide with a particular area and be enhanced by a concentration of practices, including food ones, within a particular area.

It is worth noting, as the above examples suggest, that there is no consensus among champions of local reconnection on what, exactly, counts as local. How big is the 'where' that you infer is yours from the food you are eating? The northeast of England? The Wear Valley? The village of Doddington? Sometimes the call for reconnection is one for the resurrection of traditional national dishes; sometimes, at the other extreme, for supporting one's nearest ice-cream maker or village store. Most commonly, perhaps, it is one for protecting or reinvigorating the agriculture and cuisine of a region, with the ambition of promoting or recollecting a *sense* of region, since regions, as often as not, are partly identified in terms of their produce and 'typical' dishes. But as a scheme for environmental enrichment, regionalist projects are surely limited. For one thing, it is hard to see what impact they might have on the environments of city dwellers living in places already too cosmopolitan to be much affected by practices in the market towns and villages of the geographical areas the cities happen to be within. For another thing, gastronomic 'regionalism' is easily commandeered for the global, commoditised system that it is designed to 'resist'. Supermarkets all over the country or the continent proudly sell the much-travelled 'typical' products of far-flung regions, and most of the food associated with a particular region is likely to be sold and consumed not there, but in cities scattered around the world. Most importantly, it is obscure how, except for a few producers and retailers, buying locally, eating some 'typical' dishes and the like can significantly constitute or contribute to a 'way of life', something which, as McMichael (2000, 31f) reminds us, food still does 'for the majority of the world's population', and which it once did in the countries where calls for regional reconnection are now being so loudly heard. Such practices, one feels, do not shape environments ('ways of life'), but gesture at ones already lost.

It is in a different set of practices, I suggest, that better prospects for environmental reconnection and enrichment, for 'resistance to the homogenising global', may be found – those involved in kitchen gardening, whether in private or communal gardens and whether in gardens proper or in allotments. These prospects, one likes to think, are recognised by the half-million families in the United Kingdom who, in a striking revival of the practice, now garden allotments, or by the many New Yorkers in the Green Thumb movement of community gardens, and perhaps even by some governments, such as that of Cuba with its support of intensive organic urban gardens. (That many communal gardens and allotments are found in cities means, incidentally, that the prospects for environmental reconnection afforded by kitchen gardening are not confined, as some regional initiatives are, to people living in the countryside.)

It would be a mistake to subsume these practices under the label of 'localization', and to suppose that the problem with regional food practices is that regions are not local enough. For one thing, a communal garden or family allotment need not be especially local, for it may be further away from its users than the nearest supermarket. More importantly, talk of localisation is a diversion from the main point, which is not the distance to their houses from where the produce they eat is grown, but people's active engagement with its growing and use. Several aspects of this engagement deserve mention, for each contributes to the shaping of environments and, thereby, to the good life (for a more detailed account, see Cooper 2006, chs 4–5).

First, it is hard to envisage any activities – landscape painting, for example, or back-packing in the mountains – that are available to almost everybody and which are *more* apt than kitchen gardening to engender the sense of 'communion with nature' that, as Michael Pollan recalls in his celebration of gardening in *Second Nature* (1996, 18), was his grandfather's main reason for growing vegetables. There are few forms of intercourse with natural things that require such intimate understanding of them, and perhaps none where there is such a degree of mutual dependence. What is good for the gardener is good for what he or she grows, and vice versa. Secondly, kitchen gardening engenders a further sense of communion, this time with other people. Even in the case of growing food in one's own garden, the activity is rarely solipsistic: seeds are swapped with neighbours, vegetables and fruit exchanged as gifts, other people's plots visited and learnt from, just as they visit and learn from one's own. And in the case of allotments and community gardens, as the name of the latter indicates, people are gathered into communities through their mutual interests and knowledge, as well as by their dependence on one another's cooperation. If kitchen gardening forges and shapes the relationships to nature and community that are integral to environments, to 'fields of significance', so, thirdly, it is apt to contribute to the environment of the home, of the family. It is not simply that kitchen gardening typically involves the family as a whole: in addition, the preparation and eating of one's own produce takes on a significance and invites an attention that purchased, especially pre-prepared, food rarely does. The home is enhanced – becomes, one might say, more of a home – when the preparation of food is an exercise of care and pride and the eating of it a celebration of the fruits of the earth and of shared labour alike.

What should be emphasised above all, however, about the engagement that kitchen gardening involves is that it is indeed an engagement – a long-term, active and purposive commitment that is integral, not incidental, to a 'way of life', to one's 'world'. Gardening, if engaged in seriously, lends structure and regularity to a person's life – an intelligent, 'unruffled consistency', as Goethe (1971, 224) put it, 'in doing, each season of the year, each hour of the day, precisely what needs to be done'. It is not a 'hobby', a 'bolt-on' extra to one's life, an incidental and dispensable decoration to the environment that is one's sphere of familiarity. The demands it makes – the demands of a nevertheless '*voluntary* dependence', to cite Goethe again – play a role in defining that sphere, in shaping that life and what is significant in it. This is why the cultivation of one's own food is able, more perhaps than any other food practice, to return to food its historical role in constituting or enriching environments, in taking its place within the good life.

References

Atkins, P. and Bowler, I. (2001), *Food in Society: Economy, Culture, Geography* (London: Arnold).
Barnett, A. and Scruton, R. (eds) (1999), *Town and Country* (London: Vintage).
Bell, D. and Valentine, G. (1997), *Consuming Geographies: We are Where we Eat* (London: Routledge).
Brody, H. (1999), 'Nomads and Settlers', in Barnett and Scruton (eds).
Cooper, D.E. (1992), 'The Idea of Environment', in Cooper and Palmer (eds).
Cooper, D.E. (2006), *A Philosophy of Gardens* (Oxford: Oxford University Press).
Cooper, D.E. and Palmer, J.A. (eds) (1992), *The Environment in Question* (London: Routledge).
Goethe, J.W. (1971), *Elective Affinities* (trans. R. Hollingdale) (Harmondsworth: Penguin).
Heidegger, M. (1980), *Being and Time* (trans. J. Macquarrie and E. Robinson) (Oxford: Blackwell).
Koc, M. and Dahlberg, K.A. (1999), 'The Restructuring of Food Systems: Trends, Research, and Policy Issues', *Agriculture and Human Values* 16, 109–16.
McMichael, P. (2000), 'The Power of Food', *Agriculture and Human Values* 17, 21–33.
Norberg-Hodge, H. (2005), 'The Case for Local Food', <www.isec.org.uk/articles/case/html>, accessed 30 December 2007.

Pollan, M. (1996), *Second Nature: A Gardener's Education* (London: Bloomsbury).
Powers, C.T. (1997), *In the Memory of the Forest* (London: Anchor).
Pretty, J. (2002), *Agri-Culture: Reconnecting People, Land and Nature* (London: Earthscan).
Raven, H. (1999), 'Food, Farm and Future', in Barnett and Scruton (eds).
Rose, J. (1999), 'An Organic Connection', in Barnett and Scruton (eds).
Visser, M. (1991), *The Rituals of Dinner: The Origins, Evolution, Eccentricities and Meaning of Table Manners* (New York: Grove Weidenfeld).

Chapter 17

Conversion or Co-option? The Implications of 'Mainstreaming' for Producer and Consumer Agency within Fair Trade Networks

Stewart Lockie

In October 2005, Nestlé, the largest of the world's big four coffee multinationals, launched a certified fair trade coffee in the United Kingdom. With net profits in 2005 of approximately US$6.5 billion from the sale of some 8500 product lines (Nestlé 2007), the introduction by Nestlé of a single fair trade product to just one of the countries in which it operates was bound to generate cynicism. By contrast, the involvement in fair trade of Starbucks – the world's largest 'specialty' coffee roaster and retailer – has invited a more mixed response. In the fiscal year 2006, Starbucks purchased some 8 million kilograms of certified fair trade coffee. This represented 14 per cent of global fair trade coffee imports and about 6 per cent of Starbucks' own coffee requirements, making Starbucks the largest importer of fair trade coffee in North America (Starbucks 2007). According to civil society organisations, however, Starbucks' entry into fair trade has been a slow and reluctant response to campaigning and consumer pressure (Renard 2003).

It is not the intention of this chapter to assess in detail the particular claims to corporate social responsibility of Nestlé or Starbucks, but to examine more broadly the implications of market expansion and multinational involvement for our understanding of fair trade production and consumption. The chapter will commence, therefore, with a review of debates concerning the potential social and ethical consequences of the apparent mainstreaming of fair trade food consumption before moving to an examination of what we actually know about those people who have been mobilised as fair trade consumers.

Conversion or Co-option? The Mainstreaming of Alternative Consumption

Rapid growth in demand for, and sales of, certified fair trade products has stimulated considerable debate over whether fair trade commodity chains risk co-option by the mainstream food sector; whether the opportunity for fundamental trade reform is being undermined; or whether, in fact, any form of international trade is likely to offer sustainable livelihoods to the millions of small farmers of the South

(Shreck 2005). Contemporary fair trade organisations and networks, according to Wilkinson (2006), can be categorised into three broad groups:

- Alternative trading networks that link producer groups, traders, dedicated 'world' shops, and consumers. While these networks operate often on the basis of interpersonal interaction and trust rather than on formal product guarantees, it is increasingly common for participating groups to seek certification as Fair Trade Organisations by the International Fair Trade Association (IFAT). By 2007, over 150 organisations were registered through IFAT and licensed to display the FTO Mark as a signifier of their commitment to fair trade (IFAT 2007).
- Fair trade certification and labeling schemes that focus on verification and communication of product attributes. Since 1997, most national certification schemes have been affiliated with the Fairtrade Labelling Organisation International (FLO), which sets standards encouraging long-term contracts, direct trading relationships, advanced credit, guaranteed minimum prices, and price premiums. Compliance with these standards is audited by autonomous third-party inspection and certification bodies while licenses to attach the fair trade logo to certified products are offered to manufacturers, retailers, and others. This enables certified fair trade products to move through mainstream processing and retailing channels dominated by companies that would struggle to meet the standards for Fair Trade Organisations set by IFAT in other aspects of their operations.
- Campaigning and advocacy groups whose focus is not solely on expanding the market for certified fair trade organisations and goods but on promoting more fundamental reform of the rules of international trade in order to make all trade fair and achieve more equitable and sustainable development outcomes.

Has mainstreaming the potential to undermine alternative trading networks and/ or wider projects of trade reform and poverty alleviation? According to a number of commentators, the answer is yes; for while mainstreaming may assist, in the short term, to secure more access to high-value markets for poor Southern producers, it does so by diluting, in a variety of ways, the challenge that fair trade actually poses to dominant patterns of trade and consumption. For the sake of convenience, concerns over mainstreaming will be referred to here as the 'co-option thesis', the core components of which can be summarised to include the commodification and consumption of justice, the logical contradiction of trying to work 'in and against the market', obscuring relations of production, codification and de-radicalisation, exclusion and polarisation, subsumption of control, and erosion of standards.

Commodification and consumption of justice

It is possible to argue that there is something fundamentally wrong with offering up for sale the rights of some – rights such as freedom from poverty and access to education – as items of personal consumption for others. Such an argument may seem particularly apt in the case of fair trade markets dominated by largely unnecessary luxury goods such as coffee, chocolate, and tea (Wilkinson 2006). More pragmatically, it might be argued that justice simply is not something that can effectively and efficiently be bought and sold through existing market mechanisms without: first, creating relationships of dependency between those in need of economic justice and the consumers who may, or may not, dispense it according to their own perceived needs, responsibilities, and capacities (Bryant and Goodman 2004); and, secondly, without allowing those whose labor and produce is not 'in demand' simply to fall through the gaps.

Consumer demand is both fickle and finite. It is likely, if not inevitable, that particular markets for fair trade produce will become saturated as a consequence of rising production and/or falling demand and producers will be forced to sell their goods on the conventional market as coffee producers are already forced to do (Bryant and Goodman 2004; Murray et al. 2005). And they may make other sacrifices. Getz and Shreck (2006), for example, describe how some fair trade banana networks privilege consumer expectations of consistency in supply over the careful implementation of principles such as democratic organisation at the local level.

The contradiction of working 'in and against the market'

According to Renard (2003), it is possible to discern two competing visions of the relationship between fair trade and neoliberalism. The first, and more pragmatic, vision is to use fair trade as a mechanism to insert more products from the South into global markets at a reasonable price. The second, and more radical, vision sees fair trade as a transitional strategy through which to challenge and modify dominant forms of economic organisation. While some authors refer to this later vision as a strategy to work 'in and against the market' others, like Renard (2003), see it as inherently contradictory; raising the possibility that the mainstreaming of fair trade may not only dilute its challenge to neoliberal market fundamentalism, but serve to reinforce it.

By defining poverty as an outcome of market failure – rather than of inequitable access to resources – neoliberalism identifies trade liberalisation as the only sustainable macroeconomic solution and entrepreneurial self-help as the only sustainable microeconomic solution. In what may appear something of a paradox, many proponents of fair trade move from a critique of neoliberalism, associated processes such as globalisation, and institutions such as the World Trade Organisation that promote them, to ostensibly similar solutions. Macroeconomic market reform is advocated to remove 'distortions' such as production subsidies and import tariffs that limit access to high-value Northern markets. And microeconomically, capacity building and standards development is promoted in order to enhance the ability of producers to meet market demands (Wilkinson 2006). Further, as Johnston (2001) argues, despite the benefits of capacity building programs and price premiums for fair trade producers and communities, it remains that case that the lifestyles of fair trade consumers remain hopelessly out of reach to those supplying them with coffee, handicrafts, and other signifiers of an ethical life. Not only, in this respect, can fair trade be seen to accept a degree of inequality, but by allowing the wealthy citizens of the North to buy a clear conscience through their purchase of fair trade goods it can also be seen to absolve them of responsibility to participate in campaigns for more far-reaching political and economic change (Renard 2003). This consistency between neoliberal and fair trade prescriptions for self-help and entrepreneurialism suggests that fair trade is more likely to support limited reform of dominant economic forms than it is their transformation.

Obscuring relations of production

Foods often are packaged and labeled with a range of images and pieces of information associated with spaces of production and consumption. However, as Cook and Crang (1996) point out, such imagery and information may relate to the agro-ecology and social conditions under which those foods actually have been produced, but equally it may relate to a whole set of other meanings evoked by food consumption that have little connection with the realities of production. This can be illustrated through comparison of the actual social conditions facing coffee farmers since the onset of the 'coffee crisis' (Bacon 2005) and the romanticised images of a sophisticated European café society and an exotic smiling peasantry that are made available for consumption by Northern coffee buyers (Smith 1996).

Fair trade claims to challenge this trend by focusing the attention of consumers on the impacts of their choices on the livelihoods and well-being of Southern producers. But does this result in a genuine demystification of fair trade production and exchange? There are at least two important ways in which critics assert it does not. First, any demystification is, at best, partial, as most aspects of the trading networks that supply fair trade products remain unexamined. Packaging and/or advertising for many fair trade products contains no more information than a certification logo and a generic statement of its meaning. Where more information is provided, it tends to follow a familiar narrative structure in which basic background details on the farmer or producer cooperative's location and ethnic identity are followed by a brief good-news story on the benefits they derive from fair trade (Lyon 2006; Wright 2004). More detailed information on political campaigns and the causes of global inequality are available for the consumer who wishes to go digging through fair trade organisation websites and newsletters, but the over-riding message attached directly to fair trade products is a one-dimensional and unchallenging representation of distant small farmers who benefit from the consumption of those products (Johnston 2001). Entirely unexamined are questions such as the differential between premiums paid to fair trade producers and the prices charged to consumers (Moberg 2005); the profit margins of distributors and retailers dealing in fair trade products; the success, or otherwise, of attempts to reduce the costs to farmers of dealing with transport operators and other supply chain intermediaries; the fate of farmers who are not able to comply with fair trade standards; and so on.

This brings us to the second way in which it is alleged that fair trade fails to demystify production and exchange; namely, the targeting of fair trade information and imagery towards the putative fair trade consumer. Not only is little information available to fair trade farmers on the consumers of their produce (Wright 2004), some case studies have found that few participating farmers have even a rudimentary knowledge of what fair trade is (Getz and Shreck 2006; Murray et al. 2005;

Shreck 2005). Rather than a genuine partnership for development or act of solidarity between Northern consumers and Southern producers, fair trade organisations commodify and sell opportunities for privileged Northerners to engage in consumption that they regard as at once ethical and pleasurable (Lyon 2006). For critics of mainstreaming, the point is not that fair trade has not benefited many Southern producers, but that it is misleading to argue that such benefits have been achieved by demystifying commodity exchange.

Codification and de-radicalisation

Entry of fair trade products into mainstream distribution and retail channels has been enabled by the development of clearly documented and verifiable standards. In contrast with the more informal and subjective processes possible within alternative trading networks small enough to allow direct interpersonal relationship building and trust, product-based certification requires compliance with the rules, norms and expectations associated with conventional quality assurance regimes. There are two main issues related to the codification of fair trade values in this manner. The first relates to the complexity of the social and agro-ecological issues implicated in the notion of fair trade and the impossibility of codifying these into one universally applicable set of standards (Lockie and Goodman 2006). The FLO has demonstrated an awareness of this issue through the development of differentiated standards for major varieties and regions of origin for coffee (Lockie and Goodman 2006) and of variation in the environmental standards applied to banana production (Moberg 2005) in order to reflect better the social and ecological characteristics of particular production environments.

The second issue related to the codification of fair trade values is the need for that codification to comply with rules for standards setting, auditing, and certification established by transnational bodies into which the fair trade movement has no avenue for involvement or influence and which exist principally to support market liberalisation. Certification practices have been 'profoundly restructured' since the late 1990s as a consequence of harmonisation with transnational standards established by the International Organisation for Standardisation (ISO) and World Trade Organisation (Mutersbaugh 2005, 397), specifically in relation to the use of independent third-party auditors. Networks once based on common values and self-regulation are replaced with networks based on contractual relationships governed by centrally imposed standards and specialised bureaucracies (Renard 2005).

Exclusion and polarisation

The logical corollary of auditing and certification being used to govern market access is that standards act as a barrier to entry to anybody who cannot *demonstrate* compliance with them (Guthman 2004). As we have seen, considerable debate within the fair trade movement has focused on whether standards need to be modified in order deliberately to exclude multinational food processors and retailers who are not widely perceived to operate, in the main, according to the principles of fair trade. An equally important debate has focused on what some see as the unintended potential of certified product standards to exclude large numbers of particularly marginal farmers who cannot afford the expense of auditing and certification (Lockie and Goodman 2006; Renard 2005), meet required production standards (Getz and Shreck 2006; Moberg 2005; Murray et al. 2005; Renard 2005; Shreck 2005), or otherwise establish themselves as members of fair trade networks. Particular concerns, for example, have been raised about the extent to which fair trade cooperatives have challenged traditional patterns of gender inequality and facilitated women's access to fair trade opportunities (Murray et al. 2005).

While the cost of farm auditing and certification was initially supported through the licensing fees paid by processors and retailers wishing to market fair trade products, growth in producer numbers, combined with the need to comply with ISO standards for auditing and certification, has seen these costs redirected to the cooperatives through which farmers are organised (Lockie and Goodman 2006; Renard 2005). Prior to certification, cooperatives are also required to provide evidence of a market or buyer for their produce (Lockie and Goodman 2006), a significant challenge given the generalised conditions of oversupply in the fair trade market. Obviously enough, this creates pressures to be particularly diligent about meeting market expectations and a number of researchers have detailed cases of farmers thus excluded from fair trade certification because they were unable to adopt required environmental or quality management practices. Lockie and Goodman (2006) conclude that even though FLO continues to work with donors and development organisations to support less well resourced producer organisations, the harmonisation of certification requirements with ISO standards and the increasing movement of fair trade products through mainstream retail channels have created conditions that are far more favorable to larger and more well-established cooperatives with established reputations for quality, professionalism, and adaptability.

Subsumption of control

A basic feature of production standards is the imposition of constraints on the ability of producers to implement whichever production, labor or environmental practices they might choose in response to personal goals, local knowledge, farm agro-ecologies, family needs, cultural obligations, and so on. A number of commentators have pointed to the origin of most fair trade standards in the North and the lack of genuine opportunity for the vast majority of farmers to participate in standards setting or evaluation (Lyon 2006; Shreck 2005). While it might be argued that fair trade standards have been established with the 'best of intentions' and that the membership of IFAT and FLO is gradually coming to be dominated by Southern organisations (Wilkinson 2006), it has also been argued that the need to comply with ISO procedures has eroded opportunities to democratise both the setting of standards and their interpretation and implementation at the village and field level (Mutersbaugh 2002; 2004). Even where fair trade standards do not directly impose major changes in farm management they do impose a range of organisational and administrative requirements in order to validate compliance. Further, as we have seen, access to fair trade markets is often dependent on the ability of farmers to meet additional requirements related to product quality; requirements that very likely do entail more profound changes in farm management practice.

Erosion of standards

Despite its ostensive challenge to mainstream trading relationships, fair trade is attractive to mainstream food processors and retailers for a number of reasons. First, it represents a rapidly growing niche within food markets that are generally characterised by static demand (Renard 2005). Secondly, it is consistent with the increasingly widespread response to static demand of seeking ways to compete on quality as opposed to competing on price (Renard 2005). Thirdly, it is consistent with growing interest in finding ways to demonstrate corporate social responsibility and thus to avoid public criticisms and potential liabilities (Hughes 2001). The fear is, of course, that the more fair trade networks engage with mainstream food businesses the more pressure will be created to water down those aspects of fair trade standards that are seen as unfavorable to mainstream businesses (Getz and Shreck 2006). A number of large coffee producers and importers, for example, including Starbucks, have lobbied for changes to fair trade standards to permit plantation-grown coffee (Murray et al. 2006; Renard 2005). Proponents argue that there are many more poor farm workers who could benefit from fair trade than there are small farmers; that plantation production is permitted for cocoa and tea; and that such a change would make fair trade coffee more attractive to large coffee roasters (Murray et al. 2006). In fact, some large roasters have indicated their willingness to make fair trade a centerpiece of their product lines, provided that certification is extended to the plantations that already dominate their supply chains. With small fair trade farmers struggling to sell more than 20 per cent, on average, of their coffee on fair trade markets, this is clearly a proposal more related to economies of scale than an expression of corporate social responsibility. The fear that is raised, not surprisingly, is that such a shift would see small farmers squeezed from the fair trade market (Murray et al. 2006) by plantations that are already well-placed to attract premium prices and which ought anyway to ensure reasonable pay and working conditions for their employees.

Standards may also be eroded less directly. In addition to the use of small volumes of fair trade to clean up corporate images while doing little to help the majority of suppliers (Raynolds 2002), large food processors and retailers have developed a range of competing standards and labeling schemes that are difficult for the majority of consumers to distinguish from FLO and IFAT standards (Mutersbaugh 2005; Renard 2005). Concerns about 'greenwashing' and 'image laundering' notwithstanding, the key difference between ethical trade – as such schemes are known – and fair trade is that the emphasis is shifted away from the development aspirations of fair trade and toward a conception of social responsibility based on the avoidance of illegal labor practices and other human rights abuses (Hughes 2001). The Utz Kapeh Foundation, for example, certifies coffee as socially 'responsible' against audited compliance to national labor laws, International Labor Organisation conventions, occupational safety, and access to housing, education for children, healthcare, and clean drinking water. There is no minimum price or guaranteed premium. Utz Kapeh argues that certification adds value that is explicitly determined through negotiation between the buyer and the seller (Utz Kapeh 2007). As Renard (2005) points out, some South and Central American growers' cooperatives supplying Utz Certified coffee have received half the fair trade price and barely more than the world price. Yet with large volumes of fair trade coffee failing to find a market, farmers' cooperatives are forced to look at alternatives such as Utz Kapeh and a growing range of retailer and roaster 'own-brand' quality and labeling schemes.

Limits to the Co-option Thesis

The co-option thesis is open to a number of criticisms. Proponents of ethical trade (as contrasted with fair trade), for example, argue that the imposition of minimum prices and price premiums distorts the coffee market by encouraging growers to plant more coffee at the very time that over-production is forcing down the world price and throwing small growers into poverty (see Moore 2004). Market logic suggests that these growers would be better off, in the longer term, by abandoning coffee and reinvesting their resources in more profitable enterprises.

However, there are a number of problems with this argument. First, it fails to acknowledge the extent to which buyer oligopolies lead to their own distortions in the world coffee price. Secondly, it ignores the limited opportunities that many small farmers have for diversification. Alternative crops must be suited to the agro-ecologies and human resource bases of existing small coffee farms; they must be non-perishable enough to market without access to refrigerated storage and transport; and they must themselves be in demand. Thirdly, the over-production argument ignores the extent to which the global coffee market is increasingly differentiated into a large number of specialty coffees, each with their own quality, flavor, ethical, and symbolic characteristics (Bacon 2006; Giovannucci 2001; Renard 1999). When all of these factors are taken into consideration it becomes possible to argue that instead of distorting market signals, fair trade conveys them with far greater clarity and evenhandedness than do the major alternatives (Lyon 2006). As such, those aspects of the co-option thesis related to image laundering and the erosion of standards remain legitimate concerns due to their potential to suppress market growth by stimulating consumer cynicism and/or deflecting consumer demand toward 'ethically traded' goods that provide producers with lower returns.

The more pressing criticism of the co-option thesis is that it potentially overstates the extent to which mainstreaming of distribution and retail channels actually undermines fair trade standards and, most importantly, benefits for small producers. Such a view pre-empts the need to extend the monitoring of fair trade impacts in order to inform such debates better (see Raynolds et al. 2004). It discounts the potential for even small gains in producer incomes to reduce short- and long-term threats to producers' livelihoods by helping to keep children in school, access healthcare, and so on (Bacon 2006). And it ignores the potential for fair trade products – even fair trade products accompanied by highly simplified images and information – to contribute to the development of moral economies based on what Goodman (2004) refers to as consumers' 'spatial dynamic of concern'. The issue that will be dealt with here, however, is the relative neglect within the co-option thesis of the potential for producer and consumer agency to continue shaping fair trade outcomes despite the mainstreaming of distribution and retailing.

Producer and Consumer Agency Within Fair Trade Networks

Case studies of fair trade impacts within production communities highlight the fact that, in addition to monetary and social impacts, those communities benefit in a number of ways that may be seen to enhance their influence within trading networks.

- Fair trade facilitates the organisation of producers into cooperatives and marketing associations that increase their collective economies of scale, knowledge bases, and bargaining powers (Bacon 2004).
- In so doing, fair trade reduces the number of market intermediaries with whom producers must deal in order to sell their produce (Hudson and Hudson 2003; Murray et al. 2005) and has potential both to reduce transaction costs and to improve the communication of market requirements.
- While low demand plays a major role in forcing the sale of around 80 per cent of potentially fair trade-certified coffee on the conventional market, so too do high quality requirements within the specialty coffee market in which fair trade coffee competes (Bacon 2004). Those grower organisations that have been able to use fair trade premiums to support improvements in product quality have found this to improve market acceptance and to consolidate relationships with coffee buyers (Renard 2005; see also Lyon 2006). In the absence of fair trade, it is likely that such 'preferred supplier' status would remain available only to plantations and other large growers.
- By enhancing environmental sustainability and occupational health and safety (Hudson and Hudson 2003) – both of which embody their own intrinsic value – fair trade helps producers to stabilise and improve production, to improve tangible aspects of product quality such as taste, and to highlight intangible aspects of product quality such as claims to environmental responsibility.

Notably, each of these points relates to the capacity of fair trade producers to position themselves more favorably within mainstream commodity trading networks. None of them relate to the sorts of direct and transparent relationships with consumers that are implied by notions of solidarity. This is not to say that such relationships do not exist in some alternative trading networks. It is fair to say, however, that there is very little evidence with which to challenge the argument made above that mainstreaming the distribution and retailing of fair trade products leads to an emphasis on the marketing of lifestyle choices about which Northern consumers may feel good rather than on the provision of comprehensive information about production conditions or on opportunities for direct interaction.

In contrast with other varieties of ethical consumption, relatively little is known about the consumers of fair trade products. In a Canadian study, Arnot et al. (2005) found that consumers were less price sensitive when presented with choices regarding fair trade coffee than they were when presented with other choices. Yet, in the Belgian study by De Pelsmacker et al. (2005), it appeared that price premiums for fair trade coffee (27 per cent) were higher than the majority of people otherwise interested in purchasing them were willing to pay (10 per cent). Those who did buy fair trade coffee despite the premium were not sociodemographically different to those who did not. Although these few studies do not, by themselves, move us a great deal closer to understanding whether consumer agency is likely to be a force either for or against the co-option of fair trade, it is interesting to note their consistency with research on the consumption of certified organic foods. Organic consumer research has consistently pointed toward a profile of the 'organic consumer' who, while more likely to be female than male, might come from any social class and whose consumption behaviors are influenced by a complex mix of ethical and personal motivations combined with the material opportunities for consumption afforded by market organisation and retailing practices (see Lockie et al. 2006). According to Lockie et al. (2006), the growth of organic food sales in mainstream retail channels has tended to stimulate demand and expand the organic market rather than to parasitise other outlets. For while the values that underpin organic food production (environmental protection, animal welfare, consumer safety, and so on) are not controversial, only a small number of particularly dedicated ethical consumers will actively seek out certified organic foods. With so much food purchasing influenced by habit and convenience, the visibility and availability of organic foods have been critical to expansion in sales. Further, there is some evidence that the availability of organic foods in mainstream retail outlets might play an educative role that ultimately leads more people to participate in alternative distribution and retailing networks such as farmers' markets (Lockie et al. 2006). Noting that the mainstreaming of fair trade distribution and retailing has been accompanied by a professionalisation and revitalisation of alternative trading networks, along with a dramatic rise in voluntary activism on fair trade issues, Wilkinson (2006) argues that a similar 'virtuous dynamic' may be at work in the fair trade sector.

As Holzer (2006) points out, consumer choices do little, by themselves, to challenge the ability of large retailers to control the flow of goods, since the refusal of individuals to buy a particular product does not necessarily result in the supply of a more desirable alternative. Translating the monetary resources of consumers into genuine influence depends on the involvement of organisations capable of articulating a problem, identifying its causes, suggesting solutions, and issuing calls to action that are meaningful to both consumers and retailers (Holzer 2006). In the organic sector, private certification bodies, consumer cooperatives, local food coalitions, environmental NGOs and others have thus played a significant role in the articulation and mobilisation of 'consumer demand' by organising the organic market and providing the mechanisms through which people could use consumption choices to signal support for the political project of organic agriculture (see Barnett et al. 2005). There is a clear parallel here with the articulation and mobilisation of 'consumer demand' for fair trade by civil society organisations responsible for the establishment of alternative trading networks and certification schemes.

Conclusion

It is widely accepted both that the integration of fair trade products within mainstream trading networks has facilitated the expansion of fair trade sales and that the livelihoods of many Southern producers have improved as a result. The 'co-option thesis', as it has been outlined here, does not contest the benefits that have been associated with fair trade or with the use of product-based certification to secure a wider distribution and retail platform. Instead, the co-option thesis questions whether mainstreaming might serve, ultimately, to undermine the transformative potential of fair trade by legitimating the activities of multinational food companies and by blunting political opposition to these activities in the North. Catering to the consumption cultures of the global middle and upper classes, it argues, provides a shaky foundation for just and sustainable livelihoods. On that basis, the co-option thesis certainly deserves to be taken seriously. But is it inevitable? For those who see the fair trade vision of working 'in and against the market' as inherently contradictory, the only logical answer is yes. Some producers may continue to benefit from fair trade but – in markets dominated by buyer oligopolies, economies of scale, and strict quality requirements – these producers simply will become one more elite group from which most small Southern farmers are excluded.

However, as powerful as this argument is, the potential for co-option remains dependent on a number of factors and not solely on the opportunities afforded to multinational firms by product-based certification. Of particular relevance here are those factors that, in some way or other, enhance the agency of putative fair trade producers and consumers. Perhaps most obvious among these are the alternative trading networks that continue to bypass mainstream distribution channels and which continue to provide the fair trade movement with much of its social and political vitality by engaging people not solely as consumers but as volunteers, campaign activists, educators, and so on (Wilkinson 2006). Less obvious, but no less important, are the opportunities that are afforded to enhance producer and consumer agency through product-based certification and the mainstreaming of distribution and retailing. As argued above, mainstreaming has been as much a response to pressure from consumers and advocacy groups as it has an attempt to engage in niche marketing and corporate image building. In this respect, the activities of advocacy groups have been critical in articulating and communicating to potential consumers and retailers of fair trade products the problem (unfair trade) to which they are a solution. Further, it is likely that the emergence of a greater variety of retail channels has been critical in attracting and educating a larger number of potential fair trade consumers. While it may be argued that alternative trading networks better embody the values of fair trade, the familiarity and convenience of mainstream retail channels are no doubt critical in reaching that majority of Northern consumers who are unlikely to break established shopping habits easily. The challenge is to take advantage of the opportunities multiple channels provide to enroll more people as fair trade consumers and to shift not only their ideas about food quality, but their ideas about what is familiar, what is convenient and, ultimately, for whom they are responsible when making consumption choices.

References

Arnot, C., Boxall, P. and Cash, S. (2005), 'Do Ethical Consumers Care About Price? A Revealed Preference Analysis of Fair Trade Coffee Purchases', *Canadian Journal of Agricultural Economics* 54, 555–65.

Bacon, C. (2005), 'Confronting the Coffee Crisis: Can Fair Trade, Organic, and Specialty Coffees Reduce Small–Scale Farmer Vulnerability in Northern Nicaragua?', *World Development* 33, 497–511.

Barnett, C., Clarke, N. and Cloke, P. (2005), 'The Political Ethics of Consumerism', *Consumer Policy Review* 15:2, 45–51.

Bryant, R. and Goodman, M. (2004), 'Consuming Narratives: The Political Ecology of "Alternative" Consumption', *Transactions of the British Institute of Geographers* 29, 344–66.

Cook, I. and Crang, P. (1996), 'The World on a Plate: Culinary Culture and Geographical Knowledges', *Journal of Material Culture* 1:2, 131–53.

De Pelsmacker, P., Driesen, L. and Rayp, G. (2005), 'Do Consumers Care About Ethics? Willingness to Pay for Fair Trade Coffee', *Journal of Consumer Affairs* 39:2, 363–85.

Getz, C. and Shreck, A. (2006), 'What Organic and Fair Trade Labels Do Not Tell Us: Towards a Place-Based Understanding of Certification', *International Journal of Consumer Studies* 30:5, 490–501.

Giovannucci, D. (2001), *Sustainable Coffee Survey of the North American Specialty Coffee Industry* (Philadelphia: Summit Foundation).

Goodman, M. (2004), 'Reading Fair Trade: Political Ecological Imaginary and the Moral Economy of Fair Trade Foods', *Political Geography* 23, 891–915.

Guthman, J. (2004), Back to the Land: The Paradox of Organic Food Standards', *Environment and Planning A* 36, 511–28.

Holzer, B. (2006), 'Political Consumerism Between Individual Choice and Collective Action: Social Movements, Role Mobilization and Signalling', *International Journal of Consumer Studies* 30:5, 405–15.

Hudson, I. and Hudson, M. (2003), 'How Alternative is Alternative Trade? Alternative Trade Coffee in the Chiapas Region of Mexico', unpublished working paper.

Hughes, A. (2001), 'Global Commodity Networks, Ethical Trade and Governmentality: Organizing Business Responsibility in the Kenyan Cut Flower Industry', *Transactions of the Institute of British Geographers* 26, 390–406.

International Fair Trade Association (IFAT) (2007), 'Monitoring: Building trust in Fair Trade', updated 30 May 2007 <www.ifat.org/index.php?option=com_content&task=view&id=21&Itemid=68>, accessed 4 June 2007.

Johnston, J. (2001), 'Consuming Social Justice: Shopping for Fair Trade Chic', *Arena Magazine* February/March, 42–7.

Lockie, S. and Goodman, M. (2006) 'Neoliberalism, Standardisation and the Problem of Space: Competing Rationalities of Governance in Fair Trade and Mainstream Agri-Environmental Networks', in Marsden and Murdoch (eds).

Lockie, S., Lyons, K., Lawrence, G. and Halpin, D. (2006) *Going Organic: Mobilizing Networks for Environmentally Responsible Food Production* (Wallingford: CABI Publishing).

Lyon, S. (2006), 'Evaluating Fair Trade Consumption: Politics, Defetishization and Producer Participation', *International Journal of Consumer Studies* 30:5, 452–64.

Marsden, T. and Murdoch, J. (eds) (2006), *Between the Local and the Global: Confronting Complexity in the Contemporary Agri-Food Sector* (Oxford: Elsevier).

Moberg, M. (2005), 'Fair Trade and Eastern Caribbean Banana Farmers: Rhetoric and Reality in the Anti–Globalization Movement', *Human Organization* 64, 4–15.

Moore, G. (2004), 'The Fair Trade Movement: Parameters, Issues and Future Research', *Journal of Business Ethics* 53, 73–86.

Murray, D., Raynolds, L. and Taylor, P. (2006), 'The Future of Fair Trade Coffee: Dilemmas Facing Latin America's Small-Scale Producers', *Development in Practice* 16:2, 179–92.

Mutersbaugh, T. (2002), 'The Number is the Beast: A Political Economy of Organic–Coffee Certification and Producer Unionism', *Environment and Planning A* 34, 1165–184.

Mutersbaugh, T. (2004), 'Serve and Certify: Paradoxes of Service Work in Organic Coffee Certification', *Environment and Planning D* 22, 533–52.

Mutersbaugh, T. (2005), 'Just-in-Space: Certified Rural Products, Labor of Quality, and Regulatory Spaces', *Journal of Rural Studies* 21, 389–402.

Nestlé (2007), 'Group Figures: 2006–2005 Totals', <www.Nestlé.com/Investor Relations/FinancialOverview/GroupFigures/2005_2004Totals.htm>, accessed 26 April 2007.

Raynolds, L. (2002), 'Consumer/Producer Links in Fair Trade Coffee Networks', *Sociologia Ruralis*, 42, 404–24.

Raynolds, L., Murray, D. and Taylor, P. (2004), 'Fair Trade Coffee: Building Producer Capacity Via Global Networks', *Journal of International Development* 16, 1109–21.

Renard, M.–C. (1999), 'The Interstices of Globalization: The Example of Fair Coffee', *Sociologia Ruralis* 39:4, 484–99.

Renard, M.-C. (2003), 'Fair Trade: Quality, Market, and Conventions', *Journal of Rural Studies* 19, 87–96.

Renard, M.-C. (2005), 'Quality Certification, Regulation and Power in Fair Trade', *Journal of Rural Studies* 21, 419–31.

Shreck, A. (2005), 'Resistance, Redistribution, and Power in the Fair Trade Banana Initiative', *Agriculture and Human Values* 22, 17–29.

Smith, M. (1996), 'The Empire Filters Back: Consumption, Production, and the Politics of Starbucks Coffee', *Urban Geography* 17, 502–24.

Starbucks (2007), 'Starbucks Corporation Corporate Social Responsibility/Fiscal 2006 Annual Report', <www.starbucks.com>, accessed 26 April 2007.

Utz Kapeh (2007), 'Price Policy', <www.utzcertified.org/index.php?pageID=162>, accessed 14 May 2007.

Wilkinson, J. (2006), *Fair Trade Moves Centre Stage*, Working Paper 3 (Rio de Janeiro: Edelstein Centre for Social Research).

Wright, C. (2004), 'Consuming Lives, Consuming Landscapes: Interpreting Advertisements for Cafédirect Coffees', *Journal of International Development* 16, 665–80.

Chapter 18

Towards a New Agenda

Cathy Rozel Farnworth, Emyr Vaughan Thomas and Janice Jiggins

The first section of this final chapter seeks to unearth the tensions and dilemmas implicit in the issues explored by the authors. The second section provides suggestions for principles that might be useful to guide action in the future.

Tensions and Dilemmas

The tensions and dilemmas recognised in the contributions to this book relate to the ethics of mainstreaming, to 'literacy' about food, to food and livelihoods, and to the rules of engagement and other drivers of innovation. These are explored in turn.

The ethics of mainstreaming

In the body of this book we have seen how ethical goods are goods deriving from systems of production that connect to ethical and not purely commercial considerations. Sometimes the actors in these chains of interaction have themselves a deep attachment to a set of ethical ideals that inspire them to adopt a particular production or trading system. Organic farmers are an example. Sometimes the ethical dimension derives from what others believe it is important to create and support. An example here is that of Northerners who believe it is important and right to support fair trade products because these aim to help ensure a livelihood to small producers in less economically prosperous countries.

Mainstreaming is the attempt to import the ethics that currently relate to ethical goods into the governance of the main systems of production, distribution and consumption that bring food to the majority of people. Cumulatively the readings in this book suggest that there are a number of tensions and dilemmas inherent in the idea of mainstreaming ethical goods.

There is an apparent tension between developing brands that simultaneously deliver a satisfying experience to the consumer and also educate and transform the consumer's choice, inspiring him or her to grasp new horizons. Can there really be complementarity between feeding existing consumer preferences and developing informed preferences? Does mainstreaming genuinely offer the prospect of transforming the thinking of the majority of people in Northern societies? Can the mainstreaming of ethical produce serve to shift not only consumer ideas about food quality but also their ideas about what is familiar, what is convenient and, ultimately, for whom they are responsible when making consumption choices?

An interrelated tension concerns the role of supermarkets, the most powerful retail model of our age, in all this. Are they curse, a source of salvation or some complex amalgam of these extremes?

There is also a dilemma associated with the implicit assumption that our beliefs about the situations of others are an acceptable basis for mainstreaming. To what extent and in what ways can the values of 'the other' be encompassed by Northern consumers? Farnworth's chapter inspires awareness of the tension between embracing the horizons of others and letting go of our own.

Farnworth, Guijt and van Walsum, and Lockie question whether the complex social and agro-ecological issues implicated in the notion of fair trade actually can be codified into a universally applicable set of standards. Can Organic and Fair Trade certification schemes really cope as they expand their business or are they getting too big to provide effective oversight? How can they retain the interpersonal interactions that characterised their early years of growth so that communication flows, feedback loops and dialogues enable learning to be sustained?

A separate issue concerns how far mainstreaming strategies result in a devaluation of ethical principles as these become harnessed to achieving predominantly commercial goals in an unreformed marketplace? Do they not, in turn, serve to entrench the portrayal of poverty as solely an outcome of market failure and never one of inequitable access to resources and power to affect the rules of the game? Can transactions in the unreformed marketplace become more than a one-dimensional and unchallenging representation of unequal trading relationships? Whether at the level of regional or global trade negotiations or at the level of supermarkets' supplier contracts, fundamental issues of justice are glossed over, including the differential between premiums paid to Fair Trade producers and the prices charged to consumers, the profit margins of distributors and retailers and the fate of farmers who are not able to comply with Fair Trade standards

A further dilemma concerns whether the costs of the social innovations involved in mainstreaming fair trade can be shared more evenly and not made to fall on the very poorest. Who should work towards the organisational strengthening that is the bedrock of empowering producers? How can responsibility for unexpected and adverse effects for some specific groups of people that may arise from the construction of new value chains be shared more equitably? Can these be formalised on the basis of a social precautionary principle?

A separate quandary concerns the values and approaches that should inform the process involved in the configuration of organisations that is needed to create a viable fair chain. Who should deal with the assumptions and capacities that they bring into the system?

There is a further question concerning whether and, if so, how far there is an ethical difference between mainstreaming to further economic cohesion objectives within Northern countries (for example, in Cornwall and in Prince Edward Island) and mainstreaming of fair trade produce emanating from less developed countries in the South.

These last dilemmas raise a new question: just what should mainstreaming be aiming to sustain? Should it be specific enterprises, the chain itself, or the very concept of fair, ethically clean trade as a market norm? Is it possible to support all these three dimensions simultaneously? Or is mainstreaming necessarily a transient and contingent project? Perhaps the values that are mainstreamed are not static and unchanging. Perhaps they derive from a context that is itself liable to transformation and change? As Chiffoleau and colleagues remind us in their chapter, 'the practice of ethical principles is not a universal given, but a contingent co-building product, anchored in a social context, in meso-structures such as firms and territories and in interpersonal relations'.

Food literacy

The authors share a general belief that diet matters for environmental sustainability because diet affects the extent and nature of resource use and effects environments and societies. They also share the standpoint that Northern consumers are detached from the processes involved in the production of food and often have little understanding of the origin of the food that they purchase. However, there are differences among the authors over the extent to which food literacy is seen as attainable, the methods that could effectively bring this about and even about its very nature.

One tension concerns whether food literacy is something accessible to the consumer. Duxbury reminds us that most consumers buy on price. Food shopping is considered by most people to be no different to the purchase of any other disposable commodity. In the United Kingdom up to a third of the food purchased is wasted. This suggests that the consumerist standpoint can be resistant to efforts to instil 'food literacy'. However, Duxbury also highlights how the mainstreaming of organic and fair trade produce by supermarkets have inspired many more consumers to experience Organic and Fair Trade produce than might otherwise have done. Lockie likewise anticipates that those exposed to mainstreamed fair trade goods will come to shift their ideas about food quality and come to a greater recognition of the responsibility that arises in making consumption choices.

A further tension concerns designing 'tools' to inform citizens about the origin of their food. Johansson explains how the concept of foodprint analysis aims to tackle the question: where is our food coming from and how is it getting to us? Footprinting is a way to translate the human activities associated with food production into their environmental impact, expressed in terms of the area required to support these activities. Other tools discussed by Farnworth and by Reed and colleagues go beyond the issue of resources used in production to raise issues about the nature of 'food literacy' itself.

What is food literacy supposed to be? What sort of 'origins' should we seek to unearth and convey? For some contributors, food literacy is not just about the physical origin of food but also about the social context and quality of life aspirations of those who produce it. If consumers have not grasped this then they will not have achieved food literacy. For Cooper, food literacy is not a matter of factual knowledge about the origin of food. Food literacy involves an enmeshment of one's life with the process of growth. This instils a deep sense of significance in 'things', a sense that has been largely lost in the modern world. Thus the modern citizen needs reconnecting with the environment as a field of significance.

Another dilemma concerns whether involvement in organic food chains, as a consumer, trader or producer, is an unambiguously genuine expression of food literacy. Many take this for granted. However, Reed, Butler and Lobley suggest that the form of production, whether organic or non-organic, does not necessarily change producer–consumer relations. Some forms of organic chain relations, for example in the dairy sectors, are not all that different from non-organic relations in that marketing and distribution involves the formation of direct relations to large, centralised processors. Such chains are not readily conducive to educating the consumer.

A further difference relates to whether food literacy is to be fostered best by appeal to 'intellect', such as through the use of educative tools of certification to designate organic or fair trade standards. Or is food literacy something that can come about only through action and immersion in a changing social context where new values come to life? For Cooper, food literacy is not ultimately something that can logically be brought about by tools and techniques that seek to highlight food origin or public awareness schemes aimed at educating the public about how their food gets to the table. For him, a person's life has to 'connect' with nature and with other human beings involved in pursuits that connect. Similarly, Schäfer highlights the importance of the way that organic entrepreneurs spread information and share experiences regarding environmentally sound agriculture, for example, through informal chatting while selling products in their own stores or at open-air markets. They also offer 'hands-on' experiences to (potential) customers through product tasting or bringing customers into contact with animals and plants on the farms.

Food and livelihoods

The authors also reveal tensions and dilemmas in the nature of how economic sustainability is conceived or operationalised.

One issue concerns the steps available in Northern countries to reinvigorate local economies through the provision of ethically produced food products. For some, such as Wilson, the solution involves carefully planned attempts to achieve competitive advantage from the 'brand' that capitalises on the identity of a particular locality, such as Prince Edward Island. Chiffoleau and colleagues see this in a similar light as competing in a modern market through creating an identity that can appeal to ethics-oriented consumers. In contrast, for Heath and Pearson, the preferred route is to orchestrate the public purchasing capacity of a region to target the food produce of that region at the expense of products from elsewhere. Though these strategies are not necessarily incompatible at present, new tensions could arise if the scale of action in support of regional or local purchasing grew substantially. The notion of concerted planning of a market of local scale will inevitably give rise to dilemmas over what sort of interventions are acceptable and how to avoid compromising the notion of a free market. And what happens if we find that an adjacent region has better environmental or job-creation credentials for its production methods? In which circumstance should we switch our purchasing allegiance? What principles should guide us in making trade-offs between competing ideals? Other contributors suggest a third strategy for supporting livelihoods, namely by fostering more cohesive social and commercial networks within localities. Schäfer and also Reed and his colleagues include a discussion of the potential for organic farming to contribute to these goals.

Another question concerns how far globalisation presents a threat to local or regional economies. For several authors, globalisation offers opportunities for poor producers to reach distant consumers. For others, for example Johansson, the food industry and global markets have diluted the role of local institutions and undercut the value of local knowledge. This raises the question of how far the institutions that were important to past economic and social viability of particular places should be reinvigorated by public policy in order to support local livelihoods in the future. How far might policy makers draw on the values of the past to move into the future, or is the past useful only to provide brand differentiation to the products we now produce? For some, market viability is the only test. For others, the values of the past need to be considered. Reed, Butler and Lobley highlight how a new breed of organic producers, often originating from outside a particular locality, develop innovative links to consumers and pose a challenge to the indigenous 'family farm' in parts of the United Kingdom. Should policy seek some corrective intervention here? Similarly, Chiffoleau, Dreyfus and Touzard draw attention to how the changing context of wine cooperatives, established a century ago to embed socialist principles and ethics in the everyday life of their members, raises the question of what such an ethical project means today.

An additional dilemma concerns whether livelihoods are to be enhanced by purely economic interventions or whether they require attention to a broader set of considerations that relate to the 'structures' that pertain to a particular social context. All too often an appreciation of the social basis of an economy is forgotten. Schäfer helpfully focuses attention on understanding that a combination of market and non-market motives and activities is necessary to achieve sustainable economic activity. The contribution made towards the stabilisation of social structures by becoming engaged in local or regional organisations is one key dimension that she highlights as important. Ballet, Dubois and Mahieu see the emergence of value chains as important in generating growth, employment and added value that can be assigned to all the players involved in the chain. However, they are careful to note the negative consequences that result from focusing solely on the economic dimension. Reed, Butler and Lobley suggest that the structure and directness of the links between producer and consumer may also be a significant issue affecting the propensity of a farming operation to provide a livelihood.

In the context of economically less prosperous countries, the dilemma arises of whether women's involvement in Fair Trade automatically involves a strengthening of their position. Or is involvement in formal labour merely a passive choice, not necessarily providing women a voice in making decisions? If so, how could a more active role be secured? What must be done to secure substantive gender equality?

Rules and other drivers of innovation

Berdegué and Reardon and Waples highlight the drama of market-led changes in the rules of the trading game and in the institutional relations among regulators, supermarkets and suppliers. Their evidence, together with the analysis by Thomas, confronts the role of policy as a driver of innovation. In these changing conditions, are supermarkets necessarily exploitative and damaging to the ideal of ethically produced food, or can they potentially nurture innovation? For some contributors, supermarkets represent an unstoppable, profit-oriented business model that is irreconcilable with ethical production. However, for others they are potentially invaluable in bringing innovation to a wider range of people than would otherwise be possible. If that is so, how can supermarkets become motivated to act in this spirit? Supermarkets do respond to consumer demand, suggesting a role for consumer education. They also often proactively assess future scenarios and seek to take a lead in inspiring consumption changes. They can muster vast resources capable of effecting large-scale change and some are already planning for more localised food sourcing in the face of the changes in oil pricing and availability. Supermarkets already have played an important role in introducing many to Organic and Fair Trade produce and enriching food cultures. Can supermarkets be left to 'regulate' themselves? Berdegué and Reardon call urgently for 'proactive, anticipatory strategies and policies' to deal with the global phenomenon of supermarket domination of production for the market. Waples calls for a greater role for citizens and consumer organisations in determining the governance of trade in agricultural commodities and trade, and more awareness among governments of how trade negotiators' deals can undermine policy goals directed towards sustainable farming, agro-ecologies and food systems.

What, then, is the role of policy approaches in effecting innovation in food chains? Thomas argues that we should not think in terms of aiming to effect change in one dimension of policy because there is a sluggishness in policy regimes that is the result of their irreducible multidimensionality. Which ethical spaces need to be reclaimed in policy and the rules of the game? Contributors suggest different answers. Waples highlights how free trade agreements have created systems of rules that force nations to facilitate trade on unequal terms and deter them from making independent political decisions about the level of protection they wish to embrace and the social policies they wish to promote. Such rule systems need to be subordinated to the ethical realisation that our food chain embraces much more than a system of commerce. She suggests that this has been achieved to a greater extent in European Union policy than in other multilateral governance agreements. Ballet, Dubois and Mahieu call attention to the need to recover the ethical idea of 'responsibility' and to bring this explicitly into an analysis of value chains. Heath and Pearson call attention to ways of working within existing procurement rules. Although procurement teams cannot specify the need for local produce, they can write criteria into the tender specifications – for example regarding freshness – that increase the likelihood of the tender being won by a local supplier. Schäfer focuses on the ethical spaces that the dominant tradition in modern economics has forgotten. She calls for economic frameworks that question a hard differentiation between market and non-market activities and recognises that entrepreneurs are not only acting as *homo oeconomicus* but also as citizens with individual social goals that go beyond making profits. Greater acknowledgement of the contributions of the organic sector, for instance, would result in 'prices which tell the ecological truth'.

How far is innovation supportive of ethical food production likely without public interest funding? Some contributors focus on the role of citizens and on activist groups in finding creative ways of 'using the market'. Others highlight interventions requiring the support of public funding. For example, Heath and Pearson recount how funding from the European Union's Regional Development programme in Cornwall was used to support the initiative to promote regional sourcing of hospital food. Lockie argues that translating the monetary resources of consumers into genuine influence depends on the involvement of organisations capable of issuing calls to action that are meaningful to both consumers and retailers. Such organisations will often require some public funding support. We end this section with a final as yet unresolved question: how far are practical solutions to practical problems a viable alternative to concerted action to change systems of rules and policy regimes?

Principles to Guide Action

We recognise in the concluding section of this book that the abstraction of normative principles from experience and reasoning is an act of informed judgement. The following are the principles that we, as editors of this volume, offer as important in helping to guide future action:

- Branding and certification schemes that seek to move Northern consumers out of their 'comfort zone' need to be continually refined and developed.
- Policy makers should challenge supermarkets to stimulate their customers to appreciate the social and environmental factors that relate to the production and availability of the goods sold.
- Policy makers need to ensure that they research the dynamics of the impacts of supermarket on regional economies and to devise interventions that minimise negative effects of this retail model.
- Rather than assume that markets will allocate responsibility equitably, policy makers from all sectors should undertake evaluations of value chains and identify where and by whom the responsibility and costs of social innovation might be borne. Evaluations should include an assessment of the scope for the optimal dispersion of benefits to all stakeholders.
- Tools such as the foodprinting and quality-of-life toolkits suggested in this book need to be developed continually and used to communicate with people, in an interactive discussion process, about the social and environmental issues relevant to food production and future food security.
- Innovative ways of understanding and communicating the needs of poor producers in the South need to be developed by various actors in the food chain.
- Deeper citizen involvement with the growing of food, going beyond communication to encompass hands-on experience of food cultivation and local trade, should be considered for inclusion in all new food initiatives.
- Public bodies need to promote wider use of public procurement schemes that harness the food production and processing capabilities of local and regional economies.

- Public interest funding needs to be made available to support initiatives such as local food sourcing, and also to support organisations capable of articulating a problem, identifying its causes, suggesting solutions, and issuing calls to action that are meaningful to both consumers and retailers and those seeking to improve regional or local economic development.
- Policy makers need to move to a more sophisticated understanding of economics, one that is informed by the social and environmental dimensions on which an economy depends. Consideration of environmental and social issues should be placed on a par with economic and trade issues.
- Policy makers, public interest activists and citizens need to foster more critical awareness of the way policy regimes function and how they present barriers to innovation. Ways need to be found to enable them to foster innovation and creativity.
- National legal systems should be reformed to reflect the reality of multinational corporations and international trade and should give increased authority to individuals and public interest groups to challenge the systems of rules operating in trade and other food regimes.
- In order to ensure that women truly benefit from engagement in Fair Trade, measures to encourage discussion of what 'substantive gender equality' means in a particular context needs to be developed.

Finally, we consider it vital to appreciate that learning by doing is central to any agenda for change. Innovations that transform will emerge from ongoing critical analysis of success factors and obstacles by all parties in a food chain, by experimentation and by dedicated 'acts of faith'.

Index

Figures are indicated by bold page numbers, tables by italics.

accountability of pesticide producers 33
Advocacy Coalition Framework (ACF) 47
advocacy coalitions linked with CAP 47–8
Agreement of the Application of Sanitary and Pytosanitary Measures (SPS Agreement) 28
agriculture
    commoditization of North American 98–9
    dairy farms 76
    family based in UK 67, 68–9
    land use for 60, 63, **63**, *64*
    management and performance of farms 71, 72–6
    multifunctionality in 50–1
    social life of farmers and families 69–71
    socio-economic footprint of farms 70–6, **72**, *74*
    see also Common Agricultural Policy (CAP)
Agrofair 81, 89, 90
allotments 212–13
Argentina
    Code of Good Commercial Practice 155–6
    delayed payments to suppliers 152
Arndt, S. 190
Arnot, C. 223
ASERCA, Mexico 157
Australia, economic liberalisation in 51
Averyt, W.F. 45

Ballet, J. 199
Balsevich, F. 157
Barndt, Deborah 209
Baumgartner, F.R. 48
Becker, G.S. 45
Berdegué, J.A. 158–9

Berlin-Brandesburg region, organic farming in
    consumption of produce from 110
    dissemination of information and experience 113–14, **115**, 117
    ecological engagement by 116
    economic contributions of 111–12
    market/non-market-oriented activities 116–18
    motivation of organic entrepreneurs 114–18
    protection of nature and the environment by 112–13
    and regional networks 116–17
    relations with customers and suppliers 116
    socially oriented activities of 112, **113**
bilateral treaties and environmental standards 36–7
Bimandiri 18
Biorganika 84–8
Blythman, J. 164
bonding 69–70
Borromeo, Federico 180
Boucher, F. 194
branding
    as being about trust 102
    FoodTrust initiative 104–7
    personality-based branding 103
    Prince Edward island, Canada 97, 104–7
    product branding 102–3
    values-based 103–4
bridging 69–70
Broads Grazing Marsh Scheme (BGMS) 46
Brom, J.F. 152
Brooks, J. 45
Brown, M.T. 62
budget crises as driver of CAP reform 49
Burkina Faso, fruit exports from 88, 89, 90, 91–2
business development services for suppliers 157, 159

Cajamarca cheese production in Peru 194–5
campaigning and advocacy groups 216
Canada
   Chemtura Corp. v. Government of Canada 34n6
   commoditization of agriculture 98–9
   consumerism in 99–101
   Crompton Corp. v. Canada 34–5
   households, changes in 100
   Pest Management Regulatory Authority (PMRA) 34–5
CAP. *see* Common Agricultural Policy (CAP)
capability structures 193–7
capacity development of suppliers 156–9
carbon emission reduction by supermarkets 172–3
Carimentrand, A. 194, 199
carrying capacity 61–2
Caswell, J.A. 164
catchment areas for procurement 17–18
centralisation of catchment areas for procurement 17–18
certification standards 167–9, 216
change, Solidaridad's theory of 82–4
Charles, Prince 184
cheese production in Peru 194–5
Chemtura Corp. v. Government of Canada 34n6
Chile
   decline in small shops 149
   limiting supermarket growth 154–5
   modernisation of street markets 156
   rural producer organisations 157–9
China
   supermarket food retail in 12–13
   wet markets in 21
China Resources Enterprise 18
Circle of Poisons 32
citizen enforcement mechanisms of NAFTA 30–1
co-option thesis 216–22
Coco-Cola 103
Code of Good Commercial Practice, Argentina 155–6
codification of values into standards 219
Codron, J.-M. 20
collective capability 194–5
Comité des Organisations Professionelles Agricoles (COPA) 45, 46

Commission for Environmental Cooperation (CEC) 31, 33
commodification and consumption of justice 216–17
commoditization
   of food 164
   of North American agriculture 98–9
Common Agricultural Policy (CAP)
   advocacy coalitions linked with 47–8
   change in objectives of 51–2
   and changes in discourse 50–1
   criticisms of 41–2
   defined as policy regime 42
   external pressures for reform 48–9
   institutional processes of 42–5
   interest groups associated with 45–8
   MacSharry reform 46
   modulation of payments to farmers 43–5
   and policy communities 45–6
   policy entrepreneurs linked with 46–7
   reform of 43
   Single Farm Payments (SFPs) 43–5
communities, policy 45–6
community gardens 212–13
concentration of the distributive trade 99, **100**
Concepcion, S.B. 20
conflict between supermarkets and suppliers 150, 152–3
consumer agency in fair trade 223–4
consumer segments, diffusion of supermarkets across 14
consumerism in North America 99–101
consumers
   preferences of and farming realities 89–90
   and supermarkets 163–5
consumption of justice 216–17
contracts, implicit, with suppliers 18–19
Cook, I. 218
Cork Declaration 51
Cornwall Food Programme
   aims and funding of 123
   benefits to the community 123–4
   future developments 127–8
   impact on local businesses 125–6
   origins and development of 124–5
   success in meeting objectives 128–9
   wider impacts of 126–7

Council of Agriculture Ministers (CAM) 42–3
Countryside Commission 46–7, 50
countryside products 50
Courtney, Paul 69
Coyler, D. 32
Crang, P. 218
credence labels. *see* social labels
Crompton Corp. v. Canada 34–5
customer segments, diffusion of supermarkets across 14

dairy farms 76
dairy products and supermarket penetration 15
Dawson Farm 98
De Pelsmacker, P. 224
de-radicalisation 219
Deardoff, A. 190
demand for supermarkets 15–16
determinants of diffusion of supermarkets 15–21
developing countries
   changes in food retail 11–15
   demand for supermarkets in 15–16
   determinants of diffusion of supermarkets in 15–21
   see also individual countries
Dickens, P. 190
diet and environmental sustainability 65
diffusion of supermarket product categories 14
Digal, L.N. 20
discourse, changes in and policy regimes 50–1
dispute resolution under free trade agreements 28–30
dissemination of organic farming information and experience 113–14, **115**
distributive trade, concentration of 99, **100**
diversification
   in farming 73, 75, 76
   of supermarket shop formats 14
domestic law and regulations
   as counterbalance to free trade agreements 37–8
   and supermarket diffusion 20–1
Downes, A. 48
drivers of diffusion of supermarkets 15–21

ecological footprinting 61, 64, **64**
economics of rural towns 69, 70–6, **72, 74**
ecosystem services 61
Eko-Oké 82
embeddedness 70, 71
emergy footprinting 61–2
employment, standards of in organic farming 167
empowerment through fair trade 94–5
enterprise law 38
entrepreneurs
   motivation of organic 114–15
   policy, linked with CAP 47–8
environment, the
   compared to environments 204–5
   impact on of food production 101–2
   protection of by organic farmers in Germany 112–13
   standards in free trade agreements 35–7
   sustainability and diet 65
environmental law 38
Environmental Side Agreement (ESA) 31
environments
   and the environment 204–5
   and food practices 205–7
   impoverishment of by food practices 208–10
   reconnection to food practices in 210–13
erosion of standards 221–2
Errington, Andrew 68, 69
ethical consumption, social labels as enabling 175–6
ethics
   analytical framework of 132–3
   and expansion of wine cooperatives 136–8
   and hypermodernity 138–9
   initial development of wine cooperatives 133–6
   v. commercial realities for supermarkets 169–70
   in wine cooperatives today 141–2
European Conference on Rural Development 51
European Council Regulation 44/2001 37–8
European Union (EU)
   ban on artificial growth hormones 29
   environmental standards in free trade agreements 35–6
   moratorium on approvals of GMOs 29

rural development policy changes 51–2
  see also Common Agricultural Policy
     (CAP)
exclusion and polarisation 219–20
experience, dissemination of organic
     farming 113–14, **115**
extension of catchment areas for
     procurement 17–18

fair trade
  achieving sustainable impact 93–4
  bananas in Peru 84–8
  benefits to producer communities 223
  campaigning and advocacy groups 216
  certification standards 216
  codification of values into standards 219
  concerns over mainstreaming 216–22
  de-radicalisation 219
  empowerment through 94–5
  entry of Nestlé and Starbucks 215
  erosion of standards 221–2
  exclusion and polarisation 219–20
  and gender (in)equality 84, 86, 90–1,
     92–3
  mainstreaming of 83, 84, 88, 89–90,
     92, 94–5
  obscuring relations of production
     218–19
  organisations and networks of 216
  pineapple market 89–90
  producer and consumer agency 223–4
  role of middlemen 91–2
  setting and evaluation of standards
     220–1
  Solidaridad initiatives 81–2
  standards as a barrier to participation
     219–20
  strategic choices by Solidaridad 84–94
  tensions and dilemmas around
     mainstreaming 229–31
  value chains 198–9
  West African Fair Fruit Project (WAFF)
     89–91
  as working in and aganst the market
     217–18
Fair Trade Labelling Organisations
     International (FLO) 81, 86, 87, 219
family farms
  as basis of UK farming 67
  as supermarket suppliers 150–2
Farmapine Ltd 89

Farmers on the Edge project 69
farming
  dairy 76
  different views of 67
  diversification in 73, 75, 76
  family based in UK 67, 68–9
  land use for 60
  management and performance of farms
     71, 72–6
  multifunctionality in 50–1
  realities of and consumer preferences
     89–90
  social life of farmers and families 69–72
  socio-economic footprint of farms
     70–6, **72, 74**
  see also Common Agricultural Policy
     (CAP); organic farming
fields of significance. see environments
financial services, suppliers access to 157,
     159
Fischer Boel, Mariann 48
Fischler, Franz 50
Flores, L. 151
Florida, Richard 72
food and livelihoods 232–3
food consumption in Sweden 57–8
food cultures and supermarkets 171–2
food literacy 231–2
food practices
  contribution to environmental
     impoverishment 208–10
  and environments 205–7
  growing your own food 212–13
  reconnection to 210–13
food production, environment impact of
     101–2
food retail, changes in developing countries
     11–15
food supply, changes in origins of 55–7
foodprinting 59–65, **63, 64**
foodshed approach 58–9, **59**
FoodTrust initiative 97, 98, 104–7
foot-and-mouth disease in the UK 49
footprinting
  ecological 61
  emergy 61–2
foreign direct investment (FDI) 12–13,
     16–17
forum non conveniens doctrine 33, 37–8
fragility of capability structures 195–6
fraud prevention 168

free trade agreements
    counterbalance of domestic and international law 37–8
    environmental standards in 35–7
    and investor disputes with governments 30
    lack of power over food choices for individuals 31–2
    and sovereignty 27–31
fruit exports from West Africa 88–90
Fruiteq 89, 91–2

Garcia-Barandiaran, Jack 88
Garrod, D. 191
Gasson, Ruth 68
gender (in)equality
    in fair trade 92–3
    formal/substantive equality 91n3
    and Solidaridad 84, 86, 93n4
    West African Fair Fruit Project (WAFF) 90–1
General Agreement on Tariffs and Trade 1994, Article III 28
Gereffi, G. 190, *191*
Germany. *see* Berlin-Brandesburg region, organic farming in; Regional Wealth Reconsidered research project
Getz, A. 58
Ghana, fruit exports from 88–90
Gibbon, P. 191
globalisation and Languedoc wine cooperatives 139–41
Goldman, A. 15, 156
Good Agricultural and Environmental Condition (GAEC) standards 48
Goodman, M. 220
governance of value chains 190–1, *191*
government regulations and supermarket diffusion 20–1
Granovetter, Mark 70
Grant, W. 45
Grolleau, G. 164
Guatemala
    lettuce farming 151
    procurement modernisation in 20
Gutman, G. 16, 152

harmonisation under free trade agreements 28–30, 32
Harrison, Lucy 69
Haverkamp, D.-J. 1

Henderson, J. 190
heterogeneity of procurement modernisation 19–20
holistic economies
    challenges to 118
    developing and supporting 119–20
Holzer, B. 224
Hong Kong, traditional retail in 156
Hortifruti 18
households, changes in 100
Hughes, A. 190
human rights law 38
Humphrey, J. 190, *191*
hypermodernity 138–9

Impacts Project
    intellectual roots of 68–70
    socio-economic footprint 70–6, **72, 74**
India, supermarket food retail in 12–13
Indonesia
    rising supermarket sales 149
    tomato farming 151–2
information, dissemination of organic farming 113–14, **115**
information flows for social labels 178–9
integration of catchment areas for procurement 17–18
interest groups associated with CAP 45–8
International Fair Trade Association (IFAT) 216
International Federation of Organic Agriculture Movements (IFOAM) 168
international free trade agreements. *see* free trade agreements
international law as counterbalance to free trade agreements 37–8
investment flows 16
investor disputes with governments 30

Johnston, J. 217
Jones, B.D. 48
Jordan, A.G. 45
justice, commodification and consumption of 216–17

Kast, S.W. 164
Kierzkowski, H. 190
kitchen gardens 212–13

land use for agriculture 60, 63, **63, 64**

Land Use Policy Group (LUPG) 47–8
Languedoc wine cooperatives
    ethical projects today 141–2
    expansion of 136–8
    globalisation and quality requirements 139–41
    initial development of 133–6
Latin America
    dominance of multinationals 17
    regulation of procurement 155–6
lettuce farming in Guatemala 151
liberalisation
    in China and India 13
    economic, in Australia 51
    of retail FDI 16
lindane 34–5
Lisbon Strategy 51–2
literacy, food 231–2
livelihoods and food 232–3
local sourcing
    of food by individuals 211–12
    impact on businesses 125–6
    by supermarkets 170
Locke, S. 220
Lockie, S. 164, 224
logistics, outsourcing of 18

MacSharry reform of CAP 46
Madagascar 168–9, 181, 182
mainstreaming of fair trade
    balance between business and empowerment 94–5
    and choices regarding markets 89–90
    concerns over 216–22
    need for organisational strengthening 88
    Solidaridad 83, 84
    tensions and dilemmas around 229–31
    of what and why 92
Malaysia, limitation of supermarket growth 155
marketing by farms 75
Max Havelaar Coffee trademark 81
Mazey, S. 45
McMichael, Philip 209
MD2 pineapple 91–2
Metalclad case 30
Mexico
    market promotion for suppliers 157
    procurement modernisation in 20
    trade in pesticides under NAFTA 32–3
middlemen 91–2

Midgley, G. 182
Milward, A. 45
modernisation of procurement systems 17–20
modulation of CAP payments to farmers 43–5
motivation of organic entrepreneurs 114–15
multi-stakeholders
    encompassing values of in social labels 182–4
    negotiations for social labels 179–80
multifunctionality in farming 50–1

NAFTA. *see* North American Free Trade Agreement (NAFTA)
NARAPs. *see* North American Regional Action Plans (NARAPs)
Natawidjaja, R. 151
nations, sovereignty of and free trade agreements 27–31
nature, protection of by organic farmers in Germany 112–13
neoliberalism 217
Nestlé 215
Nile perch production in Tanzania 191–3
non-organic farming
    dairy 76
    diversification in 73
    socio-economic footprint of 70–6, **72**
    see also organic farming
North America
    commoditization of agriculture 98–9
    consumerism 99–101
    households, changes in 100
    pesticides in 31–5
North American Agreement on Environmental Cooperation 30–1
North American Free Trade Agreement (NAFTA)
    citizen enforcement mechanisms of 30–1
    harmonisation and dispute resolution under 28–30
    investor disputes under 30
    pesticides in North America 32–3, 34–5
North American Regional Action Plans (NARAPs) 33–4
Nussbaum, Martha 193

Odum, H.T. 62

Oké label for fair trade bananas (later Eko-Oké) 81–2
Olson, M. 45
organic farming
    certification standards 167–9
    contribution to rural development 76–7
    dairy 76
    different views of 67
    diversification in 73, 75, 76
    economic pressures on 118
    fraud prevention 168
    impact of innovation of 76
    socio-economic footprint of 70–6, **72, 74**
    standards of employment 167
    see also Berlin-Brandesburg region, organic farming in; farming
organic food in supermarkets 164, 165
outsourcing of logistics 18

Paying for a Beautiful Countryside (Countryside Commission) 50
Penrose, E. 193–4
perch (Nile) production in Tanzania 191–3
personality-based branding 103
Peru
    Cajamarca cheese production 194–5
    fair trade bananas in 84–8
Pest Management Regulatory Authority (PMRA) (Canada) 34–5
pesticides in North America 31–5
Phan, T.G.T. 15
Philippines, procurement modernisation in 20
pineapple market 89–90
pisteurs 91–2
place of origin of food and supermarkets 170–1
polarisation and exclusion 219–20
policy
    as driver of innovation 233–5
    and supermarket diffusion, limiting growth 154–6
policy communities 45–6
policy entrepreneurs linked with CAP 47–8
policy regimes
    and changes in discourse 50–1
    Common Agricultural Policy (CAP) defined as 42
    factors influencing changes in 44–52
postmodernity 138

preferred supplier lists 18–19
Pretty, Jules 211
price as main food buying criteria 163–4
Prince Edward island, Canada
    branding approach 97, 104–7
    Dawson Farm 98
    environmental impact of potato production 101–2
    as a finite resource 97
    FoodTrust initiative 97, 98, 104–7
    marketing of potatoes 106–7
private standards 19
processed food and supermarket penetration 14
procurement
    modernisation of systems 17–20
    regulation of 155–6
producer agency in fair trade 223–4
product brands 102–3
product categories, diffusion of 14–15
public standards 19
punctuated equilibrium, theory of 48
Putnam, Robert 69–70

Reardon, T. 14, 15
reconnection to food practices 210–13
Rees, W. 61
regime shifts, factors influencing 44–52
Regional Wealth Reconsidered research project 109n1
    aim of 109
    hypothesis and key questions 110
    research methodology 110, 110n2
    see also Berlin-Brandesburg region, organic farming in
regionalism, gastronomic 211–12
regulation
    domestic, and supermarket diffusion 20–1
    as driver of innovation 233–5
    of procurement 155–6
Reliance Industries (India) 13
Renard, M.-C. 217–18, 222
Requier-Desjardins, D. 194
responsibility
    distribution of within value chains 190–3
    and the social precautionary principle 197–9, **198**
retail selling of food
    changes in developing countries 11–15

development of traditional retail 156
traditional v supermarkets 149
Richardson, J.J. 45
Ricoeur, P. 139
Rituals of Dinner, The (Visser) 207
Rose, Sir Julian 208–9
rules as driver of innovation 233–5
rural development
    contribution of organic farming 76–7
    policy changes 51–2
rural life and businesses
    different views of 67
    economics of rural towns 69
    embeddedness 70
rural producer organisations 157–9
Rural Restructuring project 69

Sabatier, P.A. 47
semi-processed food and supermarket
    penetration 15
Sen, A.K. 189, 193
shop formats, diversification of
    supermarkets 14
Single Farm Payments (SFPs) 43–5
social capital of farmers and families 69–72
social labels
    aim and functions of 176–7
    criteria for effective 185
    as enabling ethical consumption 175–6
    encompassing values of multi-
        stakeholders 182–4
    information flows for 178–9
    multi-stakeholder negotiations 179–80
    need for new kind of 176
    and values 180–2
social precautionary principle 197–9, **198**
socio-economic footprint of farms 70–6,
    72, 74
socioeconomic strata, diffusion of
    supermarkets across 14
Solidaridad
    achieving sustainable impact 93–4
    bananas in Peru 84–8
    consumer preferences and farming
        realities 89–90
    and empowerment 87–8
    funding of 82
    and gender (in)equality 84, 86, 90–1,
        93n4
    initiatives of 81–2
    mainstreaming of fair trade 83, 84,
        89–90, 92
    partners and business organisation 86–7
    programme participants 85–6
    role of middlemen 91–2
    strategic choices faced by 84–94
    theory of change of 82–4
    West African Fair Fruit Project (WAFF)
        89–91
sovereignty and free trade agreements 27–31
SPS Agreement 28
stakeholders, multi-
    negotiations between for social labels
        179–80
    values of 182–4
standards
    as a barrier to fair trade participation
        219–20
    codification of fair trade values into 219
    environmental standards in free trade
        agreements 35–7
    erosion of 221–2
    farmers's participation in setting and
        evaluation of 220–1
    Good Agricultural and Environmental
        Condition (GAEC) 48
    private and public 19
Starbucks 215
states
    investment in supermarket chains 21
    sovereignty of and free trade agreements
        27–31
    subsidies for farming 74
stress and consumerism in North America
    99–101
Sturgeon, T. 190, *191*
supermarkets
    carbon emission reduction by 172–3
    competition with traditional retailers
        149
    and consumers 163–5
    defining 164–5
    delayed payments to suppliers 152
    determinants of diffusion of 15–21
    diffusion across consumer
        socioeconomic strata 14
    diffusion of product categories 14–15
    diversification of shop formats 14
    domestic regulations and diffusion of
        20–1

ethics v. commercial realities for 169–70
family farms as suppliers 150–2
FDI by 16
and food cultures 171–2
geographic spread within countries 13–14
local sourcing by 170
organic food in 164, 165
and place of origin of food 170–1
spread across developing countries 11–15
supplier relationships 166–7
suppliers and stages of diffusion of 153–4
tension and conflict with suppliers 150, 152–3
supplier lists, preferred 18–19
suppliers
business development services for 157, 159
capacity development 156–9
delayed payments to 152
family farms to supermarkets 150–2
and stages of supermarket diffusion 153–4
supermarket relationships 166–7
tension and conflict with supermarkets 150–3, 152–3
supply-side drivers of supermarket diffusion 16–20
support areas 61
sustainable economies
challenges to 118
developing and supporting 119–20
tensions ans dilemmas around 232–3
Sutcliffe, W. 181
Sweden
agricultural land use for food 63, **63, 64**
food consumption in 57–8
foodprinting **63**, 63–5, **64**
foodshed of 58–9, **59**

table-wine cooperatives 137–8, 140–1
Tanner, C. 164
Technical Working Group (TWG) of NAFTA 32
tenders encouraging local food resourcing 125
tension between supermarkets and suppliers 150, 152–3

Tesco 14
Thailand, limitation of supermarket growth 155
Tim Hortens coffee 103
tomato farming in Indonesia 151–2
Tracy, M. 45
trade agreements. *see* free trade agreements
trade in pesticides 32–3
traditional retail
development of 156
v. supermarkets 149
Trewithen Dairy 126
Trinethra 14
TWG. *see* Technical Working Group (TWG) of NAFTA

Ulgiati, S. 62
United Kingdom
Countryside Commission 46–7
family farms in 67
foot-and-mouth disease 49
Land Use Policy Group (LUPG) 47–8
modulation of CAP payments to farmers 43–5
United States, environmental standards and bilateral treaties 36–7
Uruguay Round Agriculture Agreement (URAA) 49
Utz Kapeh Foundation 221–2

Valle de Chira Association (VCA) 85, 87, 88
value chains
and capability structures 193–6
distribution of responsibilities within 190–3
fair trade 198–9
governance of 190–1, *191*
values
branding based on 103–4
multi-stakeholder 182–4
and social labels 180–2
vegetables, fresh, and supermarket penetration 15
Vignerons Libres de Maraussan, initial development of 133–6
see also wine cooperatives
Visser, Margaret 207
VREL 89
vulnerability of agents 195–6

Wackernagel, M. 61
Wales and Single Farm Payments 44
watersheds 58, 60–1
Weible, C.M. 47
West African Fair Fruit Project (WAFF) 89–91
wet markets, regulation of 21
wholesalers, growing use of specialist 18
Wilkinson, J. 216, 224
wine cooperatives
    ethical projects today 141–2
    expansion of 136–8
    globalisation and quality requirements 139–41
    initial development of 133–6
women and equality
    formal/substantive equality 91n3
    and Solidaridad 84, 86
    West African Fair Fruit Project (WAFF) 90–1
World Trade Organisation (WTO)
    accords 28
    Agreement of the Application of Sanitary and Pytosanitary Measures (SPS Agreement) 28
    General Agreement on Tariffs and Trade 1994, Article III 28
    harmonisation and dispute resolution under agreements of 28–30

Zadek, S. 185

About the Editors

Cathy Rozel Farnworth (PhD) has lived and worked in a number of countries including Afghanistan, Syria, Zimbabwe, Tanzania, Ghana, Madagascar, Germany, China and the UK. She works on capturing local understandings of quality of life through developing indicators with people on the ground, on participatory research and development, and on ethical value chains and marketing. Cathy trained in rural development studies and gender analysis.

Janice Jiggins (PhD) trained in history and political science. She has worked in the field for many years on agricultural development policy, sustainable farming systems and natural resource management, in both developing countries and in Europe. Through her former position as Professor of Human Ecology at the Swedish University of Agricultural Sciences and currently as Guest Researcher at Wageningen University, the Netherlands, she remains actively engaged in participatory plant breeding, integrated pest management and in questions of gender equity and social inclusion. The governance of agricultural research and development organisations and in the last four years also an author's role in the International Assessment of Agricultural Science and Technology provide additional stimulation.

Emyr Vaughan Thomas (PhD) has a doctorate in methodological issues in the study of values and a Master's in environmental policy and planning. He worked for many years for an environmental agency on issues in European environmental policy. He currently works as an Associate Lecturer with the Open University, UK, and has published one book and a range of scholarly papers.

If you have found this book useful you may be interested in these other forthcoming titles from Gower

Corporate Sustainability
Güler Aras and David Crowther
978-0-566-08819-3

Corruption in International Business
Sharon Eicher
978-0-7546-7137-4

Global Perspectives on Corporate Governance
Güler Aras and David Crowther
978-0-566-08830-8

Looking Beyond Profit
Peggy Chiu
978-0-7546-7337-8

GOWER

**Making Ecopreneurs
2nd Edition**
Michael Schaper
978-0-566-08875-9

New Work Ethics
Peter Kelly
978-0-7546-4963-2

**Spirituality and Corporate
Social Responsibility**
David Bubna-Litic
978-0-7546-4763-8

For more information on any of these titles visit www.gowerpublishing.com

GOWER